글로벌 사서를 위한
도서관 영어회화
Essential English for Global Librarians

발간사

『글로벌 사서를 위한 도서관 영어회화』를 발간하며

'글로벌'이라는 단어는 이제 우리에게 익숙한 용어가 되었습니다. 각 대학에서 외국어 강의가 늘어나고 있고, 국제화가 대학의 평가지표가 되고 있으며, 우리나라에 수학하기 위해 온 많은 외국인들을 교정 곳곳에서 볼 수 있습니다. 대학도서관은 이들이 도서관을 이용하는데 어려움이 없도록 각종 서비스 안내에 외국어를 병기하고 있습니다. 나아가 외국 학생들이 학습 및 연구 활동을 좀 더 편안하게 하고, 도서관에 대한 친밀한 이미지를 갖도록 외국인 학생을 위한 도서관 축제를 개최하거나 외국인 전담사서를 배치하는 곳도 있을 정도입니다.

이제 사서에게 외국인과의 소통을 위한 회화는 기본적인 사항이 되었고, 때문에 영어회화능력을 키우기 위한 노력을 게을리 할 수가 없는 형편입니다.

『글로벌 사서를 위한 도서관 영어회화』는 대학도서관에 근무하는 사서들이 현장에서 일어날 수 있는 모든 상황을 미리 가정하여 대화 내용을 정리하였고, 외국대학도서관을 이용한 경험이 있는 사서들이 기초 대화문을 만들었습니다. 그리고 이를 실제 외국인(외국인 교수, 대학원생, 교환학생 등)들에게 현장감 있는 용어로 점검하였습니다.

『글로벌 사서를 위한 도서관 영어회화』는 지난 2004년에 우리 학술정보교류협의회에서 발간한 『사서실무영어회화(Practical English for Librarians)』에서 취급하지 못했던 새로운 서비스를 내용에 포함시켰고(SNS서비스, 주제서비스,

이용자교육, 전자자료 서비스 등), 도서관에서 알리는 각종 안내문도 영어로 만들어 보았습니다. 또한 스토리텔링형식의 실용적인 내용을 기본으로, 외국인 아나운서의 녹음을 CD에 담음으로써 기존의 영어회화 책자로서의 부족한 점을 보강하였습니다.

학술정보교류협의회는 1998년 경희대학교, 고려대학교, 성균관대학교, 연세대학교, 한양대학교 등 5개 대학교의 도서관들이 해외학술지 공동구독 및 이용을 통한 예산절감을 목적으로 결성되었고, 최근에는 회원 간의 유대강화와 상호 협력증진 그리고 다양한 학술정보의 교류 등으로 그 기능을 확대하였습니다.

나아가 학술정보교류협의회가 대학도서관계의 발전을 위하여 일익을 담당해야 한다는 회원교 사서들의 공감대와 사명감으로 번역서인『대학도서관·변화와 발전』그리고『사서실무영어회화』, 또한 5개 대학의 도서관 현황 분석 및 평가를 담은『학술정보교류협의회 Annual Report 2010』등을 출간하기도 하였습니다.

이번에 발간하는『글로벌 사서를 위한 도서관 영어회화』는 2011년 학술정보교류협의회 연구출판 사업의 일환으로 1년간 준비하여 세상에 내 보내게 되었습니다. 회원교 도서관 현장에서 실제로 일어나는 현장의 상황을 담으려고 애썼으며, 고려대학교 국제어학원에서 1차 감수하였고, 미국 USC 동아시아 도서관 한국학 전문사서 이선윤 선생께서 최종 감수를 하는 등 현지 외국인들의 감각을 살리려고 힘썼습니다.

그럼에도 불구하고 다소 아쉬운 점은 시간적 제약으로 권말에 색인과 도서관 전문용어 해설을 삽입하지 못하였다는 점입니다. 그러나 향후 도서관계의 빠른 변화에 맞추어 새로운 개정판이 발간되어야 한다고 생각하며, 이때에 E-Book 등 다양한 매체로의 출판과 더불어 보다 충실한 내용으로 보강될 것을 기대해 봅니다.

이번 『글로벌 사서를 위한 도서관 영어회화』의 초고를 담당한 학술정보교류협의회의 각 대학 담당자인 경희대 황일원 사서, 고려대 오태호 사서, 성균관대 민경승 사서, 연세대 채정림 사서, 한양대 안신섭 사서에게 고마움을 표합니다. 그리고 이 책의 발간을 위하여 처음부터 끝까지 기획과 편집을 직접 담당하고, 실무팀을 이끌어 준 고려대학교 서진영 부장의 노고에 진심으로 감사 드립니다.

이 책이 도서관에 근무하는 모든 사서들에게 필독의 영어회화 지침서가 될 수 있을 것이라는 기대와 함께 전국의 문헌정보학 전공 학생들에게도 좋은 자료로서 활용되기를 바랍니다.

2012년 2월
학술정보교류협의회장
고려대학교 도서관장 유관희

Contents

Contents • •

4. 시설 / Library Facilities (한양대학교 학술정보관) • 233

5. 수서 / Acquisition (연세대학교 중앙도서관) • 287

Contents • •

6. 정리 / Cataloging (성균관대학교 학술정보관) • 379

Contents • •

7. 전산 / Library Systems (한양대학교 학술정보관) • 413

부록 : 공지 / E-mail 영어 예문 • 463

[일러두기]

Situation(상황)의 대화 상대자는 다음과 같은 이니셜을 사용하였다.

A : Student Assistant
D : Donator
L : Librarian
P : Publisher
R : Research Institute
U : User
V : Vendor

Information Retrieval

검 색

경희대학교 중앙도서관

1 검색 / Information Retrieval

U : 도서관 홈페이지에 대해 질문이 있는데요.

L : 어떤 점이 궁금하시죠?

U : 이용법이 복잡한데, 죄송하지만 전반적으로 설명을 해주시겠어요?

L : 우선, 지금 보시는 화면이 도서관 홈페이지 메인 화면입니다.

　　메인 화면은 도서관에 대한 이용안내, 문헌검색시스템, 원문제공서비스, 개
　　인정보관리, Q&A등으로 구성되어 있습니다.

　　또한 유용한 학술자원들을 연결시켜 놓았습니다.

U : 저는 맥북을 이용하는데요, 사파리 브라우저로도 도서관 홈페이지를 이용
　　할 수 있나요?

L : 물론입니다. 인터넷 익스플로러 뿐만 아니라 파이어 폭스, 구글 크롬 등 다
　　른 브라우저에서도 이용할 수 있습니다.

U : 알겠습니다. 감사합니다.

L : 천만에요.

Situation 1   Library Website 1

U : I have some questions about your library's website.

L : What sort of questions?

U : Your homepage is quite complicated. Could you show me how to use it?

L : Sure, why don't you come over here and I can show you. OK, now you
are looking at the main screen of the library homepage.

Our main page includes the library user's guide, online catalog, full-text
service, user information and Q&A. It also serves as a gateway to many
useful academic resources.

U : I'm using a MacBook. Can I access the library website using the Safari
browser?

L : Sure, you can. In addition to Internet Explorer, you can connect to our
website via Firefox, Google Chrome and other web browsers.

U : I got it. Thank you.

L : You're welcome.

상황 2 　💬 홈페이지 안내 2

U : 홈페이지를 통해 도서 검색, 구입신청, 예약 등을 이용할 수 있나요?

L : 물론이죠. 검색시스템을 통해서 소장자료에 대한 검색이 가능하고, 도서 신청이나 예약 등은 '이용자서비스' 메뉴를 통해 가능합니다.

U : 원문제공서비스는 무엇을 의미하죠?

L : 원문제공서비스에서는 국내외 70여종의 웹 데이터베이스를 통한 원문제공 과 상호대차 및 원문복사 서비스를 제공하고 있습니다.

U : 이용에 관련된 규정도 있나요?

L : '도서관 이용안내'를 클릭하면 도서관 역사, 규정 및 이용안내, 조직 등에 대해 자세히 볼 수 있습니다. 또한 새로운 서비스나 이용자 교육에 관한 소 식은 'Web Magazine'을 통해 제공하고 있습니다.

U : 많은 도움이 되었습니다. 감사합니다.

Information Retrieval • 검색

 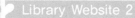

U : Can I search, recommend a book, or place a hold from the library website?

L : Of course, you can search for our holdings through the online catalog. You can also recommend a book, or place a hold from the 'User Services' page.

U : What is the full-text service?

L : Our full-text service includes loans and copies of material not otherwise accessible in our library, with more than seventy full-text databases, both domestic and foreign, directly accessible on the web.

U : Are there any library policies I should be aware of when I'm using the full-text service?

L : Yes, there are. 'The Library User Guide' explains the history, policies, searching techniques and library organization in detail. Also, 'The Web Magazine' provides you with news about our new services and user instructional programs.

U : You were very helpful, thanks!

상황 3   ▶ 도서관 목록 검색 1

U : 검색 시스템에서 결과물이 나오지 않는데요?

L : 제가 한번 해볼까요? 어떤 자료를 찾고 계시죠?

U : 중소기업에 관련된 단행본 자료를 찾고 있습니다.

L : 검색 시스템에서 서명란에 '중소기업'을 입력하시고, 자료형태에 '단행본'을 두고 검색하시면 됩니다.

　　(잠시 후) 검색 결과가 너무 많은데요. 559건이나 검색이 되네요.

U : 검색범위를 좁힐 수 있나요?

L : 구체적으로 찾으시는 자료가 있습니까?

U : 경문사에서 나온『중소기업론』이라는 책은 있나요?

L : 검색창에서 출판사 항목에 '경문사'를 추가하여 검색해 보면, 2건이 검색되네요. 그 중 하나가『중소기업 개론』이란 책입니다.

U : 어디에 가면 볼 수 있죠?

L : 청구기호 '338.642 지65ㅈ'에 가면 볼 수 있습니다.

상황 3   Library Catalog 1

U : My search is not yielding any results.

L : I'll try it for you. What are you looking for?

U : I'm looking for a book on small and medium enterprises.

L : Type in 'small and medium enterprises' in the search box, select 'Books'
for the material type, and click on search.
(After a little while) I got too many results — 559 books.

U : Can you narrow the search?

L : Are you looking for a specific book?

U : Yes, do you carry a book called The Theory of Small Medium Enterprises,
published by Kyungmoonsa?

L : Let me add Kyungmoonsa in the Publisher field. (After a little while) I see
two books; the first one is The Theory of Small and Medium Enterprises.

U : That's it. Where can I find it?

L : Please check the call number 338.642 지65ㅈ.

상황 4　　　💬 도서관 목록검색 2

U : 검색시스템의 검색방법을 잘 모르겠습니다.

L : 데스크 안쪽으로 들어오시면 설명해 드리겠습니다. 우선 도서관 홈페이지 검색 시스템에 접속하셔서, 첫 화면의 검색 항목란에 보시자 하는 자료를 입력하신 후 검색하시면 됩니다.

U : 검색 항목란에 대해 좀 더 설명해 주세요.

L : 검색 항목란은 기본적으로 서명, 저자, 출판사 등의 항목으로 검색하실 수 있으며, 자료 형태에 의해서 검색할 수도 있습니다.

U : 일본어는 어떻게 입력하죠?

L : 검색화면 하단에 일본어와 다국어 입력 항목이 있습니다.

U : '소장 도서관'은 무엇을 의미하는 거죠?

L : 도서관 별 소장자료를 나타내는 건데, 선택 항목에 따라 도서관 별로 자료를 검색할 수 있습니다.

Situation 4  Library Catalog 2

U : I don't know how to search for library resources.

L : Would you come over here so that I can explain it in detail? First, click 'Online Catalog' from our library homepage. Then type in the search terms.

U : Can you show me some searching techniques?

L : You can search by title, author, publisher and so on. You can also limit your search by format.

U : How can I input Japanese words?

L : There are language options at the bottom of the search screen.

U : What does 'Holdings Library' mean?

L : It shows which library owns an item. You can choose different libraries on campus to search items held by those libraries.

상황 5　♥ 학술지 논문 검색

U : 어떤 논문이 어느 저널에 있는지 쉽게 찾을 수 있는 방법은 없습니까?

L : 검색창에서 통합검색을 하거나 기사검색을 지정하여 검색하면 됩니다. 저자명, 기사명, 주제명, 잡지명 등으로 검색이 가능합니다.

U : 우리 도서관에 소장하고 있는 것만 검색이 가능한가요?

L : 예. 그렇습니다. 혹시 소장자료 이외의 자료를 검색하고자 한다면 한국교육학술정보원 DB나 NDSL에 접속하여 검색하시면 됩니다.

U : NDSL이요?

L : 한국과학기술정보연구원에서 제공하는 서비스인데요, 국내 도서관에서 소장하는 외국저널의 기사검색을 할 수 있습니다.

U : 기사 원문은 어떻게 하면 얻을 수 있나요?

L : 원문복사서비스를 이용하시거나, 우리 도서관이 해당 저널의 온라인 버전을 구독하고 있는 경우 기사 원문에 바로 접속할 수도 있습니다.

U : 감사합니다. 많은 도움이 되었습니다.

Situation 5 Journal Articles

U : How can I search for journal articles?

L : You can search articles either from the integrated search screen or from the journal article search screen. Just type in the author, article title, subject, journal title, etc.

U : Can I search for articles held by our library only?

L : Yes. You can also search for materials held by other libraries using the journal database of the Research and Information Sharing Service (RISS) or National Discovery for Science Leaders (NDSL).

U : What is the NDSL?

L : The NDSL is provided by the Korea Institute of Science and Technology Information. It includes foreign journal articles held in domestic libraries.

U : How can I get the articles in full-text?

L : You can apply for Document Delivery Service. You may be able to directly access the full-text of articles if our library subscribes to the journal 's online version.

U : Thanks for your help.

상황 6　　　♥ 한국학 데이터베이스 검색 1

U : 한국학에 관련된 연구 자료를 찾고자 하는데, 혹시 도움이 될만한 데이터 베이스가 있습니까?

L : 현재 저희 도서관에서는 한국학 관련 데이터베이스로 ABC미디어에서 제 공하는 국학 데이터베이스를 서비스하고 있습니다.

U : 좀더 상세히 말씀해 주세요. 이용방법이라든가 제공목록이라든가.

L : 화면을 보면서 설명하는 게 좋을 것 같은데, 안쪽으로 들어오세요. 우선 도 서관 홈페이지에 접속하신 후 왼쪽 메뉴에서 'Web Databases'를 선택하세 요. 보여지는 목록에서 아래쪽으로 이동하시면 'ABC 미디어 한국학 DB'라 고 있죠? 이 중 원하시는 곳을 클릭하시면 됩니다.

U : 제가 찾고 있는 자료는『고려사』인데, 여기 있네요.

L :『고려사』말고도 35종의 한국학 자료를 이용하실 수 있습니다.

U : 혹시 집에서도 이용이 가능한가요?

L : 집에서는 이용이 불가능하고, 교내에서만 가능합니다.

Situation 6  Korean Studies Database 1

U : I'd like to find some resources on Korean Studies. Is there any database
for that?

L : We now have Korean Studies Database offered by ABC Media.

U : Can you show me the content of the database and how to use it?

L : It is easier to demonstrate on the screen. Please come in. First, open the
library website, and select 'Web Databases' from the menus on the left.
Scroll down and you will see ABC Media's Korean Studies Database. Click
on a title you want from the Korean Studies Database.

U : I am looking for *Koryosa*. Here, I found it.

L : Besides *Koryosa*, there are 35 different titles in that database.

U : Can I access them from my home computer?

L : You can only use these databases on campus.

상황 7  한국학 데이터베이스 검색 2

U : 검색했던 검색결과를 다시 볼 수 있나요?

L : 메뉴에 있는 검색 목록 메뉴를 이용하시면 됩니다.

U : 이쪽 검색 메뉴를 말하는 건가요?

L : 맞습니다. 검색 목록을 여시면 현재까지 검색했던 검색어들의 검색 결과 목록이 올라옵니다.

U : 저는 국문 번역본이 아닌 원본을 보고 싶은데, 가능한가요?

L : 상단 메뉴에 보면 '원문보기' 버튼이 있습니다. 이 버튼을 클릭하면 원본 이미지를 볼 수 있습니다.

U : 도움을 주셔서 감사합니다.

L : (명함을 건네며) 다른 도움이 필요할 경우 여기에 있는 연락처로 연락해 주세요.

Situation 7 Korean Studies Database 2

U : Can I go back to previous search results?

L : Yes. You can do that by using the search history menu.

U : Is this what you are talking about?

L : Yes, that's it. If you open the search history, you'll see all results for your previous searches.

U : I'd like to find the original Chinese text instead of the translated Korean version.

L : Click on the 'Full-text' button at the top, and you will get a full-text image of the original text.

U : Thank you for your help.

L : (Giving a business card) If you need my help, feel free to contact me at this number.

상황 8 　　♥ 학회지 원문 제공

U : 『대한내과학회지』를 보고 싶은데요. 어디로 가야 하나요?

L : (검색 후) 60번 서가에서 볼 수 있는데, 『대한내과학회지』는 인쇄저널뿐만 아니라 전자저널로도 이용이 가능합니다.

U : 아! 그래요. 검색하는 방법에 대해 알려주시겠습니까?

L : 예. 우선 도서관 홈페이지에 접속하신 후 검색메뉴의 'E-Journal' 버튼을 클릭합니다. 검색어 입력란에 저널의 완전명이나 일부를 입력합니다. 'Go' 버튼을 클릭한 뒤, 결과 리스트가 화면에 나타나면, 해당 저널명을 클릭합니다. 그러면 원하는 권, 호를 제공하는 DB를 선택할 수 있는 새로운 창이 나타나는데, 여기서 KISS 데이터베이스로 연결되는 'Go' 버튼을 선택하면 됩니다. 새로운 창에서 원하는 연도를 선택하면, 그 해의 모든 권, 호의 리스트를 볼 수 있습니다.

U : 혹시 기사명으로도 검색이 가능한가요?

L : 예. 가능합니다. 여기 검색어 입력란에다가 해당 기사명을 입력하시면 됩니다.

U : 의학과 관련된 다른 학회지도 제공되나요?

L : 이 DB는 약 1,000개 학회의 학회지 원문을 Full-text 형태로 제공하고 있으며, 그 중 의학 관련 학회는 약 100여 개 정도입니다.

U : 잘 알겠습니다. 제가 직접 검색해 보도록 하겠습니다.

U : I'd like to use the *Journal of Korean Internal Medicine*. Where can I find that?

L : (After searching) You can find a hard copy in stack number 60. You can also browse an electronic full-text version of the journal.

U : Oh, really? Can you show me how to find the electronic version?

L : Yes. First, go to our library website and click the 'E-Journal' button in the search menu. Enter the full journal title or part of the title in the search box. After clicking the 'Go' button, the search results will appear on the screen. Click on a title to open the e-journal and a new window may appear, offering different volumes of the journal. Click on the 'Go' button to connect to 'Korea Information Science Society (KISS) Journals. Select the year from the new screen that appears and you will see a list of that journal year's volumes and issue numbers.

U : Can you search by article title as well?

L : Yes, just type the title of the article in the search box of this page.

U : Do you also offer other medical journals?

L : We provide access to the full-text of approximately one thousand scholarly society journals online. About one hundred of them are related to medicine.

U : I see. I'll try it.

상황 9 　시범 서비스

U : 저는 물리학과 박사 과정의 학생인데, 전자저널에 대해서 문의할게 있습니다.

L1: 전자저널 관련한 질문은 저쪽에 앉아 계신 선생님에게 문의하시면 됩니다.

L2: 무슨 일로 오셨죠?

U : 어제 *Science* 전자저널에 접속해보니 사용자 인증을 요구해서요. 혹시 서비스가 중단된 건가요?

L : 죄송합니다. 4월 22일까지 이용하셨던 서비스는 시범 서비스라서 무료로 이용이 가능했던 것입니다.

U : 그럼 앞으로 이용할 수 없습니까?

L2: 아니요, 많은 이용자들의 요청이 있어서 현재 온라인 구독을 추진 중입니다.

U : 좋은 소식인데요. 그럼 언제쯤 이용이 가능할까요?

L2: 정확히 말씀 드리기는 어렵지만 2주 정도 후에 정식 서비스를 제공할 예정입니다. 진행사항은 홈페이지 게시판을 통해 공지하도록 하겠습니다.

U : 잘 알겠습니다. 인쇄저널은 어디에 있죠?

L2: 저쪽 코너를 돌아가시면 서가가 있는데, 쉽게 찾을 수 있을 것입니다.

U : 감사합니다.

Situation 9　Trial Services

U : I am a doctoral student in physics. I have questions about electronic journals.

L1 : The library staff behind that desk can answer your questions regarding electronic journals.

L2 : What can I do for you?

U : I had a problem accessing *Science* yesterday. Unexpectedly, it asked for authorization. Has the service been discontinued?

L2 : I am sorry. *Science* was a free trial version and it ended on April 22.

U : So, is it no longer available?

L2 : Not at present, but we are planning to subscribe to it online because many people have requested it.

U : That sounds good. When will I be able to use it?

L2 : I am not quite sure yet, but we can provide service in two weeks. We will make an announcement on our website.

U : Okay. How about print journals? Where can I find them?

L2 : Make a left at that corner, and you won't miss them.

U : Thank you.

상황 10 SSCI

U : 예전에 도서관 이용교육을 통해 SSCI라는 것이 있다고 들었는데, 사용을 하지 않다 보니 검색 방법이 잘 기억이 나지 않네요.

L : SSCI는 현재 Web 데이터베이스 또는 CD Net을 통해 이용이 가능합니다.

U : 거기까지는 저도 알고 있는데요, 첫 화면에서 어디로 가야 할지 알 수가 없습니다.

L : 1998년 이후의 SSCI 수록 논문 및 피인용 횟수에 관해서 검색하시려면 Web 데이터베이스 메뉴에서 이용하시면 됩니다.

U : 제가 찾고자 하는 자료는 1995년 자료입니다.

L : 1998년 이전자료는 CD Net 목록에서 SSCI를 선택하시면 됩니다.

U : 감사합니다. 검색 방법과 관련해서 좀 더 자세한 교육을 받을 수는 없나요?

L : 마침 내일 정기교육이 있군요. 도서관 홈페이지에서 교육참가 신청을 하시면 됩니다.

Situation 10  SSCI

U : I learned about the Social Science Citation Index (SSCI) during a library instruction class some time ago. However, I have not used it for a while and have forgotten how.

L : You can use SSCI through the web database or CD Net.

U : Yes, but I don't know what to do on the first screen.

L : If you want to search for articles and citations data published after 1998, use the web database.

U : I am looking for resources from 1995.

L : Use CD Net for data published prior to 1998.

U : Okay. Are there any instructional courses to learn more about searching databases?

L : We have a class tomorrow. You can sign up for the class from our library website.

상황 11 　전자저널 검색

U : 안녕하세요? *Journal of Psychosomatic research*를 보려고 하는데요.

L : 온라인으로 검색해 보셨나요?

U : 의학도서관에 자료가 있다고 나오는데, 그럼 의학도서관까지 가야 하나요?

L : 항상 그렇진 않습니다. 전자저널로도 이용 가능한지 확인해 봅시다.

U : 그래요? 어떻게요?

L : 모니터를 봐 주시겠습니까? 여기에 전자저널이라는 버튼이 있죠? 버튼을 누르시면 원문이 제공되는 전자저널로 연결됩니다.

U : 집에서도 전자저널을 이용할 수 있습니까?

L : 물론입니다. 현재 한국대학교 재학생, 직원, 교수라면 누구라도 교외접속을 통해 거의 대부분의 도서관 전자자원들을 이용할 수 있습니다.

U : 어떻게 하면 되죠?

L : 자료검색 또는 데이터베이스에 접속하기 전에 도서관 홈페이지에 로그인만 하면 됩니다. 캠퍼스 밖에서 도서관 홈페이지에 로그인함과 동시에 도서관 프록시 서버에도 로그인 됩니다. 이는 도서관 홈페이지 링크를 통해서 해당 전자자원에 접속하거나, 프록시 서버에 캐시된 링크를 사용해야 한다는 것을 의미합니다. 만약 브라우저 세션이 새로 시작되면, 다시 로그인을 해야 할 수도 있습니다.

Situation 11 Electronic Journals

U : Hi, I'd like to find the *Journal of Psychosomatic Research*.

L : Did you try searching our online catalog?

U : It says that the Medical Library has the journal. Should I go there?

L : Not necessarily. Let's check whether an electronic version is available for this journal first.

U : Really? How do I do that?

L : Please look at the monitor. You can find an 'Electronic Journal' button on the result screen. Click the button and you'll see the full-text of the journal.

U : Can I use it from home?

L : Yes. License agreements for most of the library's electronic resources permit access from off-campus to currently enrolled Hankook University students, staff and faculty.

U : How do I use it?

L : Just log in to the library website before accessing your database or online catalog. When you log in to the library website from outside the campus, you are simultaneously logged in to our proxy server. This means you must access the resource through the link in the library website or use a proxy link. You may need to log in again if you start a new browser session.

상황 12　♥ 접속이 제한된 전자 저널

U : *Nature*지에 대해 온라인 검색이 되지 않네요. 상세정보를 보면 검색이 원문
　　보기가 가능하다고 나오는데, 클릭하면 볼 수가 없어요.

L : 지금 계신 곳이 어디죠?

U : 전산실습실에 있는데요. 여기서는 전문을 볼 수 없습니까?

L : *Nature*지 같은 경우는 교내라고 하더라도 일부 제한된 곳에서만 볼 수 있습
　　니다. 현재 5개 PC에서만 검색할 수 있습니다.

U : 그럼 어디로 가야 하지요?

L : 도서관 전자정보실의 학술정보검색전용 PC와 의료원 도서실 등에서 검색
　　이 가능합니다.

U : 보통 다른 저널들은 교내 어디서나 접근이 가능한 것으로 알고 있습니다.
　　이 저널은 많은 사람들이 이용하는 저널일 텐데, 상당히 불편하네요.

L : 예산과 관련된 문제여서 보통 다른 저널처럼 구독하기에는 어려운 점이 있
　　습니다. *Nature*지 외에도 이러한 저널이 몇 종 더 있는데, 내년에는 좀 더
　　많은 곳에서 이용할 수 있도록 노력하겠습니다.

Situation 12 Electronic Resources with Limited Access

U : I cannot view the full-text for *Nature*. On the instruction page, it says that I should be able to get the full-text if Iclick the button.

L : Where are you trying to access online journals?

U : I am at the computer lab. Is that a problem?

L : Even though you find the full-text of *Nature* available online, it is limited to certain locations on campus. Only five PCs can access *Nature*.

U : Where are the five PCs?

L : Some are at the hospital library and there are some PCs strictly designated for searching scientific journals in the Information Commons.

U : We usually can use the online full-text service for many other journals anywhere on campus. *Nature* is a popular one, but it's very in convenient to use.

L : It's a budget-related problem. We have some other journals besides *Nature* with limited access. We will try to improve this situation next year.

상황 13 　♥ 전자저널 접속에러

U : 잠깐만 여기 좀 도와주세요.

L : 네, 무슨 일이신가요?

U : *Harvard Journal of Law & Public Policy*란 저널의 한 기사를 찾고 있습니다. 그런데 전자저널 페이지에서 찾아 접속했더니 에러 메시지가 뜨는데요.

L : 출판사로부터 현재 시스템 업그레이드로 인해 일부 저널에 대해 서비스가 어렵다는 통보를 받았습니다. 홈페이지 공지사항을 통해서 접속장애에 대한 내용을 공지했는데 보지 못하신 모양이군요.

U : 네. 그럼 언제부터 이용이 가능할까요?

L : 4월 28일 오후 1시 이후부터 이용이 가능합니다.

U : 알겠습니다.

Situation 13 Connection Errors for Electronic Journals

U : Would you please help me?

L : Sure. How can I help you?

U : I am looking for an article from the *Harvard Journal of Law & Public Policy* but there is an error message on the Electronic Journals page.

L : We received a notice from the vendor regarding some technical difficulties for certain journals due to its system upgrade. You seem to have missed the announcement on our website.

U : When is it going to be back up?

L : Please try after 1 p.m. on April 28.

U : OK.

상황 14　　　♥ 학위논문 원문검색 1

L : 네, 중앙도서관 전자정보실입니다.

U : 여보세요? 여기는 여수인데요, 그곳 학위논문을 좀 보고 싶습니다.

L : 원문제공이 되는지 검색해 보셨습니까?

U : 아니요, 이곳에서도 원문을 볼 수 있는 건가요?

L : 네, 일부 논문에 한해서 외부에서도 원문제공이 가능합니다. 어떤 논문을 찾으시나요?

U : 노인복지에 관한 논문을 찾고 있어요.

L : 잠시만 기다리세요. 검색결과가 꽤 되는군요. 직접 한번 검색해 보시겠습니까?

U : 그렇게 하지요. 어떻게 하면 될까요?

L : 검색에서 '학위논문'을 선택하고 키워드를 "노인복지"로 넣어 검색해 보세요. 그리고 검색결과가 나오면 "원문보기"라는 버튼을 누르세요.

U : 감사합니다. 한 번 해보고 모르는 점이 있으면 다시 전화 드리겠습니다.

Situation 14　Full-text Theses 1

L : Hello, this is the Information Commons at the Central Library.

U : Hello. I am calling from YeoSu. I'd like to use theses and dissertations from your university.

L : Did you check whether you can view the full-text?

U : No, I did not. Can I view the full-text from my location?

L : Yes. You can. We provide some online full-text theses that people outside campus can have access to. Which theses are you looking for?

U : I am looking for theses regarding senior welfare.

L : Wait a minute⋯ I see quite a few. Do you want to try your own search?

U : Yes. How can I do that?

L : First, select 'Thesis' in the search box and type 'senior welfare' for the keyword. From your results screen, click the 'Full-text' button.

U : Thank you. If I have a problem, I will call you again for your help.

상황 15 학위논문 원문검색2

L : 네, 중앙도서관 전자정보실입니다.

U : 안녕하세요? 조금 전에 전화했었는데 원문보기가 잘 안돼서요.

L : 혹시 원문 뷰어를 설치하셨나요?

U : 아니오. 그것 때문에 볼 수 없었군요. 어디서 다운로드 받을 수 있나요?

L : 도서관 홈페이지의 뷰어 다운로드에서 받아서 설치하시면 됩니다. 지금 한 번 해 보시겠어요?

U : 네, 찾았습니다. 지금 설치하겠습니다. 잠시만요. 아, 이제 되네요. 원문이 보이는군요. 감사합니다.

L : 원하시는 논문은 찾으셨나요?

U : 네, 찾았습니다. 이것을 다운로드 하면 되겠군요.

L : 죄송하지만 다운로드는 되지 않습니다. 화면에서 보시고 필요한 부분만 인쇄하세요.

U : 그렇군요. 도와주셔서 감사합니다.

L : 별말씀을요. 언제든지 도움이 필요하면 연락 주십시오.

Situation 15  Full-text Theses 2

L : Hello. This is the Information Commons at the Central Library.

U : Hello, I made a phone call a little while ago but I still cannot get the full-text.

L : Did you install the full-text image viewer?

U : Oh, I did not. That is the problem, isn't it? How can I install it?

L : You can download the viewer from our library website and install it. Would you like to try it now?

U : Yes. I got it. Wait a second. (After a little while) Wow, now I can see the full-text. Thank you.

L : Did you find what you were looking for?

U : Yes. I will download it.

L : I am sorry but you cannot download it. You can only print the part you need.

U : I see. Thank you for your help.

L : You're welcome. Give me a call whenever you need my help.

상황 16 　　학위논문 원문검색 3-국회도서관소장

L : 자료를 찾는데 어려움이 있으세요?

U : 예. 다름이 아니라 국회에서 제공하는 학위논문을 보고 싶은데 어떻게 해야 될지 모르겠습니다.

L : 국회에서 제공하는 학위논문은 전자정보실에 가셔야 보실 수 있습니다.

　　(전자정보실에서)

U : 국회학위논문 원문을 보려고 왔는데요?

L : 그래요. 그럼 이쪽으로 오시겠습니까?

U : 국회학위논문 원문보기는 다른 곳에서 볼 수가 없나 보죠?

L : 예. 아직까지는 협약에 의해서 지정된 PC에서만 원문보기가 가능합니다.

U : 출력은 가능하죠?

L : 물론이죠. 출력비는 장당 50원입니다.

U : 고맙습니다.

L : 검색하시다가 어려운 것이 있으시면 말씀하세요.

Situation 16 · Full-text Theses 3–National Assembly Library

L : Are you having any problems finding materials?

U : Yes, I am. I'd like to use the thesis database provided by the National Assembly Library, but I do not know how.

L : You need to go to the Information Commons to use the NAL database.

(In the Information Commons)

U : I'd like to use the National Assembly Library's full-text thesis database.

L : Okay. Please come this way.

U : Is this the only place I can use it?

L : Yes. Due to the contract, the database is only available on designated computers.

U : Can I print the materials out?

L : Of course you can. Each page costs 50 won.

U : Thank you.

L : Feel free to talk to me anytime if you are having difficulties with a search.

상황 17 　🗨 해외 석박사 학위논문 1-PQDT

U : 해외박사학위 논문을 찾는데 어떻게 해야 하죠?

L : 해외박사학위 논문은 PQDT서비스를 통해 검색 및 제공이 가능합니다.

U : 좀 더 자세히 설명해 주시겠습니까?

L : PQDT서비스는 과거 CD-ROM으로 제공되어왔던 DAO(Dissertation Abstracts Ondisc)의 web 버전으로서 북미지역 및 유럽 등 전세계 주요 1,000여 개 대학에서 수여된 석박사학위 논문의 서지정보 및 초록을 제공합니다.

U : 모든 자료에 대해 Full-Text제공이 되나요?

L : 1997년 이후의 논문에 대하여는 PDF 파일형태로 논문의 원본을 인터넷상에서 직접 주문을 할 수 있을 뿐 만 아니라, 논문을 다운로드 받으실 수 있습니다.

U : 검색은 어떻게 하죠?

L : PQDT 검색방법에는 Basic Search와 Advanced Search가 있는데, Basic Search는 검색 필드를 선택하신 후 검색하시면 됩니다. Advanced Search는 Basic Search 기능 외에 Query Box를 이용한 조합 검색이 가능합니다.

Situation 17　Overseas Theses 1—PQDT

U : How can I find overseas doctoral dissertations?

L : You can find them using the ProQuest Dissertations and Theses Service.

U : Would you please explain what the PQDT Service is?

L : The PQDT Service is a web version of the CD-ROM DAO (Dissertation Abstracts Ondisc). It provides bibliographic information and abstracts of masters and doctoral theses from about one thousand major universities in North America and Europe.

U : Are they all available as full-texts?

L : For theses published after 1997, you can either download full-texts or order them as PDF files on the internet.

U : How can I search them?

L : There are basic and advanced search methods. In basic search, you select a search field. In advanced search, you can combine different fields using the Query Box.

상황 18 　해외 석박사 학위논문 2-DDOD

U : PQDT에서 제가 찾고자 하는 논문이 없는데요?

L : DDOD(Digital Dissertations On Demand) 서비스에서도 검색해 보셨나요?

U : DDOD서비스에 대해서도 설명해주세요.

L : DDOD 서비스는 US News & World Report 와 The Gourman Report 등의 권위 있는 대학 평가기관에서 인정하고 있는 각 학문 분야별 'Top Ranking School'의 박사학위논문들을 선별하여 제공하고 있습니다.

U : DDOD 서비스를 이용하고 싶은데 특별한 절차나 방법이 필요합니까?

L : DDOD 서비스는 KERIS에서 운영하는 RISS4U.net 회원들을 대상으로 한 서비스이기 때문에 회원 등록 후 이용이 가능합니다.

U : 감사합니다.

Situation 18   Overseas Theses 2-DDOD

U : I couldn't find the thesis I am looking for in PQDT.

L : Have you tried Digital Dissertations On Demand (DDOD) as well?

U : What is DDOD?

L : The DDOD service provides doctoral theses from top ranking schools in each subject area, assessed by such publications as *US News & World Report* and the *Gourman Report*.

U : How can I use the DDOD Service?

L : Since it is available only to members of Korea Education and Research Information Service (KERIS), you need to register at RISS4U.net, which is a service provided by KERIS.

U : I see. Thank you.

상황 19 ♥ 학위논문 원문구축 방법

U : 디지털 원문 데이터베이스는 주로 어떤 자료들을 대상으로 구축하십니까?

L : 도서관에서는 학위논문을 우선적으로 디지털화하고 있습니다. 대상 자료를 수집하기가 쉽기 때문이죠.

U : 책을 스캔해서 이미지를 만드나요?

L : 과거에 수집한 자료들은 그렇게 하기도 합니다. 하지만 요즘에는 논문을 책과 더불어 문서파일로 제출 받기 때문에 원문DB작성이 더 쉬워졌습니다.

U : 어떤 방식으로 원문DB를 구축하고 계신가요?

L : 문서파일을 중심으로 실제 책과 비교를 통해 검증한 후 PDF형식 등으로 변환하여 서버로 업로드합니다.

U : 검증이라면?

L : 문서파일의 내용이 책자형태로 된 논문과 페이지, 삽입된 그림, 목차 등이 일치하는지를 확인하는 것입니다.

U : 검색은 어떻게 합니까?

L : 원문 파일을 서버로 업로드할 때 메타데이터를 생성하고 초록도 별도로 저장합니다. 이들을 대상으로 학위논문 검색을 제공하고 있습니다.

U : 감사합니다. 많은 도움이 되었습니다.

Situation 19   Full-text Theses Databases

U : Which materials get prioritized to become digitally available for full-text service?

L : We digitize our university's own theses first because it is more convenient to collect them than any other material.

U : Do you scan them?

L : We scan old ones retroactively. Current theses are, however, submitted in both hard copies and computer text files, so it is much easier to build a full-text database.

U : Can you explain the process in detail?

L : We compare the digital content with the hard copy, then transfer to PDF format and load them onto a server.

U : How do you compare them?

L : We check the tables of content, illustrations and pages of the file to be certain they match with those of the printed copy.

U : How can I search them?

L : The full-text theses are loaded onto the server along with metadata and abstracts.

U : Thank you. That was very helpful.

상황 20　연속간행물실 안내

U : 중앙도서관에는 국외 잡지가 얼마나 있습니까?

L : 이 곳에는 인문과학과 사회과학분야 주제의 국외 잡지가 700종 있습니다.

U : 전자저널은 얼마나 됩니까?

L : 전부 5,400종의 전자저널을 구독하고 있습니다.

U : 연속간행물의 정리는 어떻게 합니까?

L : DDC 분류법을 사용하고 있습니다.

U : 아, 그 듀이 십진분류법을 말하는군요. 그런데 이전에 있던 목록함이 안 보이네요.

L : 예, 데이터가 모두 컴퓨터 시스템에 입력되어 이제는 PC로 검색하게 되었습니다.

U : 그렇군요. 연속간행물은 어떻게 관리 합니까?

L : 신간이 입수되면 바로 기록을 하고 신착서가에 알파벳순으로 배열합니다. 일정한 시간이 지나면 등록하고 분류를 하고 서고에 넣습니다.

U : 그래서 이곳 신착서가에는 과월호가 없군요. 과월호는 어떻게 보죠?

L : 먼저 검색하여 청구기호로 서가 위치를 확인한 다음 서고에서 직접 자료를 찾아보면 됩니다.

Information Retrieval • 검색

Situation 20  Periodicals Room

U : How many Western journals do you have here?

L : We have seven hundred Western journals in the humanities and social sciences in the Central Library.

U : How many electronic journals do you have?

L : We have about 5,400 e-journals.

U : How do you classify serials?

L : We classify serials using the DDC system.

U : Are you talking about the Dewey Decimal Classification system? I don't see the card catalog that used to be here.

L : You can find them on the computer since we keep all data electronically now.

U : I see. How do you manage so much data?

L : We check in new serials as they arrive, and then they are arranged in the new arrivals stacks alphabetically. After a period of time in the new arrivals section, we register, classify, and shelve them in the regular stack.

U : That's why the past issues are not in the new arrivals area. How do I find them?

L : Search for the call number first and then go to the stacks.

상황 21 　💬 신착저널 이용

U : 제가 *International Marketing Review* 라는 잡지를 찾고 있거든요. 서가에 가보았는데, 제가 찾고 있는 해당 권호 전체가 없어요.

L : 찾고 있는 자료의 권호가 어떻게 되죠?

U : 예, 21권 2호입니다. 교수님이 이번 과제에 참고하라고 하신 자료인데, 아마 다른 친구들도 찾고 있을 겁니다.

L : 알겠습니다. 확인해 보죠.
　　찾고 계신 저널의 21권은 2012년도 자료군요. 최근 자료는 신착 서가에 따로 배열되어 있습니다.

U : 왜 이렇게 하시죠? 한 군데 모아 두면 편할 것 같은데요.

L : 저널은 신간이 많이 이용되는 자료이기 때문에 신간 이용이 편리하도록 가까운 곳에 모아 두고, 상대적으로 이용률이 낮은 구간은 서고에 두어 도서관 공간을 효율적으로 활용하도록 한 것입니다.

U : 아, 그렇군요.

Situation 21  Current Periodicals

U : I am looking for the journal *International Marketing Review*. But I cannot find the volume I am looking for in the stacks.

L : Which volumes are you looking for?

U : Volume 21 number 2. My professor recommended it for a class project. I guess all my classmates are looking for the same journal.

L : I see. I'll check.

The volume you are looking for is from 2012. The most recent issues are in the New Journals Section.

U : Wouldn't it be more convenient if you kept them in the same place together?

L : Current issues are kept in a more easily accessible place separated from the old issues. It's more efficient that way, since new journal issues are far more popular than old ones.

U : Ah, I got it.

상황 22 　제본저널 이용

U : 이 잡지의 과월호는 어디에 있습니까?

L : 1년 정도 지난 자료는 제본되어 서고에 있습니다.

U : 제본하지 않아도 되지 않나요?

L : 잡지는 얇기 때문에 관리와 이용에 편하도록 제본합니다.

U : 과월호는 대출할 수도 있나요?

L : 아니요, 신착과 마찬가지로 열람과 복사만 할 수 있습니다.

U : 복사는 어디서 할 수 있습니까?

L : 카드 복사기가 자료실과 서고 안에 있습니다.

U : 그런데 이 저널이 서고 어디에 있는지 잘 모르겠는데요.

L : 청구기호가 'P 020.5 도서관' 이니까 서고 2층 중간에 있습니다. 서고 안에
　　자료배치도가 있으니까 그걸 보면 쉽게 찾으실 수 있을 것입니다.

U : 고맙습니다.

Information Retrieval • 검색

Situation 22 — Bound Journals

U : Where are the back issues of this magazine?

L : We bind past issues that are older than one year and keep them in the stacks.

U : Is there any problem if they are not bound?

L : We have to bind them for preservation and ease of management.

U : Can I check them out?

L : No, you can only use them in the library or copy them like current journals.

U : Where can I make copies?

L : There are copy machines in each subject room and in the stacks.

U : By the way, I don't know where I can find this journal in the stacks.

L : The call number is 'P 020.5 도서관' and it should be in the middle of the second floor stacks. Please check a 'Stacks Map' and it will help you find the journal easily.

U : Thank you.

상황 23　　💬 목차정보 제공 서비스

U : 안녕하세요? 저는 사학과 김경희 교수의 조교인데요, 교수님께서 이 자료
　　를 복사해 오라고 하셔서 왔습니다. 어디서 이 자료를 찾을 수 있지요?

L : *History and Theory*이군요. 오른쪽에 있는 신착서가에 있습니다.

U : 그 책을 잘 기억하고 계시네요.

L : 교수님께서 목차정보 제공 서비스를 신청해 놓으셔서 어제 목차를 복사해
　　서 보내드렸거든요.

U : 그렇군요. 목차정보제공서비스 등록은 어떻게 하죠? 학부생도 가능한가요?

L : 예, 홈페이지를 통해 등록할 수 있습니다.

U : 이메일로 전송 받을 수도 있나요?

L : 일부 전자저널의 경우는 가능합니다. 예를 들어, *Emerald Journals* 같은 전
　　자저널 플랫폼에 들어가면, TOC Alert 같은 서비스가 제공됩니다.

U : 그게 뭐죠?

L : 지시에 따라 Alert 시스템을 등록해 놓으면 저널이 업데이트 될 때마다 정
　　기적으로 목차를 제공받을 수 있는 서비스입니다.

U : 그런 게 있었군요. 어떻게 신청하면 되나요?

L : 여기 양식에 성명, 소속, 학번, 연락처와 수령 주소를 기입해 주세요.

Situation 23  TOC Service

U : I'm a TA in the history department. Professor Kyunghee Kim asked me to copy some materials. Where can I find this book?

L : Oh, you are looking for *History and Theory*. This book is in the New Arrivals Section on your right.

U : Why do you know that so well?

L : Since Professor Kim requested TOC service, I send him copies of tables of contents whenever we get new materials.

U : I see. Can undergraduates request the service?

L : Yes, you can register for the service through our website.

U : Can I receive the service by e-mail?

L : It is possible for some e-journals. For example, TOC Alert is available on *Emerald Journals*.

U : What is that?

L : A service that provides tables of contents regularly whenever new journals of your choice come in.

U : That's fantastic. How can I apply for that?

L : Please fill out your name, your department, ID number, contact information and the address where you want to receive the information.

상황 24 💬 도서관 이용자교육 신청

U : 이용자교육을 신청하고 싶은데요. 어떻게 해야 하죠?

L : 이용자교육은 정기교육과 맞춤교육이 있습니다. 홈페이지를 통해서 신청 하실 수 있습니다.

U : 정기교육과 맞춤교육의 차이점이 있나요?

L : 정기교육은 미리 계획된 교육과정을 월, 분기 별로 진행하는 교육으로, 주 로 도서관 자원과 서비스와 관련된 주제입니다. 만약 특정 주제나 과제해 결을 위한 맞춤교육을 원한다면, 그 요구에 부합하는 교육프로그램을 개설 할 수도 있습니다.

U : 그렇군요. 어떻게 신청해야 되죠?

L : 도서관 홈페이지 또는 전화로 신청할 수 있습니다. 자세한 교육일정을 확 인 하시려면 담당 주제사서에게 문의하시기 바랍니다.

U : 감사합니다.

Situation 24 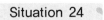 Library Instruction Programs

U : I'd like to apply for library instructional classes. What should I do?

L : We have regular classes and specially customized classes.

U : What's the difference?

L : We offer regular monthly and quarterly instructions with a predesigned curriculum, mainly about the use of library resources and services. If you would like something tailored for your specific subject or assignment, we may design a program tailored to your specific needs.

U : That's very convenient. How can I apply?

L : You can apply via our library website or by phone. To schedule a library session, please contact the librarian responsible for your subject area.

U : Thank you.

상황 25　　스캔

U : 『한국동식물도감』을 검색해서 찾았습니다. 원하는 페이지를 스캔할 수 있습니까?

L : 참고열람실 스캐너를 이용하시면 됩니다.

U : 스캐너를 사용해 본 적이 없는데요.

L : 스캔할 분량이 어느 정도 되죠?

U : 30페이지 정도 될 것 같습니다.

L : 그러면 이미지 스캐닝하는 방법을 시범으로 보여드리겠습니다.

　　자료를 스캐너에 올려놓고 스캔 버튼만 누르면 됩니다. 스캔한 자료를 저장 하려면 USB 메모리가 필요합니다.

U : 쉽게 이용할 수 있네요. 감사합니다. (잠시 후) 스캔작업을 모두 끝냈습니다. 그런데 파일 크기가 너무 커서 USB 메모리 용량이 부족합니다. 파일을 제 스마트폰으로 옮겨주실 수 있나요?

L : 그럼요, 스마트폰을 주시겠어요?

U : 감사합니다.

Situation 25 Scanning

U : I found the Illustrated Guide to Korean Plants and Animals. Can I scan the pages I need?

L : You can use the scanner in the reference room.

U : But I've never used a scanner before.

L : How many pages do you need?

U : About thirty.

L : I'll show you. Put your book on the scanner, and press the Scan button. You will need a USB memory stick to save your scanned documents and images.

U : That's easier than I thought. Thank you. (After a little while) I finished scanning, but the size of the files is too large for me to save on my USB memory stick. Is it possible to transfer the files to my smart phone?

L : Of course, just give me your smart phone and I'll take care of it.

U : Thank you.

상황 26 　♥ 노트북 사용

U : 실례합니다. 도서관에서 노트북을 사용할 수 있는 곳을 찾습니다.

L : 도서관 로비에 노트북을 사용할 수 있는 시설이 있습니다. 전원과 랜 포트가 있으니까 그곳에서 사용하시면 됩니다.

U : 이전에 사용해 본 적이 없기 때문에 사용방법을 모르겠습니다.

L : 제가 알려드리겠습니다. 절 따라오세요. (사용방법을 가르쳐 준다)

U : 사용 방법을 알겠네요. 감사합니다.

L : 이제 인터넷 접속은 되었습니다. 원문을 보려면 도서관 홈페이지에서 원문 뷰어와 CD Net 플러그인을 다운받아 설치하세요.

U : 그러면 이제는 원문까지 바로 볼 수 있는 겁니까?

L : 네, 도서관에서 제공하는 모든 데이터베이스들을 원문까지 제대로 검색해 보실 수 있습니다.

Situation 26  Using Laptops

U : I'm looking for a place where I can use my laptop computer in the library.

L : There are electrical outlets and LAN ports in the lobby.

U : Well, I don't know how to hook it up since I've never used it before.

L : I'll do it for you. Would you follow me please?

U : I got it. Thank you.

L : You're now connected to the internet. You need to install the viewer for full-text and the CD Net plug-in from our library website.

U : Is it now possible to view the full-text?

L : Yes it is. You can now use our online full-text databases with your laptop.

상황 27　　대학교 논문집

U : 대학에서 발생되는 논문집의 기사내용을 내용을 알고 싶습니다.

L : 인용정보를 가지고 있나요?

U : 한국대학의『여성문제 연구』에 실린 특정 교수님의 논문을 찾고 있습니다.

L : 현재 타 대학교 논문에 대한 기사색인은 하고 있지 않아서 검색이 되지 않습니다. 다른 대학에서 발간한 논문집의 기사정보는 국회도서관에서 발행하는 정기간행물 기사색인을 참조하시면 되는데, 저희 홈페이지에서 바로 연결해 보실 수 있습니다.

U : 잘 알겠습니다. 다른 대학 논문집은 어디에서 열람할 수 있죠?

L : 대학논문집 코너에 가면 볼 수 있습니다. 배열은 대학명의 가나다순으로 배열되어 있습니다.

Situation 27　University Research Papers

U : I want to search research papers published by universities.

L : Do you have a citation?

U : I'm looking for a paper in the *Studies of Women's Issues* by Hankook University.

L : You cannot search articles from other universities' publications on our system because we only index our own publications. For other universities' publications, you need to search the Periodicals Index of the National Assembly Library. You can find its information through a link on our website.

U : I see. Where can I read other universities' papers?

L : Go to the Universities Publications section. They are arranged alphabetically in Korean by name of university.

상황 28 　　　신문자료 이용

U : 신문은 어디에 있나요?

L : 어떤 신문을 찾으시는데요?

U : 한겨레 신문을 찾습니다.

L : 오늘 신문은 도서관 1층 로비에 있는 신문 코너에서 보시면 됩니다.

U : 그곳에 The Korea Herald나 The New York Times도 있나요?

L : *The Korea Times*는 신문 코너에 있고, *The New York Times*는 연속간행물실에 있습니다.

U : 작년 신문도 볼 수 있나요?

L : 지난 신문은 대학원도서관에 가셔서 보시면 됩니다.

U : 대학원 도서관은 어디에 있나요?

L : 중앙도서관 옆, 대학원 건물 2층에 있습니다.

U : 왜 신문을 한 군데 놓지 않고 따로 두나요?

L : 신문 코너에 있는 신문은 단순히 열람을 위한 것이라서 시간이 지나면 폐기합니다. 대학원도서관에 있는 신문은 지난 신문을 제본하여 보존하고 있으며, 외국신문은 저널처럼 체크인과 클레임 처리를 합니다. 중앙도서관 2층 전자정보실에서는 터치스크린 키오스크를 통해 전자신문도 읽을 수 있습니다.

U : 잘 알겠습니다.

Situation 28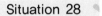

U : Where are the newspapers?

L : Which papers are you looking for?

U : I am looking for *The Hankyoreh*.

L : Today's papers are in the Newspaper corner of the first floor lobby.

U : Do you also have *The Korea Herald* or *The New York Times*?

L : *The Korea Herald* is in the News paper corner and *The New York Times* is in the Periodicals Room.

U : Do you have last year's newspapers as well?

L : Past issues are at the Graduate Library.

U : Where is the Graduate Library?

L : It is on the second floor of the Graduate School building next to the main library.

U : Why don't you keep all the newspapers together?

L : We discard newspapers in the Newspaper corner after a set period of usage. Ones in the Graduate Library are bound to be kept. We check in and classify foreign newspapers as journals. We also offer touch screen kiosks so that users can read electronic newspapers. Those are in the Information Commons on the 2nd floor of the main library.

U : I see.

상황 29   ♥ 마이크로 자료 이용

U : 1930년대 동아일보 기사를 찾는데, 혹시 소장하고 있습니까?

L : 1930년대 동아일보는 마이크로 자료로 보관하고 있습니다. 몇 년도 자료가 필요하시죠?

U : 1993년 자료가 필요합니다.

L : 잠시만 기다려 주세요. 마이크로 자료 보관함에서 찾아 드리겠습니다. 여기 있습니다. 좌측에 있는 판독기를 사용하시면 됩니다.

U : 판독기 사용법을 알려주시겠어요?

L : 이쪽 홈에 필름을 넣고 스위치를 켜세요. 그리고 화살표 버튼을 누르시면 됩니다.

U : 복사 하려면 어떻게 합니까?

L : 원하는 화면에서 복사 버튼을 누르세요.

U : 감사합니다.

Situation 29 Microfilms

U : Do you have the *Dong-A Ilbo* from the 1930's?

L : We have the 1930's *Dong-A Ilbo* on microfilm. What year are you looking for?

U : 1933.

L : Could you wait while I get the films for you? (After a little while) Here they are. You could use a reader on the left there.

U : Could you please show me how to use it?

L : Insert the end of the film in this groove and turn on this switch. Press the arrow buttons to move the film.

U : How can I make copies?

L : Press the Print button to print the screen.

U : Thank you.

상황 30   ♥ 제본중인 저널 이용

U : 도서상태에 '제본중'이라는 메시지가 나오는데, 무슨 뜻이죠?

L : 현재 제본 작업 중이라서 이용할 수가 없다는 뜻입니다.

U : 그럼 언제쯤 이용할 수 있습니까?

L : 3주 후면 이용이 가능합니다.

U : 다른 이용방법은 없나요?

L : 원문복사서비스를 신청하시면 보실 수 있습니다.

U : 알겠습니다. 신청하도록 하겠습니다.

Situation 30 Journals in Binding Process

U : What 's the message 'In-binding' mean?

L : The message means you cannot use the materials because they are in the bindery.

U : When can I use them?

L : In about three weeks.

U : Is there any way to access them?

L : You could request document delivery service.

U : Thank you. I'll do that.

상황 31 분관 소장 자료

U : 검색해 보니 의학도서관 소장자료라고 나오는데, 어떻게 하면 이용할 수 있습니까?

L : 소장위치에 의학도서관이라고 나오면 중앙도서관이 아닌 의학 도서관에 소장되어 있다는 것을 의미합니다. 우리는 4개의 분관 도서관이 있는데, 의학도서관은 이 중 하나로서 의학, 약학, 간호학 분야의 자료를 소장하고 있습니다.

U : 해당 주제의 저널도 분관 도서관에 소장되어 있습니까?

L : 물론입니다.

U : 중앙도서관에서도 중복 소장하는 게 좋지 않을까요? 중앙도서관에서도 소장하고 있으면, 이용자들이 분관까지 갈 필요가 없을 텐데요.

L : 그럴 수 있으면 좋겠습니다만, 현재는 예산과 공간의 제약으로 인해 어렵습니다.

U : 잘 알겠습니다.

Situation 31 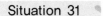 Branch Library Holdings

U : I searched the online catalog and some books indicate 'Medical Library' for their location. How can I use them?

L : If the location says 'Medical Library,' it means it is not held by the Central Library but by the medical branch library. We have four branch libraries and the Medical Library is one of them. It has books on medicine, pharmacy and nursing.

U : Are journals and magazines held by the branch libraries?

L : Yes.

U : Why don't you keep duplicates in the Central Library? If there's a copy in the Central Library, people don't have to walk all the way to the branch library.

L : That would be ideal, but we have limited budget and space.

U : Right. I see.

상황 32 　　 청구기호

U : 청구기호가 '154.63 F889프'이라고 나왔는데, 이 기호는 어떤 의미이며 어떻게 찾아야 할까요?

L : 청구기호는 자료가 주제에 따라 서가에 배열될 수 있도록 부여된 기호입니다. 청구기호는 '별치기호', '분류기호', '저자기호', '저작기호' 등으로 구성되어 있으며, '145.63'은 분류기호로 '꿈'이라는 주제를 의미합니다.

U : 체계적이군요. 그럼 '154.63' 분류기호가 붙어있는 서가에 가면 이 책을 찾을 수 있겠군요.

L : 네. 자료는 서가에서 청구기호에 따라 좌에서 우로, 그 다음 위에서 아래로 배열되어 있기 때문에 쉽게 찾을 수 있을 겁니다.

Situation 32  Call numbers

U : The system says that the call number is '154.63 F889 ㅍ.' What does that
mean and where can I find it?

L : Each book gets a unique call number for shelving according to its subject.
Call numbers consist of location code, classification number, author
number and work number. The notation '154.63' is a classification
number for dreams.

U : That's a good system. So I can find the book if I go to the stack labeled
with call number '154.63'?

L : Yes, you can. You can easily find materials in the stacks, as they are
arranged sequentially from left to right and from top to bottom.

상황 33 ꞏ 기타 참고질의 1

U : 법학 관련 자료를 찾고 싶습니다.

L : 구체적으로 주제를 말씀해주세요.

U : 문화재보호법 2011년 개정안이 필요합니다.

L : 온라인목록에서 검색해 보셨어요?

U : 검색시스템을 이용해보지 않아서 어렵습니다. 도와주시겠습니까?

L : 물론입니다. 키워드 검색을 이용해서 문화재보호법을 검색해보겠습니다.
검색결과가 없는데 이번엔 『대한민국 현행법령집』을 검색해보죠. 여기에
문화재보호법이 수록되어 있을 것입니다. 검색결과 청구기호는 'R340.9151
한17ㄷ' 입니다.

U : 감사합니다. 그런데 문화재보호법은 있는데 2011년 개정안밖에 없군요.

L : 그렇습니까? 그러면 웹 데이터베이스를 통해서 최근 개정안을 검색해 보도
록 하죠. 법누리에서 제공하는 대한민국 현행법령집 온라인판을 이용해 검
색하겠습니다.

U : 2011년 개정안이 있습니까?

L : 예, 검색용PC를 이용해서 대한민국 현행법령 웹 데이터베이스에서 검색하
는 방법을 가르쳐 드리겠습니다.

U : 감사합니다.

Situation 33 Other Questions 1

U : I am looking for materials on law.

L : Do you have something specific in mind?

U : I need 2011's revised proposal of the Cultural Properties Protection Law.

L : Did you search the online catalog?

U : I have never used it before. Would you show me how to use it?

L : OK. I will search the Cultural Properties Protection Law by keyword.
There are no results with this search. Let's try the complete collection of
current laws and regulations, *Taehan Minguk hyonhaeng pomnyongjip*.
This should cover the Cultural Properties Protection Law. I found it in
'R340.9151 한173ㄷ.'

U : Great, but do you have the most current proposal?

L : Most current? Then let's try the online database 'Bubnuri' for the most
current proposal.

U : Is 2011's revised proposal there?

L : Yes. I will show you how to use this web database.

U : Thank you.

상황 34 　 기타 참고질의 2

U : 실험기자재 관련 설명서를 찾고 있습니다.

L : 좀더 구체적으로 검색 주제를 말씀해 주시겠습니까?

U : 생물학 관련 실험서를 보고 싶습니다.

L : 생물학실험을 주제로 검색한 결과『일반생물학실험』이라는 자료가 있습니다. 청구기호는 '574.028 일42'입니다. 자연과학 자료실로 가셔서 해당 청구기호를 찾아 열람하시면 됩니다.

U : 감사합니다. (잠시 후) 그런데 이 자료에는 제가 원하는 전기영동에 관한 실험자료가 미비합니다. 좀더 구체적으로 설명된 자료는 없을까요?

L : 전기영동으로 검색한 결과『전기영동실험법』이란 일본어자료와 학위논문이 있습니다.

U : 학위논문을 보고 싶은데요.

L : 학위논문실은 3층에 있습니다.

Situation 34 Other Questions 2

U : I am looking for a manual for lab equipment.

L : Can you give me more information about what you are looking for?

U : I am looking for biology lab books.

L : Using 'biology lab' as a search term, I found *Biology Lab*. Its call number is '574.028 일42.' You can find this book in the Science Library.

U : Thank you. (After a while) This book is about lab work but it does not have enough information for 'electrophoresis.' Can you find one that explains electrophoresis in more detail?

L : Let's search for 'electrophoresis.' We have a book in Japanese and a dissertation.

U : I'd like to see the dissertation.

L : The dissertation is on the third floor.

상황 35   메타검색과 링킹서비스

U : 저는 경영대학원 학생입니다. 전자자료 검색에 대해 문의할게 있습니다.

L : 어떤 것을 도와드릴까요?

U : 홈페이지에 경영학과 관련된 DB가 다양하게 있는데, 모든 DB에 접속해서 검색하려니 불편합니다. 어떻게 간편한 방법이 없을까요?

L : 네, 좋은 질문입니다. 이런 불편함을 해소하고자 도서관에서는 올해부터 '메타검색' 시스템을 신규로 도입하여 홍보하고 있습니다.

U : 저와 같은 이용자들에게는 좋은 소식인데요. 어떻게 이용하죠?

L : 현재 도서관 홈페이지에 접속해 있으신가요?

U : 잠시만요. 네 접속했습니다.

L : 이용방법을 간략히 말씀드리면, 먼저 도서관 홈페이지에 로그인 하시고, 메타검색 또는 멀티 데이터베이스 검색이라는 메뉴 아이콘을 클릭해 보시겠어요?

U : 새로운 팝업창이 뜨네요

L : 네, 검색어 입력란 아래쪽을 보시면 한꺼번에 검색 가능한 DB리스트가 보이실 것입니다. 원하는 DB 들을 먼저 선택 하시고 검색을 하면 됩니다.

U : 혹시 검색 한 후에 원문을 보려면 해당 DB에서 다시 검색해야 하나요?

L : 아닙니다. '메타검색' 결과에서 'Find It@Hankook Univ' 라는 아이콘이 보이실 것입니다. 그 아이콘을 클릭하시면 해당 아티클 원문에 관한 여러가지 정보를 확인하실 수 있습니다. 도서관에서 구독하고 있는 자료는 원문을 바로 보실 수 있고 그렇지 않은 자료일 경우 원문복사 신청을 할 수 있습니다.

U : 우아, 이거 편리한 기능이네요?

L : 혹시 '구글 스칼라'라고 알고 계세요?

U : 네 얼마 전에 한번 접속해봤습니다.

L : 구글 스칼라 자료 검색결과에 화면에서도 'Find It@Hankook Univ' 라는 아이콘을 클릭하시면 동일한 기능을 경험할 수 있습니다. 이를 링킹 서비스라고 하지요.

U : 그래요? 오늘 들은 내용이 너무 많은데, 나중에 한번 찾아가서 다시 한번 들을 수 있을까요?

L : 네! 언제든지 먼저 연락주시고 오시면, 상세하게 안내해 드리겠습니다.

U : 감사합니다. 좋은 하루 되세요.

Situation 35 — Meta-Search and Linking Service

U : Hello, I'm a MBA student. I have a question about searching for electronic resources.

L : How can I help you?

U : It's quite inconvenient that there are various databases about business administration on the library website, which gives me too many sources. Is there an easier way?

L : That's a good question. In order to resolve the problem of excessive information, our library has adopted a 'meta-search' system this year.

U : That's good news! How can I use it?

L : Are you on the library website now?

U : Wait… Yes, now I am.

L : Let me explain briefly how to use it. Log on to the library website first, and click either the 'Meta-search' or 'Multi-database search' menu.

U : A new pop-up appears.

L : OK, under the search box, you can see the database lists that can be searched. Then select the database you want and do the search.

U : Should I search again if I want to view the full-text of a certain database?

L : No, you can see the 'Find It@Hankook Univ' icon with the results by the meta-search. Click that icon and you can find the information regarding the full-text of the article you've searched. You can view the full-text immediately if the library subscribes to it, otherwise please request a document delivery service

U : Wow, how convenient!

L : Have you heard about Google Scholar?

U : Yes. I have tried it.

L : You can also experience the same function by clicking the 'Find It@Hankook Univ' icon shown as with Google Scholar. This function is called 'linking service'.

U : Amazing! I've learned a lot today. I might have more questions next time.

L : Sure, contact me anytime you want and I'll be happy to help you!

U : Thank you. Have a nice day!

상황 36 교외접속

U : 안녕하세요! 학교에서 *Journal of Philosophy*라는 저널을 검색해서 원문을 볼 수 있었는데요. 집에서 원문을 보려고 사이트 URL을 메모해서 그 URL로 접속을 했더니 로그인을 하거나 돈을 지불하라고 하는데 어떻게 된 거죠?

L : 대부분의 전자저널 출판사들이 IP인증방식으로 원문을 서비스하고 있어서 해당 저널 홈페이지에 바로 접속을 하시면 원문을 이용하실 수 없습니다.

U : 집에서도 이용할 수 있으면 훨씬 도움이 될 텐데요.

L : 그래서 교외에서도 도서관에서 구독하고 있는 대부분의 전자자원을 이용할 수 있도록 proxy 시스템을 도입하여 운영하고 있습니다. 이용방법은 아주 간단합니다.

U : 어떻게요?

L : 해당 저널 사이트에 접속하기 전에 먼저 도서관 홈페이지에 로그인 하시고, 원하는 저널을 도서관 홈페이지에서 검색 또는 메뉴를 이용하여 자료를 선택한 후에 'URL' 아이콘을 클릭해서 해당 저널 사이트로 접속하면 자동으로 전자정보원교외접속 서비스가 이루어집니다.

U : 정말 간단하네요. 한번 해보고 안되면 다시 연락드릴께요.

L : 잠시만요. 참고로 브라우저의 즐겨찾기에 저장한 주소로는 전자정보원교외접속이 적용되지 않습니다. 반드시 도서관 홈페이지를 통해 데이터베이스 및 전자저널을 이용하시기 바랍니다.

Situation 36　Off-Campus Access

U : I was able to search the *Journal of Philosophy* and view the full-text of the article. I wrote down the URL to connect to it at home, but when I tried at home it asked me for a login or to pay money. What's wrong with it?

L : Most of the e-journal publishers offer the full-text service via IP authorization. So if you access the website from a non-authorized IP, you cannot use the text service.

U : I wish I could use it at home.

L : That's why we adopted the proxy system to make it possible for e-resources to be used off campus. It's easy to use!

U : How can I use it?

L : First, log on to the library website before you access the journal website. Then, select the resource that you want by search or menu at the library website. Lastly, click the 'URL' icon and connect to the journal website. Then, off-campus access service will automatically be provided.

U : It sounds really simple! I'll contact you later if it doesn't work.

L : Wait a moment. You cannot use this service with the address saved at your bookmark. Make sure that you use the databases and e-journals only via the library website.

Circulation

대 출

● ● ●

고려대학교 도서관

2 대출 / Circulation

U : 신입생인데요, 도서관 대출 절차에 대해 알고 싶습니다.

L : 우선 도서관에 원하는 자료가 있는지 그리고 어느 곳에 소장되어 있는지 검색해야 합니다.

U : 검색했어요. 그런데 필요한 자료가 단행본실과 보존서고에 각각 위치해 있었어요.

L : 단행본실은 본인이 직접 책을 서가에서 골라 대출할 수 있습니다. 보존서고에 소장된 책은 '도서대출신청서'에 기록하여 사서에게 제출하면 책을 받아 볼 수 있습니다.

U : 얼마나 기다려야 하지요?

L : 한 5분 정도입니다. 기다렸다가 호명되면 학생증을 제시하면 됩니다. 그리고 신입생 오리엔테이션에서 상세한 도서관 이용안내를 하고 있으니 참석하시기 바랍니다.

Situation 1   Circulation

U : Hello. I'm a new student. I'd like to know about the library's lending
procedure.

L : If you wish to borrow books, you have to find out whether we have them
and, if so, their locations.

U : I have already done searching. One of the books I need is in the closed
stacks and the others are in the open stacks.

L : You can retrieve monographs from the open stacks by yourself and check
them out here. If you wish to read a book from the closed stacks, you
have to fill out the form and then a librarian will get it for you.

U : How long will that take?

L : About five minutes. When your name is called, show your ID at the
circulation desk. If you attend the student orientation, you will learn more
about library services.

상황 2 　　♥ 대출 규정

U : 책을 몇 권이나 빌릴 수 있어요?

L : 학부생은 7책까지 빌릴 수 있습니다.

U : 얼마 동안 볼 수 있지요?

L : 대출 기한은 15일입니다.

U : 만일 15일을 넘기면 어떻게 되지요?

L : 연체한 일수만큼 대출할 수 없습니다.

U : 7책 다 연체하면 어떻게 되지요?

L : 그 중에서 가장 오래 연체한 기간을 대출 중지 기간으로 합니다.

U : 대출 중지 대신 돈으로 변상하면 안되나요?

L : 대출 중지 제도가 시작되기 이전에 빌린 책인 경우에만 하루에 100원씩 연
　　체료를 부과합니다.

U : 계속해서 반납을 하지 않으면 어떻게 되지요?

L : 각종 증명서를 발급받을 수 없습니다.

Situation 2 Loan Policy

U : How many books can I borrow at a time?

L : Undergraduates are allowed to borrow seven books at a time.

U : And how long can I borrow them?

L : The lending period is fifteen days.

U : What happens if I return my books late?

L : Then your borrowing privilege is suspended for the same number of days
that they were late.

U : What if all seven volumes are late?

L : The penalty period is equal to the number of late days of the most
overdue book.

U : Can I pay fines instead?

L : Yes. But only for the books borrowed before the new system was in
place. The fine is 100 won per day per book.

U : What if they aren't returned for a really long time?

L : In that case, restrictions will be imposed on your university transcripts,
certificates and the like.

상황 3 　　대출 연장

U : 대학원생입니다. 대출 책 수와 기간이 어떻게 되나요?

L : 석사/박사과정은 15책 30일 입니다.

U : 대출 책 수가 너무 적은 것 같네요.

L : 다른 책을 더 보고 싶을 때는 관내 열람과 복사기를 활용하기 바랍니다.

U : 대출 기간도 너무 짧습니다.

L : 대출한 책을 더 보고 싶을 때는 대출 연장을 신청할 수 있습니다.

U : 대출 연장은 몇 번이나 가능합니까?

L : 1책당 1회이며, 대출 중지 기간이거나 연체된 도서가 있을 경우에는 연장할 수 없습니다.

U : 연장 신청은 어떻게 하나요?

L : 일반적으로 도서관 홈페이지에 접속하여 연장하거나, 직접 방문이나 전화를 통해 연장하실 수 있습니다.

Situation 3　Renewal Policy

U : Hi. I'm a graduate student. I'd like to know how many books I can borrow, and for how long.

L : If you're a master's or doctoral student, you can borrow up to fifteen volumes for thirty days.

U : It seems to me that the number of books that I can borrow is insufficient.

L : If you've already reached the limit, you can either use a book in the library or copy it.

U : The loan period seems too short.

L : It's also possible to renew.

U : How many times am I allowed to renew?

L : You can renew a book once, but only if you don't have any overdue materials.

U : How can I renew?

L : Normally, it's possible to make a renewal request via the library website. Also you can renew materials in person at the library or contact us by phone.

상황 4 ▶ 대리 대출

U : 교수님 심부름으로 책을 빌리러 왔는데요.

L : 교수님 신분증을 가지고 왔습니까?

U : 아니요. 신분증이 필요한가요

L : 대출은 본인 확인을 해야 합니다. 그렇지 않으면 문제가 생길 수 있거든요.

U : 알겠습니다. 신분증을 가지고 다시 오겠습니다.

L : 대리인 신분증도 필요합니다.

U : 왜죠?

L : 대리 대출을 할 때는 대리인의 신분도 기록해 놓아야 합니다. 그래야 나중에 사고를 방지할 수 있습니다.

U : 무슨 사고가 발생합니까?

L : 대출자 본인이 대출한 사실을 잊어버리고 있는 경우가 종종 있습니다.

U : 잘 알겠습니다.

Situation 4 Proxy Borrowing

U : My professor sent me to get some books for him.

L : Did he give you his library card?

U : No. Do you need his ID?

L : We need a borrower's ID to identify the borrower. If we don't, there might be a problem later on.

U : I see. I'll come back with it.

L : We'll need your student identification also.

U : Why's that?

L : We need to know who checked a book out in the professor's name in order to prevent future problems.

U : What kind of problem?

L : We have had professors who denied that they ever borrowed books on proxy. We need to document everything.

U : I see what you mean.

상황 5   서고 이용

U : 폐가실 서고는 학부생도 출입할 수 있습니까?

L : 죄송합니다만, 대학원생 이상만 들어갈 수 있습니다.

U : 우리는 왜 출입할 수 없습니까?

L : 자료 보존을 위해서 출입자 수를 제한하고 있기 때문입니다.

U : 그렇다면 책을 확인하고 빌려야 할 때는 어떻게 하지요?

L : 그런 특수한 경우에는 담당사서의 확인을 받고 들어갈 수 있습니다.

U : 고맙습니다. 서고에 들어갈 때 가방은 어떻게 하지요?

L : 개인 소지품은 보관함에 넣고, 직원에게 신분증을 맡긴 후 서고에 들어가
세요.

U : 보관함은 어떻게 사용하지요?

L : 100원짜리 동전을 넣고 열쇠를 잠그면 됩니다. 다 사용한 후에 열쇠를 열면
동전이 다시 나옵니다.

U : 이 자료는 서고 어디에 있죠?

L : '자료배치 안내도'를 보면 청구번호에 따라 자료를 찾을 수 있습니다.

Situation 5  Closed Stacks

U : Can an undergraduate enter the closed stacks?

L : I'm sorry, but only graduate students, faculty and staff are permitted in the closed stacks.

U : Why aren't we allowed in?

L : We limit the number of users for preservation.

U : What if I want to look at the books to see if I actually need them or not?

L : In special circumstances, you can get permission from the circulation librarian.

U : That's nice. If I enter the closed stacks, what should I do with my backpack?

L : You should put your personal belongings in a locker and leave your ID card with the library staff over there.

U : How do I use a locker?

L : Insert a 100 won coin and turn the key to lock. When you come back, open the locker and you'll get your coin back.

U : Where can I find the materials that I need?

L : Refer to the Stacks Map on the wall over there. The materials are shelved by their call numbers.

상황 6　　불명도서

U : 검색을 해 보면 대출 가능하다고 와 있는데 왜 책이 없어요?

L : 반납된 책이 아직 배열되지 않아서 그럴 겁니다.

U : 며칠 전에도 없었는데요.

L : 그렇다면 다른 자리에 잘못 꽂혀 있을 수 있습니다.

U : 왜 그렇죠?

L : 책이 한번 잘못 꽂히면 찾을 수 없습니다. 그래서 한번 뺀 책은 도서관 직원이 제자리에 꽂을 수 있도록 직접 서가에 꽂지 말고 북트럭에 두게 하고 있는 겁니다.

U : 꼭 필요한 책인데.

L : 원래 자리의 주변 서가를 잘 찾아 보면 책이 나오는 경우도 있습니다.

U : 혹시 책이 없어진 것은 아닌가요?

L : 지금으로서는 단언할 수 없습니다. 추적을 해 보겠습니다. 연락처를 알려 주면 책을 찾는 대로 연락 드리겠습니다.

Situation 6  Missing Materials

U : The computer shows that the book I am looking for is in our library, but I could not find it in the stacks.

L : It is possible that the book has been returned but not yet processed.

U : But it also wasn't there when I checked several days ago.

L : The book might have been mis-shelved.

U : What do you mean by that?

L : If the book was shelved in the wrong place, there's no way to find it. That's why we tell our patrons not to re-shelve the books themselves but to put them on the book trucks.

U : But I still need the book.

L : Why don't you browse the shelves in that area?

U : Could it be missing?

L : It's hard to tell for sure right now. I'll have it searched for. Please leave your contact information and we will notify you of the result.

상황 7   장서 이전

U : 제가 찾는 책이 검색은 되는데 '정리중'으로 뜨는군요. 일주일 전에도 그랬
   는데 언제쯤 그 책을 대출할 수 있죠?

L : '정리중'이라는 메시지는 자료가 입수되어 목록작업을 하고 있다는 의미입
   니다. 잠시만요, 제가 한번 알아 보겠습니다. 아! 정리가 완료되어 이용할
   수 있는데도 상태코드를 바꾸지 않았군요. 죄송합니다. 곧바로 정정할 테
   니 대출하셔도 되겠습니다.

U : 일전에 개가실에서 빌렸던 책이 이제는 꽂혀 있지 않군요. 혹시 보존서고
   로 이전되었나요?

L : 네. 개가실에는 최근 자료를 비치하고, 오래된 자료는 서고로 모두 이전합
   니다. 한번 검색해 보세요. 다른 곳으로 이전되어있을 겁니다.

U : 아! 그렇군요. 이전되었군요. 감사합니다.

Situation 7 Change of Location

U : The library catalog indicates that the book is 'In Process.' This message
   has appeared for a week. When will it be available?

L : 'In Process' means that a material is being cataloged. Let me see. Oh, I
   see what happened. The book has already been cataloged and is
   available in the stacks, but we have not changed the status in the system.
   I'm sorry. I'll update it now so that you can borrow the book.

U : There's also a book that I checked out before, but now it isn't on the
   shelf. Has it been moved to the closed stacks?

L : Probably. Recent materials are in the open stacks and older materials are
   sent to the closed stacks. Why don't you check on the computer? It must
   have been relocated.

U : (After a little while) You were right. The book has been transferred.
   Thanks for helping me.

상황 8　　🍵 미입력 자료 대출

A : 이 책을 대출시키려는데 시스템에 서지사항이 나타나지 않네요.

L : 한번 봅시다. 등록번호에 착오가 있을 수 있어요.

A : 등록번호는 맞는데요.

L : 그럼 서지 데이터가 누락된 거 같아요.

A : 대출하려는 학생이 기다리고 있는데 어떻게 처리할까요?

L : 화면의 '비고란'에 해당 도서의 서명을 입력하고 대출시키세요. 나중에 반납되면 오류를 수정하도록 하지요.

A : 만약 등록번호가 틀린 경우에는 어떻게 하지요?

L : 그때는 저에게 알려주세요. 오류를 먼저 수정한 다음 대출시키면 됩니다.

A : 알겠습니다.

Situation 8 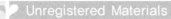 Unregistered Materials

A : I tried to check out this book but I cannot find the bibliographic information in the system.

L : Let me see. There might be a mistake with the registration number.

A : No. The registration number is correct.

L : Then, it's likely that the bibliographic data is missing.

A : What should I do with the student who is waiting to check it out?

L : Just input the title in the Remarks and check the book out. When the book is returned, we'll straighten it out.

A : If the registration number is incorrect, what should I do?

L : Then just let me know. I'll fix it and you can check it out afterwards.

A : All right then.

상황 9   대출 제한

U : 이 책 대출해 주세요.

L : 죄송합니다. 이 책은 대출이 안됩니다.

U : 왜죠?

L : 이 책은 참고도서로, 많은 이용자가 수시로 찾는 책이라서 관내 열람만 가능합니다.

U : 그밖에 대출이 되지 않는 책이 또 있나요?

L : 대출 제한 도서는 참고도서를 비롯하여 귀중본, 희귀본 및 그림책 등입니다.

U : 귀중본이나 희귀본은 이해가 갑니다만, 그림책은 왜 대출이 안됩니까?

L : 예전에는 그림책을 대출해 주었으나, 책이 훼손되는 사례가 많아서 지금은 대출을 제한하고 있습니다.

U : 그렇지만 저는 미술학과 학생이라서 이 책을 꼭 봐야 하는데요.

L : 관내에서 열람하거나 사진 촬영을 하면 안될까요?

U : 알겠습니다. 촬영은 어떻게 합니까?

L : 접사대가 있으니까 그걸 사용하세요.

Situation 9 Library Use Only

U : I'd like to borrow this book.

L : I'm sorry, it's not loanable.

U : Why not?

L : This is a reference book and reference books are used so frequently that they are for in-library use only.

U : Are there any other books that can't be checked out?

L : Rare books, valuable books and art books are not allowed out of the library.

U : I understand why the rare and valuable books cannot be checked out, but why can't you lend out the art books?

L : We have loaned them out in the past, but so many pages were torn out that we only allow them to be used in the library.

U : But I'm an art student and I need to borrow the art books.

L : Why don't you look them over in the library or, if necessary, take a photograph of what you need?

U : Alright. How can I do that?

L : There's a copy stand over there.

상황 10 연체도서

U : 반납이요.

L : 책이 연체되었습니다.

U : 그래요? 몰랐네요. 반납일을 알려면 어떻게 하지요?

L : 도서관 홈페이지에서 아이디와 비밀번호를 넣으면 어떤 책을 대출했는지, 반납일이 언제인지 알 수 있어요.

U : 연체자는 어떤 제재를 받게 되나요? 연체한 일수만큼 대출이 안되나요?

L : 맞습니다. 연체자는 제재 중 하나를 선택할 수 있습니다. "연체 기간 만큼 대출 금지" 혹은 "1일당 100원의 연체료 부과"를 이용자 스스로 선택하실 수 있습니다.

U : 레포트 작성 때문에 꼭 봐야 할 책이 있습니다. 연체료를 납부하겠습니다.

Situation 10  Overdue Materials

U : I'm returning this.

L : This book is late.

U : Really? I didn't know that. How can I find out the due date?

L : You can check the library website. Enter your ID and password, and you
can see which books you have borrowed and when they are due.

U : What is the penalty for overdue books? Is it true that I can't borrow books
for the same amount of time as this book is late?

L : Actually, you can choose one of the following penalty options

  : Either you can't borrow any library materials for the number of days
you're late, or the library will charge you a late fee of 100 won per day.

U : I didn't know that. I have a report that is due very soon, so I will pay the
late fee.

상황 11　　분실도서

U : 대출한 책을 분실했는데요, 어떻게 하지요?

L : 우선, 분실한 책과 동일한 책을 구해 가져오시면 됩니다.

U : 절판된 책이라서 구할 수 없거든요.

L : 그렇다면 유사한 책으로 대신 변상하세요.

U : 유사한 책이란 게 뭔가요?

L : 같은 주제의 책을 가격이 잃어버린 책과 동등한 책을 말합니다.

U : 돈으로 변상하면 안되나요?

L : 가능합니다만, 책으로 변상하는 편이 유리할 겁니다.

U : 언제까지 변상하면 되나요?

L : 대출 기한을 넘기면 연체한 일수만큼 대출이 중지되니까 되도록 빨리 변상 하는 게 좋습니다.

U : 알겠습니다.

Situation 11　Lost Materials

U : I lost a book that I borrowed. What should I do?

L : One thing you could do is bring another copy of the book.

U : But it's out-of-print.

L : Another option is to bring a similar book to replace the lost one.

U : What do you mean by a similar book?

L : It should be about the same subject and cost the same amount as the lost book.

U : Could I just pay for it instead?

L : That's possible, but you'll end up paying less money if you replace the book.

U : By when do I have to replace the book?

L : If the book is overdue you will be blocked from borrowing materials, so you had better replace it as soon as possible.

U : I see.

상황 12   ♥ 자료이용 협조 의뢰서

U : 우리 도서관에 없는 자료를 보려면 어떻게 합니까?

L : 구입 요청을 해 보셨습니까?

U : 절판이라고 합니다.

L : 그러면 자료를 소장한 다른 도서관에 직접 찾아가 볼 수 있습니다.

U : 소장 도서관을 어떻게 알 수 있습니까?

L : KERIS의 종합목록 RISS를 이용하여 검색하면 알 수 있습니다.

U : (검색 후) 한국대학교 도서관에 있다고 나왔는데요.

L : 그러면 자료이용 협조 의뢰서를 발급해 드리겠습니다. 이걸 가지고 한국대
학교 도서관에 가서 제출하면 자료를 볼 수 있습니다.

U : 대출도 되나요?

L : 대출은 되지 않습니다. 관내 열람 및 복사는 할 수 있습니다.

Situation 12  Referrals

U : I'd like to use some materials that are not in this library.

L : Did you fill out a request form for the library to purchase it?

U : I heard that it is out-of-print.

L : You can visit a library that has that item.

U : How can I find which library has it?

L : You can find it in RISS, the Union Catalog of the Korea Education &
Research Information Service (KERIS).

U : (After a short search) I found that the Hankook University Library has that
book.

L : I'll provide you with a referral for that university, which will then let you
use their library.

U : Can I check out books from that library?

L : I don't think so. You can only use or copy it in that library.

상황 13 　휴학생 및 졸업생

U : 저는 휴학생인데, 대출할 수 있나요?

L : 물론 가능합니다.

U : 어떤 절차가 있나요?

L : 학부생입니까? 대학원생입니까?

U : 저는 학부생이고 친구는 대학원생입니다.

L : 학부생은 주소와 연락처를 확인하면 되고, 수료 중인 대학원생은 보증서를
받아 오면 됩니다.

U : 보증서가 뭡니까?

L : 지도교수로부터 대출 보증 확인을 받아오면 바로 대출할 수 있습니다.

U : 대출 책수와 기한은 어떻게 되나요?

L : 재학생과 같습니다.

U : 졸업생도 대출할 수 있나요?

L : 안됩니다. 대신 열람실 이용과 자료 열람은 가능합니다.

Circulation • 대출

Situation 13　Students on Leave and Alumni

U : Hello. I'm currently taking this semester off. Can I still borrow materials?

L : Yes, you can.

U : Are there any special requirements?

L : Are you an undergraduate or graduate student?

U : I'm an undergraduate myself, but I'm asking for my friend who is a
　　graduate student.

L : Well, undergraduates need to supply us with an address and a phone
　　number that we can verify, and doctoral candidates need to hand in a
　　written referral.

U : What kind of written referral?

L : We need a written recommendation signed by your friend's academic
　　advisor. As soon as we receive that, he can check out materials.

U : How many books are we allowed to borrow and for how long?

L : The same rules for undergraduates and graduates apply.

U : Can alumni also borrow materials?

L : No. That is not permitted. But they are allowed to use the reading room
　　and they may browse the materials.

상황 14   외부인 이용

U : 저는 이 대학 학생이 아닌데요, 자료 좀 볼 수 있을까요?

L : 대학생이세요?

U : 그렇습니다.

L : 혹시 자료이용 협조 의뢰서 가지고 왔나요?

U : 아니요. 그게 뭐죠?

L : 대학 도서관 간에는 협력관계를 맺고 있어 자료이용 협조 의뢰서를 가지고 오면 다른 도서관 자료도 이용할 수 있습니다. 오늘은 자료이용 협조 의뢰서를 가지고 오지 않았으니 신분증을 확인한 후 출입 시켜드리겠습니다. 다음부터는 의뢰서를 가지고 오세요.

U : 고맙습니다. 그런데 대출은 됩니까?

L : 관외 대출은 안되고, 자료 열람실에서 열람 및 복사는 가능합니다.

U : 일반 열람실 이용은 가능합니까?

L : 일반 열람실은 외부 이용자에게 개방되지 않습니다. 하지만 한국대학교 근방 지역주민이라면, 지역주민 이용제도를 신청하셔서 이용하실 수 있습니다.

U : 신청방법을 알려주세요.

L : 학기 시작 전에 지역 주민에 한정하여 신청을 받고 있습니다. 자세한 사항은 도서관 홈페이지의 공지를 참고하여 주십시오.

Situation 14 Visitors

U : Excuse me, I'm not a student here, but I'd like to look at some of your materials.

L : Are you a university student elsewhere?

U : Yes, I am.

L : Did you happen to bring a referral from your university library?

U : No. What's that?

L : University libraries have mutual relationships with one another, so students can use other university libraries. But they need to bring referrals from their respective university library. Even though you didn't bring one, I'll let you use our library this time after checking your ID. Please bring the referral next time.

U : I appreciate you letting me use your library. Can I borrow books?

L : I'm sorry. You can only use them on our library premises.

U : How about using the study rooms?

L : Visitors are usually not allowed to use the study rooms; however, you can still use a study room by registering for 'the library program for local residents' if you live near Hankook University.

U : Please let me know how to apply for the program.

L : Before the start of each semester, we usually receive applications from local residents. Please refer to the library website for further information.

상황 15　　복사

U : 이 책을 전부 복사하고 싶은데요.

L : 그건 곤란합니다.

U : 왜 안되죠?

L : 저작권 때문에 그렇습니다.

U : 그렇다면 대출을 해서 복사하겠습니다.

L : 대출은 해 주겠습니다만, 외부에서도 전체 복사를 할 수는 없을 겁니다.

U : 그렇습니까? 그러면 어떻게 하면 좋겠습니까?

L : 보고자 하는 곳을 일부만 복사하세요.

U : 그러면 날마다 조금씩 복사를 해서 전체를 다 하면 어떻겠습니까?

L : 그것도 저작권법 위반입니다.

U : 저작권법을 위반하면 어떻게 됩니까?

L : 많은 벌금을 내야 합니다.

Situation 15  Photocopying

U : I'd like to copy this entire book.

L : That's not permitted.

U : Why not?

L : Because of copyright law.

U : Then I'll just check it out and have it copied on my own.

L : OK. I'll lend it to you, but I don't think any copy shop will do that.

U : Really? What should I do?

L : Just copy the part that you really need.

U : What if I copy it little by little each day until I'm finished?

L : That's still in violation of copyright law.

U : What happens if I get caught breaking copyright law?

L : There's a very stiff fine.

상황 16 · 대출증 발급

U : 아세아문제연구소 소속 연구원입니다. 책을 대출할 수 있습니까?

L : 먼저 소속 기관에서 개인 정보를 포함한 협조문을 보내주셔야 합니다. 그리고 대출증에 붙일 증명사진 1매가 필요합니다.

U : 알겠습니다. 대출증 발급은 시간이 얼마나 걸립니까?

L : 즉석에서 발급해 드립니다.

U : 대출 책수와 기한은 얼마나 됩니까?

L : 연구원은 박사과정 대학원생과 같습니다.

U : 그러면 교내 다른 도서관도 이용할 수 있는 거죠?

L : 그렇습니다. 이용자 데이터는 전체 도서관에서 공유하기 때문에 대출증 하나면 모든 도서관을 다 이용할 수 있습니다.

Situation 16  Issuing Library Cards

U : Hi. I'm a researcher at the Asiatic Research Center. Am I allowed to borrow books?

L : Yes, you are. First, however, we need a letter with your background information from your research center. We also need a small ID photo for your card.

U : OK. How long does it take to get a library card?

L : We can make the card as soon as we get the letter and the photo.

U : How many books am I permitted to borrow and for how long?

L : A researcher is allowed to borrow under the same conditions as doctoral candidates.

U : Can I use the university's other libraries as well?

L : Of course. The user data is shared by all of our libraries. With one library card you can use any of our libraries.

상황 17　　학생증 분실 1

U : 학생증을 분실했는데요.

L : 잠시만요, 학번이 어떻게 되죠?

U : 20100020입니다.

L : 다른 사람이 학생증을 주워 무단 사용하면 안되니까, 일단 대출 중지를 걸
　　어 놓겠습니다. 학생증 재발급 신청을 해 놓았나요?

U : 그렇습니다. 그런데 그 동안 어떻게 대출하죠?

L : 창구에 본인임을 증명할 수 있는 증명서만 제기하면 학생증 없이도 대출할
　　수 있습니다.

U : 운전면허증이 있습니다.

L : 그것으로 가능합니다.

Situation 17 Lost Student ID Card 1

U : I lost my student ID card.

L : Just a moment. What's your ID number?

U : It's 20100020.

L : I'll block your check-out privileges so someone else can't use your card.
Did you try to get your card reissued yet?

U : Yes, I did. How can I borrow books in the meantime?

L : Show the librarian at the circulation desk your picture ID to prove who
you are. You may then check out books again.

U : I've got a driver's license. Is that alright?

L : Sure. That's fine.

상황 18   ♥ 학생증 분실 2

U : 제가 대출한 책이 아닌데 대출한 걸로 나와 있어요. 어떻게 된 겁니까?

L : 혹시 학생증을 분실하셨나요?

U : 네, 그래서 재발급 받았습니다.

L : 학생증 분실 후 도서관에 신고 하셨습니까?

U : 안했는데요.

L : 학생증을 잃어버리면 바로 도서관에 신고해야 피해가 발생하지 않습니다.
   학생의 경우는 분실된 학생증으로 다른 누군가가 대출을 한 것 같습니다.

U : 본인 확인을 하고 빌려 주지 않나요?

L : 사진 대조를 정확히 하기가 어렵습니다.

U : 어떻게 해야 되죠?

L : 일단은 반납이 될 때까지 기다려 보고 차후에 반납이 되지 않는다면 그때
   는 책에 대한 변상을 하셔야 합니다.

Situation 18   Lost Student ID Card 2

U : The computer indicates that I have borrowed a book which I never did.
Could you tell me what's going on?

L : Did you ever happen to lose your student ID card?

U : Yes, I did. But I had it replaced.

L : Have you notified the library that you lost the old one?

U : Nope.

L : When you lose your student ID, you should report it to the library
immediately. Otherwise, you're asking for trouble. It sounds like
someone else might have used your old ID card.

U : Don't you verify who is borrowing?

L : It's hard to recognize the person with the small ID photo.

U : What should I do then?

L : You had better wait a few days and see if the book is returned. If it isn't,
you'll have to replace it.

상황 19 　　 예약제도

U : 원하는 자료가 항상 대출되어 있어 도저히 볼 수 없는데 어떻게 합니까?

L : 그렇다면 예약을 해 놓으세요.

U : 예약은 어떻게 합니까?

L : 검색한 다음 예약 버튼을 클릭하세요. 그리고 다음 화면에 이메일 주소와 휴대폰 번호를 입력하면 됩니다.

U : 그 책을 언제 볼 수 있는지 어떻게 알 수 있나요?

L : 반납되면 바로 이메일과 휴대폰으로 알려 드립니다.

U : 누가 먼저 대출해 가면 어떡하죠?

L : 반납된 후 2일 동안은 예약자 외에는 대출하지 못합니다.

U : 편리한 제도군요.

L : 그렇지만 예약해 놓고 찾아가지 않는 이용자가 많습니다.

U : 꼭 찾아 가도록 하겠습니다.

Situation 19  Hold Process

U : A book that I'd like to use is always checked out. What should I do?

L : You should place a hold on it.

U : How do I do that?

L : After you search the record, click on the 'Hold' button and enter your
e-mail address and cell phone number on the next screen that pops up.

U : How will I know if it has been returned for me to check out?

L : You'll be notified automatically via both e-mail and cell phone when the
book is returned.

U : What if someone else checks out the book before I have a chance to?

L : The book will be held for you for two days after it is returned.

U : That's quite convenient.

L : You're right. Unfortunately, many students place holds on books but
never come to pick them up.

U : Don't worry about that! I really need that book.

상황 20　　과제도서

U : 이거 빌려 주세요.

L : 이 책은 과제도서라서 대출이 안됩니다.

U : 과제도서라는 게 뭔가요?

L : 교수님이 학기마다 개설되는 과목에 필요한 교재라고 지정해 주면 도서관
　　에서 따로 비치하여 관내 이용만 되도록 한 책입니다.

U : 저 말고도 보려는 사람이 많겠네요.

L : 그렇습니다. 그렇기 때문에 과제도서로 지정한 겁니다.

U : 그럼 언제 대출할 수 있습니까?

L : 이번 학기가 끝나 과제도서에서 해제되면 그 때는 대출할 수 있습니다.

U : 알겠습니다.

Situation 20 Course Reserves

U : I'd like to check this out.

L : I'm sorry. This is a course reserve item and is not allowed to be out of this room.

U : What do you mean by course reserve?

L : Course reserves are textbooks and other essential materials that professors have assigned their students to read. We buy multiple copies and students use them inside the library only.

U : There must be many users required to use the same materials.

L : You've got that right. That's why we assign course reserves in the first place.

U : Then when will it be possible for me to borrow these books?

L : At the end of each semester, we reshelve them.

U : I see.

상황 21　무인 대출반납기

U : 이것은 무엇입니까?

L : 무인 대출반납기입니다.

U : 어떻게 사용합니까?

L : 대출할 때는 학생증을 먼저 스캔한 후 책의 바코드를 스캔하세요.

U : 반납할 때는 어떻게 합니까?

L : 반납 모드에서 책의 바코드를 스캔하면 됩니다.

U : 이 기계를 안 거치고 그냥 책을 가지고 나가면 어떻게 됩니까?

L : 출입관리 게이트에서 경보음이 나면서 문이 열리지 않습니다.

U : 셀프 서비스를 위한 기계군요.

L : 그렇습니다. 은행의 현금자동지급기와 유사하죠.

U : 신기하네요.

Situation 21 Self Check-out

U : What is this machine for?

L : It's an automatic check-out machine.

U : How do I operate it?

L : The first thing you do is scan your ID and then you scan the book's barcode.

U : How can I check in books?

L : Just scan the barcode on the book with the automatic check-in module.

U : What if I try to walk out of the library without checking out the book?

L : The alarm will sound and the gate will not open.

U : So these are self-service machines!

L : You could say that. Like an ATM at the bank.

U : That's fantastic.

상황 22   RFID

U : 최근 도서관에서 RFID 시스템을 도입한다는 공지를 봤습니다.

L : 네. RFID는 Radio Frequency Identification 의 준말로, IC에 내장된 tag로부터 전파를 이용하여 정보를 주고받는 기술입니다. 도서관 자료에 tag를 부착하고 새로운 시스템을 도입할 예정입니다.

U : 그럼 자료를 이용할 때 변경되는 점이 있나요?

L : 네. 무인 대출 / 반납기를 교체하여, 시간을 절감하고 보다 손쉽게 자료를 이용 하실 수 있습니다.

U : 그렇군요.

Circulation • 대출

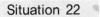**Situation 22** RFID

U : Recently, I saw a notice about installing an RFID system in the library.

L : Yes. RFID is the acronym for 'Radio Frequency Identification' and it is a technology that uses radio waves to transfer data from a tag that includes integrated circuits. We will attach RFID tags to library materials and install a new system.

U : What is the advantage for us when the library installs the RFID system?

L : The self check-out & check-in system will be newly installed. As a result, users' time will be saved and it will be easier to use resources.

U : Oh, I see.

상황 23 　　대출/반납 가능 시간

U : 대출반납은 몇 시까지인가요?

L : 평일엔 오후 10시, 토요일은 오후 3시이며 일요일은 휴무입니다.

U : 방학 기간에는요?

L : 방학 기간에는 평일 오후 7시, 토요일은 오후 1시이며, 일요일은 평소와 같습니다.

U : 야간 근무와 주간 근무의 담당자가 다른 사람인 것 같아요.

L : 그렇습니다. 야간업무 담당직원이 따로 있습니다.

U : 야간에도 학생들이 많이 이용하나요?

L : 아무래도 주간보다는 이용자 수가 적습니다.

U : 야간과 주간 서비스에 차이가 있나요?

L : 야간 업무는 대출반납 중심의 열람업무만 합니다.

Situation 23 | Library Operating Hours

U : Until what time can I return and borrow books?

L : On weekdays we're open until 10 p.m. On Saturdays we're open until 3 p.m., and we're closed on Sundays.

U : What about during the vacation breaks?

L : During the vacation breaks, we're open until 7 p.m. on weekdays. On Saturdays we're open until 1 p.m. Sundays are the same as during the regular semester.

U : It seems that your day staff and night staff are different.

L : You're right. We have day staff and night staff.

U : Do many students use the library at night?

L : There aren't as many users as during the day.

U : Are the night services different from the day services?

L : In the evening, we provide circulation services only.

상황 24 　　♥ 반납처리 실수

U : 제가 일전에 반납한 책이 '대출중'으로 나오는데요.

L : 학생증을 줘 보세요. (검색 후) 『경제사』라는 책인가요?

U : 예. 10일 전에 반납했거든요.

L : 잠시 기다려 주세요. 서고에서 찾아 보겠습니다. (잠시 후) 서가에서 발견 되었습니다. 반납 처리해 드리겠습니다.

U : 어째서 이런 일이 발생한 거죠?

L : 많은 학생들이 한꺼번에 몰려와서 착오가 생긴 듯 싶습니다. 죄송합니다.

U : 만일 서가에 없을 경우에는 어떻게 합니까?

L : 그런 경우에는 며칠 후에 다시 찾아 봅니다.

Situation 24　Check-out Mistakes

U : I have returned a book, but the computer says that it is still being checked out.

L : Give me your student card, please. (After a brief search) Is the book titled *Economic History*?

U : That's correct. I returned it 10 days ago.

L : Just a moment please. I'll go check and see. (After a while) I found it in the stacks. I'll correct the record.

U : Why did this happen?

L : Sometimes we're swamped with students and mistakes can happen. I'm sorry about that.

U : What if you hadn't found the book in the stacks?

L : In that case we would do a special search after a few days.

상황 25 　　♥ 딸림자료 이용

U : 이 책은 CD-ROM도 같이 봐야 하는데요.

L : 책의 청구기호가 어떻게 됩니까?

U : '325.4 A123c'입니다.

L : 잠깐만 기다리세요. (딸림자료를 가져 온다.) 여기 있습니다.

U : 이것도 대출 권수에 포함되나요?

L : 아닙니다. 포함되지 않습니다.

U : 제가 딸림자료를 대출했다는 기록은 남습니까?

L : 그렇습니다. 개인정보 조회 화면에서 확인할 수 있습니다.

U : CD-ROM 은 어디서 볼 수 있습니까?

L : 멀티미디어 코너에 가시면 담당자가 자리를 배정해 줄 겁니다.

U : 고맙습니다.

Situation 25   Accompanying Materials

U : I believe there is a CD-ROM that goes with this book.

L : What's the book's call number?

U : It's 325.4 A123c.

L : Just a moment. (The librarian returns with the CD-ROM.) Here it is.

U : Does this count as a separate item?

L : No, it doesn't.

U : Then will the record show that I checked out the accompanying materials as well?

L : Yes. You can check the record on your personal information page.

U : Where can I use the CD-ROM?

L : Go to the Multimedia Center and tell the librarian, and she'll assign you a CD-ROM booth.

U : Thank you.

상황 26 한적 열람 : 분류 및 열람 절차

U : 제가 보고 싶은 책을 찾지 못하겠습니다. 찾아 주실 수 없을까요?

L : 예, 찾아 드리겠습니다. 서명이나 저자를 아십니까?

U : 모릅니다.

L : 한적은 經史子集 4部로 분류되어 있습니다. 이 중에 어디에 해당됩니까?

U : 史에 해당됩니다.

L : 그럼 찾을 자료가 이 한적 목록에 있는지 보세요.

U : (잠시 후) 이거 같습니다.

L : (특정자료 열람 신청서를 주면서) 여기에 청구기호, 서명, 열람목적, 연월일, 소속, 성명 등을 기록하여 주십시오.

U : 왜 이런 걸 써야 되나요?

L : 한적은 도서관에서 특별히 관리하는 장서라서 도서관장의 허가 없이는 열람할 수 없기 때문입니다. (특정자료 열람 신청서를 접수한 후) 잠시만 기다려 주시시오. 결재를 올리겠습니다. (결재를 받은 후) 여기 있습니다. 한적은 반드시 지정된 곳에서만 열람하시기 바랍니다.

Situation 26   Classics Archive : Classification and Reading Procedure

U : I couldn't find what I was looking for. Can you help me?

L : Sure. Could you tell me the title or the author?

U : I don't know either of them.

L : Classic works are classified into four categories : Classics, History, Philosophy, and Collected works. Which one of these subjects does the material fall under?

U : History.

L : OK. Then why don't you check in this catalog?

U : (After a while) I think I've found it.

L : (The librarian passes the user a request form for special collections.) Please fill out the form, including the call number, title, your purposes for use, the date, your affiliation and your name.

U : Why do you need all this information?

L : Since the Classics collection is a part of the Special Collections, you need to obtain a permit from the director. (After receiving the request form) Wait a minute while I get approval. (He returns with the approved form.) Here is the book. Please use the material at the designated place only.

상황 27　　한적열람 : 소장 규모 및 현황

U : 소장하고 있는 한적은 총 몇 책입니까?

L : 약 100,000책입니다.

U : 분류는 어떻게 합니까?

L : 기본적으로 經史子集의 四部分類를 따르되, 우리 학교에서 叢書類를 하나 더 만들어 사용하고 있으니 실은 五部分類인 셈입니다.

U : 文庫라는 게 있네요.

L : 한적을 1,000책 이상 기증할 경우 기증한 분의 뜻을 기리기 위하여 문고를 설치합니다. 주요 문고로는 崔南善선생의 六堂文庫, 金完燮선생의 晩松文庫등이 있습니다.

U : 귀중서는 얼마나 있으며, 어떻게 책정합니까?

L : 5,000여 책입니다. 학교마다 다르겠지만 우리는 임진왜란(1592년) 이전 자료와 唯一本 등 가치 있는 자료를 귀중서로 선정합니다. 이 중에는 국보도 있습니다.

Situation 27 ❯ Classics Archive : Collection Layout

U : How many volumes do you have in this collection?

L : We have about 100,000 volumes.

U : How do you classify them?

L : We follow the four-category system, but also have an additional general category. So, in fact, we have a five-category system.

U : I noticed that there's also a special collection called Mungo. What's that?

L : If someone gives us a thousand or more documents, we set up a special collection named after the donor's pen name. In this library we have the Yuktang Mungo in honor of Nam-seon Choe, and the Mansong Mungo in honor of Wan-seop Kim. These are the premier Mungo in our library.

U : How many rare or valuable volumes of precious materials do you have in your library, and how do they become designated as rare materials?

L : There are more than 5,000 volumes. Each library has a different policy for selecting precious materials, but those printed before the Japanese invasion of Korea in 1592 are considered rare. Materials that were printed after 1592 are designated rare if they are the only remaining copy. Some of these are even recognized as national treasures.

상황 28 자료 보존

U : 오래된 자료의 보존은 어떻게 하십니까?

L : 중앙서고에 비치하여 폐가제로 운영하면서 서고의 출입자 수를 제한하고 있습니다.

U : 서고에 희귀서라는 레이블이 붙어 있는 책이 있군요.

L : 특별히 보존할 만한 가치가 있는 자료로 선정된 자료입니다. 희귀서는 대출할 수 없고 관내 열람 및 복사만 할 수 있습니다.

U : 검색해 보면 귀중서라는 것이 있던데요?

L : 귀중서는 귀중서 관리 규정에 의해 선정, 관리되는 자료입니다.

U : 특별히 관리되겠네요.

L : 그렇습니다. 귀중서고에 보관하면서 항온항습을 유지합니다. 그리고 열람은 물론, 복사도 제한됩니다.

U : 그러면 어떻게 이용하지요?

L : 마이크로필름으로 제작하거나 디지털화하니까 그것으로 대신 볼 수 있습니다.

U : 이용 중에 자료가 훼손되기도 하지요?

L : 그렇습니다. 훼손된 자료는 발견되는 대로 수리하고, 수리할 수 없는 경우에는 동일본이나 대체본을 구해 놓고 폐기합니다.

Situation 28   Preservation

U : How do you preserve your aging collection?

L : One thing that we do is move older materials to the closed stacks and limit the usage.

U : I noticed that some of the books in the stacks have a Rare label on the spine.

L : Those books were designated as rare books worthy of preservation. Rare books are not allowed to be checked out. Users can use or copy them only in the library.

U : When I do a computer search, I sometimes see that certain books are designated as a Precious Book. What does that mean?

L : Those are special materials which are selected and maintained in accordance with the Precious Book Maintenance Guidelines.

U : Oh! I bet they must be managed specially.

L : Yes, they are. We keep them in the Precious Book Stacks, which has a special climate control system. Those materials can't be circulated or copied.

U : Is there any way we can use them?

L : Most of these materials have been microfilmed or digitalized.

U : Do some of the materials get damaged from usage?

L : Yes. We attempt to repair the damage, and if we can't, we try to make a replica or get another copy before discarding the item.

상황 29 반납 독촉

U : 보고 싶은 책이 장기간 반납이 안되고 있는데 방법이 없을까요?

L : 잠깐 기다리시겠습니까? (잠시 후) 이미 반납 독촉을 했는데도 반납을 하지 않고 있군요.

U : 반납 독촉은 어떻게 합니까?

L : 반납 기일이 지나면 자동적으로 이메일로 반납 독촉이 됩니다.

U : 그래도 반납을 하지 않은 건가요?

L : 이용자의 양심에 대한 문제라고 생각합니다.

U : 장기 연체를 하면 저처럼 피해자가 생길 텐데요.

L : 그 때문에 연체자에게 각종 증명서가 발급되지 않도록 제재를 가하고 있습니다.

U : 자료를 빨리 보고 싶은데, 어떻게 좀 해 주세요.

L : 그러면 전화를 걸어 직접 독촉해 보겠습니다.

Situation 29 Overdue Notices

U : A book I want to borrow has been out for a long time. Can you help?

L : Would you wait for a moment, please? (After a short while) The book has
not been returned yet, even with an overdue notice.

U : How do you send an overdue notice?

L : When a book is overdue, an e-mail is automatically sent out.

U : But he didn't return the book!

L : It's up to his conscience.

U : People like him cause problems for others.

L : That's why we place a block on transcripts, certificates and the like for
them.

U : Anyway, I need this book right away. Please do something.

L : Let me call him and see what I can do.

상황 30　사물함

L : 학생, 잠깐만요.

U : 왜 그러시죠?

L : 이 자료실에는 가방을 가지고 들어가면 안됩니다. 입구에 있는 사물함에 넣고 들어가세요.

U : 왜 가방을 가지고 들어가면 안됩니까?

L : 자료 분실을 방지하기 위해서입니다.

U : 이 책은 참조하는 데 필요한데 가지고 들어가면 안될까요?

L : 좋습니다. 나중에 나갈 때 확인 받고 나가세요.

U : 고맙습니다. 그런데 사물함은 어떻게 이용하죠?

L : 학생증을 맡기면 사물함 열쇠를 지급합니다. 퇴실할 때 가방을 찾고 열쇠를 주면 학생증을 돌려줍니다.

Situation 30 Lockers

L : Excuse me, just a moment please.

U : What is it?

L : You may not enter this room with your bag. Please leave your bag in the locker at the entrance.

U : Why can't I bring my bag with me?

L : In order to prevent the loss of materials, bags are not allowed. That's our policy.

U : I need this book in order to work on my report. Can I bring it in with me?

L : That's not a problem. But please show me the book when you go out.

U : OK. How can I use the locker?

L : Give your student card at the desk and get a key for a locker. Hand in the key when you leave and you'll get your ID back.

상황 31　분실물 신고

U : 열람실에서 지갑을 분실했어요.

L : 이런, 안됐군요. 언제 어디서 분실했습니까?

U : 언제 어디에서 잃어버렸는지 잘 모르겠어요.

L : 주변을 찾아 보셨습니까?

U : 예, 아무 데도 없어요.

L : 그럼 수위 아저씨한테 여쭈어 봤어요?

U : 예, 없다고 하시던데요.

L : 혹시 모르니까 습득물 진열장에서 찾아 보세요.

U : 그러죠. (10분 후) 거기에도 없어요.

L : 그러면 여기 분실물 신고대장에 기록해 놓으세요.

U : 발견되면 알려 주나요?

L : 그렇습니다.

Situation 31 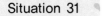 Lost and Found

U : I lost my wallet somewhere in the library.

L : I'm sorry to hear that. When and where did you lose it?

U : I don't know exactly.

L : Did you retrace your steps and look over where you might have lost it?

U : Yes, but I could not find it anywhere.

L : Did you check with the security guard at the front gate?

U : I already checked. There hasn't been any report.

L : Did you happen to check the Lost and Found?

U : Let me try that. (After 10 minutes) I didn't have any luck.

L : I'm sorry. Why don't you fill out this Lost Items Report?

U : Will you let me know if someone finds it?

L : Of course we will.

상황 32 💬 검색 결과

U : 이 자료는 어디에 있어요?

L : 잠시만요, 먼저 검색해 봅시다.

U : 여기서 검색하면 어느 도서관에 있는지 다 알 수 있어요?

L : 교내 여러 도서관의 모든 자료는 데이터베이스로 입력되어 있어 어디서 검색해도 알 수 있답니다.

U : 대출가능 여부도 알 수 있나요?

L : 그렇습니다. 그리고 도서관의 어느 자료실에 있는지도 알 수 있습니다.

U : 어떤 자료는 대출불가로 나타나네요.

L : 그런 자료는 참고도서나 연속간행물같이 관내에서만 열람할 수 있는 자료입니다. 자, 검색 결과가 나왔습니다. 자연과학도서관에 소장되어 있고, 현재 대출 가능합니다.

U : 고맙습니다. 빨리 가서 빌려야겠습니다.

Situation 32  Search Results

U : (Holding a library slip) Where can I find this?

L : Please show me the slip so that I can do a search.

U : If I do a search here, can I find out which library has it?

L : This database includes the holdings for all of this university's libraries.
You can access the same information at any of the terminals on campus.

U : Does the system say whether it is available for check-out?

L : It does. It also indicates the location within the library.

U : I noticed that some materials are not loanable.

L : Those are reference books or periodicals which can only be used within
the library. Ah-ha, I found your book. It's in the Science Library and it is
ready to be checked out.

U : I appreciate your help. I'll go get it right now.

상황 33　　개인정보 조회

U : 제가 대출한 책이 어떤 책인지 확인하고 싶은데요.

L : 먼저 학생증을 보여 주시겠어요? (스캔 후) 3책 대출하였고, 그 중 1책은 연체했군요.

U : 예? 연체했다고요? 제가 직접 조회할 수도 있습니까?

L : 도서관 홈페이지의 이용자 조회 서비스를 이용하세요.

U : 어떻게 하는 건지 가르쳐 주세요.

L : 아이디는 본인의 학번이고, 초기화된 비밀번호는 주민등록번호 뒷번호니까 그걸로 로그인하세요.

U : 비밀번호를 바꿀 수 있나요?

L : 그렇습니다. 비밀번호 변경 버튼을 클릭한 후 지시에 따라 하면 됩니다.

U : 집에서도 제가 대출한 책이 무엇인지, 언제 반납해야 하는지 알 수 있겠네요.

L : 그렇습니다. 그 밖에도 과거에 어떤 책을 대출했는지도 알 수 있습니다.

U : 아주 편리하네요.

L : 도서관은 알면 알수록 편리하게 이용할 수 있답니다.

Circulation • 대출

U : I'd like to check and see which books I've borrowed.

L : Let me have your student ID, please. (After scanning the card) You have checked out three books. One of them is overdue.

U : Excuse me? One of them is overdue? Is there any way I can check myself?

L : Check your user account on the library website.

U : Could you show me how to use it?

L : Log in with your student number as your ID and the last seven digits of your national identification number as your password.

U : Can I change my password?

L : Of course you can. Click on the Change of Password button and follow the instructions.

U : Then I'll be able to find out at home what I have borrowed and when they are due.

L : You can also see all books borrowed in the past.

U : That's really great!

L : The more you know about the library, the more convenient it becomes to use.

상황 34　　♥ 메일 전송 에러

U : 도서관에서는 반납 예정일 전에 알림 서비스를 하지 않나요?

L : 시스템을 통해서 반납 예정 3일 전에, SMS와 E-mail로 알려 드립니다.

U : 이상하군요. 전혀 안내를 못 받았습니다.

L : 도서관 홈페이지에 접근하여 개인 계정으로 로그인 해주세요. 그리고 개인 정보를 확인하여, 개인 정보가 정확하게 입력되었는지. 등록하신 E-mail과 핸드폰 번호를 확인해 주세요.

U : 아. 그렇군요.

L : 연락처에 잘못된 정보나 휴면 계정을 입력하고 방치하는 이용자 분들이 종종 계십니다.

U : 곧바로 수정하겠습니다. 감사합니다.

Situation 34   E-Mail Delivery Errors

U : Does the library send a notice before due dates?

L : The library system automatically dispatches e-mail and SMS alarms to your account 3 days before the due date.

U : It seems strange to me because I didn't receive any messages.

L : Please access the library website and log in to your account. Then make sure your contact information, such as e-mail address or cell phone number, is correct.

U : I see.

L : Users often input wrong or old contact information and neglect the account.

U : I'll check it right now. Thanks a lot.

상황 35　　메일 서버 다운

U : 도서 반납 예정일인데, E-mail 안내를 받지 못했습니다.

L : 아. 그렇지 않아도 도서관 홈페이지에서 E-mail 전송 에러에 대한 공지를 올렸는데 아직 못 보셨군요.

U : 네. 무슨 일이죠?

L : 실은 도서관 메일 서버에 문제가 있어서, 지난 이틀간 제대로 서비스를 해 드리지 못했습니다.

U : 이틀이나요?

L : 또 어제 정전으로 e-mail 서버가 정상 작동하지 못했습니다. 하지만 오늘 복구가 완료되어, 내일부터는 정상적으로 서비스 될 예정입니다. 이용에 불편을 드려 죄송합니다.

U : 다행이군요. 잘 알겠습니다.

Situation 35 — E-Mail Server Down

U : Today is the due date but I haven't received any messages from the library.

L : You seem to have missed an announcement on our homepage that there is a problem with e-mail delivery.

U : What happened?

L : There has been a problem with the university e-mail server for the last two days.

U : There has been no service for two days?

L : Not only that, but there was also a power outage yesterday that made the E-mail server inoperable. The server just got back online today. Starting tomorrow, it will be back to normal service. I'm sorry for any inconvenience this may have caused you.

U : Don't worry about that. I'm just glad everything's OK now.

상황 36 　　전자책 이용 1

U : 전자책 이용 방법에 대하여 문의하고 싶습니다.

L : 말씀하세요. 구체적으로 찾으시는 전자책 자료가 있습니까?

U : 네, 제목은 *Protocells : Bridging Nonliving and Living Matter* 이고 2009년 출판 자료입니다. 도서관 홈페이지에서 검색해보니, NetLibrary에서 이용할 수 있다고 하더군요.

L : 해당 검색결과 화면에서 URL 아이콘만 클릭하시면 곧바로 원문으로 연결됩니다.

U : 원문 저장이나 출력은 가능한가요?

L : 저작권 보호를 위해 1쪽씩 출력할 수 있습니다. 그러나 저장 기능은 지원하지 않습니다.

U : Can I ask you a question about how to use e-books?

L : Sure, go ahead. Is there any specific e-book you want to read?

U : Yes. The title is *Protocells : Bridging Nonliving and Living Matter*, and it was published in 2009. I searched on the library website and found this material is available via NetLibrary

L : Then all you need to do is click the URL icon from the search result. You can access this e-book directly.

U : Is it possible to save or print?

L : You can print a single sheet at one time due to copyright. But NetLibrary service does not support a save function.

상황 37　　♥ 전자책 이용 2

U : 해외 문학 관련 수업 때문에 파울로 코엘료의 『연금술사』책을 보고 싶은데, 모두 대출 중이라 빌릴 수가 없습니다. 혹시 다른 방법이 있을까요?

L : 해당 도서는 우리 도서관에서 전자 책으로 보유하고 있습니다.

U : 자세한 이용 방법을 알려주세요.

L : 혹시 스마트폰이나 태블릿 PC를 보유하고 계신가요?

U : 네.

L : 전자책 도서관은 어플리케이션을 통해 손쉽게 접근할 수 있습니다. 어플리케이션 스토어에 접근하여, 전자책 어플리케이션을 검색하여 설치해 주세요. 설치 후에 간단한 보안 인증절차를 거친 후, 대출하여 이용하실 수 있습니다.

U : 대출기한은 어떻게 되나요?

L : 일반 단행본과 동일합니다.

Circulation ● 대출

Situation 37 e-Book 2

U : I want to read The *Alchemist* written by Paulo Coelho for my foreign literature class, but there is no copy available. Is there any way to read this book?

L : The requested item is available via e-book in the Hankook University Library.

U : How does one access an e-book?

L : Do you have any multimedia devices, like a tablet or smart phone?

U : Yes.

L : The e-book library can be easily connected by an application. Please search and install the e-book program through the application store. After a simple security certification, you can borrow an e-book.

U : How long is the loan period for e-books?

L : It's the same as for monographs.

상황 38　　　전자책 단말기 대여

U : 안녕하세요, 전자책을 보고 싶은데 스마트폰이나 태블릿 PC를 보유하고
　　있지 않습니다. 다른 방법은 없을까요?

L : 도서관에서 제공하는 전자책 단말기를 이용해 보시는 것은 어떠세요?

U : 대여 절차에 대해서 간단하게 소개해주세요.

L : 우선 각 분관별 담당 사서에게 대출 가능 단말기 여부를 문의하세요. 대여
　　가능한 단말기가 있을 경우, 간단한 서약서를 작성하신 후에 단말기를
　　대여 받으실 수 있습니다.

U : 서약서는 왜 작성하죠?

L : 단말기 대여에 대한 간략한 소개와 이용 지침을 안내하고 있으며, 이에
　　동의하는 내용을 담고 있습니다.

Situation 38 Borrowing an E-book Reader

U : Hello, I wish to read an electronic book but I don't have any mobile device, such as a smart phone or tablet PC.

L : Why don't you borrow an e-book reader from the library?

U : Please let me know the procedure.

L : First, check for available readers in your branch library. Then, fill out a loan form and rent an e-book reader.

U : Why do I need to fill out a form?

L : It includes brief guidelines and terms of use to which you have to agree when you make a loan for an e-book reader.

상황 39 ♥ 분관 대출 안내

U : 논문 작성을 위해 필요한 도서가, 세종캠퍼스 학술정보원에 소장되어있습니다. 분관 도서관에 소장된 자료를 빌릴 수 있는 방법은 없을까요?

L : 분관 대출 서비스를 권해 드립니다. 다른 캠퍼스에 소장되어 있는 도서의 경우, 도서관 홈페이지를 통해 분관 대출을 신청해 주세요. 주기적으로 운영하는 셔틀을 통해 전달 받을 수 있습니다.

U : 편리한 서비스군요.

L : 단, 주의하실 점이 있습니다. 신청하신 분관 대출 도서는, 도착 안내 후 3일 안에 수령하셔야 합니다. 만약 지정된 기일 내에 수령하지 않으실 경우, 한 달 동안 해당 서비스를 이용하실 수 없게 됩니다.

U : 잘 알겠습니다.

L : 아울러 신청을 하셔도, 현재 대출 가능 도서가 0권이라면 자동으로 취소됩니다.

U : 아. 우선 도서 반납부터 해야겠네요. 안내 감사합니다.

Situation 39   Loan from Branch Libraries

U : I need a book for my thesis but I found this item is located at Sejong Academic Information Center. Is there any way to get it to a library on Anam Campus?

L : I recommend using the 'Loan from Branch Libraries' service. Please make a request via the library website. Requested materials will be delivered by a shuttle that goes daily between Anam campus and Sejong campus.

U : Oh, that's very handy!

L : But you must remember that users must pick up requested materials within 3 days after receiving an arrival notice. Users will get a one-month suspension from the service if they don't pick up materials on time.

U : OK. I see.

L : Also, you can't use the service if your maximum number of loan items is full.

U : Then, first, I need to return some materials I have on loan. Thank you.

상황 40 ♥ 도난 방지 시스템

(경보음 소리)

U : 이게 무슨 소리지요?

L : 놀라게 해드려 죄송합니다만, 도난 방지 시스템의 알람 소리입니다. 혹시 대출하지 않은 자료를 갖고 계시지 않은가요?

U : 아니요. 모두 대출한 도서입니다.

L : 이 두 권의 책은 한국대학교 도서관에서 빌린 도서가 아닌 듯 하군요. 다른 도서관에서 빌린 책을 갖고 계신가요?

U : 네. 동네 도서관에서 일주일 전에 빌린 책입니다.

L : 그렇다면 이 책들이 원인일 수도 있겠군요. 이 책을 잠시 놔두시고 지나가 보시겠어요?

U : 경보음이 멈췄네요. 앞으로 주의 해야겠네요.

Situation 40 Book Detection System (BDS)

(Beep Sound)

U : What's that sound?

L : I am sorry to embarrass you but this is an anti-theft alarm. Do you have any un-checked materials?

U : No, they are all borrowed items.

L : But those two items do not belong to the Hankook University Library. Are they from another library?

U : Yes, I've borrowed them from a library in the neighborhood.

L : Then, they might be the cause for the alarm. Would you please pass through the gate without them? I'll hand them back to you.

U : OK, I will be careful next time.

Interlibrary Loan

상호대차

● ● ●

성균관대학교 학술정보관

Essential English
for Global Librarians

3 상호대차 / Interlibrary Loan

U : 안녕하세요. 찾고 싶은 저널의 기사가 있는데요.

L : 네. 일단 학교도서관 홈페이지에서 저널이 학교에 있는지 검색부터 하셔야 합니다.

U : 어떻게 하는지 가르쳐 주시겠어요?

L : 도서관 홈페이지의 통합검색 창을 통해 검색해보면, 찾고자 하는 저널의 소장 여부를 알 수가 있는데요. 만약 저널이 미소장으로 나타나면 다른 기관에 복사 신청이 가능합니다.

U : 절차가 좀 복잡한 것 같아요

L : 검색을 한번 해 보시고 잘 모르는 부분들이 있으면 다시 한번 질문을 해 주시겠어요?

U : 네. 알겠습니다.

Interlibrary Loan ● 상호대차

U : Hi. I'm trying to find a journal article.

L : All right. I suggest that you first search the library catalog to see if the university has the journal.

U : Can you show me how?

L : Visit the library website and do a book search. Enter the name of the journal you're looking for to see if the library has it. If it shows that the library doesn't have it, we can order a copy of it from another library.

U : It seems a bit complicated.

L : Give it a try and if you get stuck, come back and I'll try to help you.

U : All right. Thanks.

상황 2 　원문복사 서비스 신청

U : 대학원생인데요. 원문복사를 신청을 하고 싶은데 어떻게 해야 할지 모르겠습니다.

L : 서비스 신청 방법으로는 두 가지 방법이 있습니다.

U : 어떤 방법이 가장 빠르게 접수가 되겠습니까?

L : 홈페이지의 원문복사 메뉴를 통하여 신청하는 것이 가장 빠릅니다. 그 외에는 직접 방문을 하여 신청하는 방법이 있으나 불편해서 대부분 홈페이지를 통한 신청을 합니다.

U : 그럼 홈페이지에서 바로 신청을 하면 되는 건가요?

L : 그렇습니다. 원문복사 메뉴를 선택 후 내용을 기입해주세요.

U : 저널명과 기사명 외에 또 달리 써야 할 부분들이 있나요?

L : 발송방법을 선택해 주시고요. 소장기관을 기재해주시면 됩니다.

U : 네 알겠습니다. 다 기재했는데요.

L : 예. 그렇습니다. 신청해서 의뢰하도록 하겠습니다.

U : 언제쯤 받아 볼 수 있을까요?

L : 전자전송의 경우엔 근무일(business day) 기준 1~2일, 일반우편의 경우엔 한 3-4일 정도 걸리고, 빠른 우편의 경우엔 한 2~3일정도 걸립니다. 자료가 도착을 하면 문자로 연락을 드리겠습니다.

U : 네. 수고하세요.

Situation 2 Document Delivery Orders

U : I'm a graduate student. How would I go about ordering a copy of an article?

L : Well, there are two ways to order copies.

U : Which is the quickest?

L : Placing an order through the library homepage is the quickest. Placing an order in person is also possible, but less convenient. Usually users use the library website to request an article.

U : So I can order copies through the website directly?

L : Yes. Choose the 'Request Article' menu and fill in the form.

U : Do I need to give any other information besides the journal article name?

L : You will also need to specify how you want the journal delivered to you as well as where the journal is held.

U : All right. I think I'm finished.

L : Good. We'll process your order.

U : When can I expect the copies to be delivered?

L : About 1-2 business days by electronic transfer, about 3-4 days by regular mail and about 2-3 days by express mail. We'll contact you as soon as your order confirmation arrives through SMS.

U : Sounds good. Thanks for your help.

상황 3 　　　전자전송 시스템

U : 원문복사도 온라인으로 주고받을 수 있습니까?

L : 네. KERIS, NDSL기관에서는 각자 전자전송 시스템을 구축해서 기관간 논문이 온라인으로 전송되도록 하였습니다.

U : 전자전송의 장단점이 있을까요?

L : 전자전송은 기존 우편배송보다 쉽고 빠른 것이 장점입니다. 근무일 기준 1일 안에 대부분 처리가 되고, 스캔하여 업로드하면 되니 쉽습니다. 다만, 보통우편에 비해 장당 비용이 비싼 것은 단점이라고 할 수 있겠죠.

U : KERIS, NDSL 각 비용은 어떻게 되나요?

L : KERIS는 장당 100원입니다. NDSL은 1-10P까지는 1,000원이고, 추가는 장당 100원이 부과됩니다.

U : 그렇다면 이용자도 PDF형태로 받아볼 수 있나요?

L : 아니요. 이용자에게 PDF를 전송하는 것은 저작권에 위배됩니다. KERIS, NDSL의 시스템을 통해서 전자형태로 전송만 될 뿐이지 파일을 다운받을 수는 없습니다. 따라서 이용자에게는 페이퍼로 드리게 됩니다.

Situation 3　　Electronic Transfer System

U : Is it possible to get an article online?

L : Sure. KERIS and NDSL recently built their own electronic transfer system to deliver articles to libraries online.

U : What are the advantages of the electronic transfer system?

L : Electronic transfer is much easier and faster than mail. Almost every request is handled in about one business day. They are just scanned and uploaded. However, it's more expensive than mail.

U : How much does KERIS or NDSL cost?

L : KERIS is 100 won per page. NDSL is 1,000 won for articles up to 10 pages. Extra pages cost 100 won per page.

U : Is it possible to get a PDF file?

L : No. It's illegal to give PDF files to users. Through KERIS or NDSL, it's just an electronic transfer like mail. But there's no way to download a file. So we should give a copy of the article to users.

상황 4　♥ 저널 소장기관 문의

U : 신청서를 보면 소장기관을 기재하는 란이 있는데요. 그게 어디에 있는지 잘 모르겠어요.

L : 그러세요? 그럼 www.ndsl.or.kr 이나 www.riss.kr 로 들어가 저널들을 검색하시면 됩니다.

U : 그 사이트를 이용하는 방법을 알려주시겠어요?

L : 먼저 이용자 등록을 하세요. 그리고나서 저널명을 검색하는 화면에서 원하는 저널명이나 기사명을 치면 곧바로 그 저널이 소장되어 있는 학교나 기관들에 대해 알 수가 있습니다.

U : 무료로 등록이 가능한가요?

L : 그렇습니다. 저널검색 같은 서비스는 언제든지 무료로 이용하실 수 있습니다.

U : 바로 가서 검색을 해 봐야겠군요. 감사합니다.

Interlibrary Loan • 상호대차

U : On the order form, there is a space for the holding institution, but I don't
know who holds this journal.

L : I see. Then log in to www.ndsl.or.kr or www.riss.kr. You can search for
the journal there.

U : Can you show me how to search?

L : First, log in to the site. Then in the journal search window, type in the
name of the journal or the name of the journal article you're looking for
and it will show you where the journal is located.

U : Is that free?

L : Yes. Searching on those websites is always free.

U : I'll try that. Thanks.

상황 5 　본교 이용자 확인

U : 금방 온라인 상에서 원문복사 신청을 했는데요. 이용자를 인증받으라고 하던데 그건 뭔가요?

L : 원문복사 서비스는 우리 학교 학생들만 사용할 수 있기 때문에 이용자를 확인해야 합니다.

U : 아하! 그러면 어떻게 인증을 받죠?

L : 학생증을 보여 주시겠어요.

U : 여기 있습니다.

L : 정보통신 대학원에 다니시는군요. 저희 이용자 관리 시스템에 등록이 되어 있는지 확인을 한 후에 곧바로 온라인 상에서 인증작업을 하도록 하겠습니다.

U : 이제 원문복사 서비스를 이용할 수 있나요?

L : 예 KERIS나 NDSL 같은 사이트에서 직접 원문복사 신청을 하셔도 되고요. 도서관을 통해서 신청을 하셔도 서비스를 받을 실 수 있습니다.

U : 예, 알겠습니다.

Situation 5 Student Verification

U : I just placed a request online for Document Delivery Service. It says that my user status has to be verified. What does that mean?

L : Only students from our school are allowed to use this service, so we need to verify the status of our users.

U : Really? Then what do I need to do?

L : Can you show me your student ID?

U : Here it is.

L : I see you are a student at the IT graduate school. I'll check to see you are in the user management system and verify you online.

U : Can I use the document delivery service now?

L : Yes. You can order through KERIS or NDSL. You can also order through the library.

U : I see. Thanks.

상황 6   원문복사 신청 1

U : 원문복사 신청을 했는데요. 빠른 우편과 일반 우편으로 말고. E-mail로도 원문을 받아 볼 수 있나요?

L : 저작권법 관계상 이용자에게 이메일 자료 전송하는 것은 불법입니다. 대신 전자전송 방식이 있어서 학교간 시스템을 통해서 전송됩니다. 제일 빠른 방법이죠. 이용자는 근무일 기준 1일 이내 자료를 받을 수 있으며, 복사 형태로 전달받게 됩니다.

U : 그럼 전자전송 방식으로 해주세요.

L : 그런 제일 빠른 방식인 반면에 가격이 좀 비쌉니다. 장당 100원의 요금입니다.

U : 자료가 도착하면 어떻게 연락이 오나요?

L : 도착하면 저희가 SMS를 발송합니다

U : 네 기다리고 있겠습니다. 감사합니다.

Situation 6   Processing Document Delivery Requests1

U : I placed a request for Document Delivery Service. Instead of regular and express mail, can I receive journal articles by e-mail?

L : No. It's illegal to download PDF files because of copyright. Instead, there's an electronic transfer system that connects each library. It's the fastest way. Users can get a copy of an article within 1 business day.

U : OK, then I would like to use electronic transfer.

L : While the electronic transfer service is the quickest way, it is costly at 100 won per page.

U : How will you contact me?

L : We'll contact you either by cell phone or by e-mail.

U : OK, I'll use electronic transfer.

상황 7 　 원문복사 신청 2

L1 : 안녕하세요. 한국대학교 도서관 김성균입니다. 원문복사 서비스 담당하시는 분 좀 부탁드립니다.

L2 : 전데요. 무슨 일이시죠?

L1 : 예 안녕하세요. 어제 저희 학교 학생이 신청한 자료에 대해서 물어 볼 게 있어서요.

L2 : 예. 그러세요.

L1 : 어제 신청했다고 하는데 아직까지 신청 접수가 되지 않았습니다. 저희 학생이 급하게 원하는 자료라서요.

L2 : 죄송합니다. 실은 어제 시스템이 다운이 되었거든요. 지금 한번 확인해 보도록 하겠습니다. 학생 이름이 어떻게 되죠?

L1 : 예. 홍길동입니다. 신청한 저널은 *Journal of construction engineering*, vol. 12. n 4 page 22-46입니다.

L2 : 예. 접수는 되어 있네요. 곧바로 소장 여부를 확인해서 접수완료로 바꾸어 놓도록 하겠습니다.

L1 : 확인 후에 곧바로 전화 주시겠어요. 제 이름은 김성균이고, 전화번호는 012-345-6789입니다.

L2 : 예. 알겠습니다.

L1 : 감사합니다.

Interlibrary Loan • 상호대차

Situation 7 Processing Document Delivery Requests 2

L1 : Hi. This is Sungkyun Kim at Hankook Library. I'd like to speak with someone who's in charge of Document Delivery Service.

L2 : Yes, this is he. How can I help you?

L1 : Hello. I'd like to ask you about a document that one of our students requested yesterday.

L2 : OK. Go ahead.

L1 : We submitted a request yesterday but it's not shown as 'Registered' in the system yet. Would you please check it out?

L2 : Sorry. The system went down yesterday. Let me try to connect now. What's the student's name?

L1 : His name is Gil-dong Hong. He asked for pages 22 to 46 from the *Journal of Construction Engineering*, vol. 12 no. 4.

L2 : OK. His request has been registered. I'll check the availability and change the request status to 'Completed'.

L1 : Would you please call me back after you check? By the way, my name is Sungkyun Kim and my cell phone number is 012-345-6789.

L2 : OK.

L1 : Thank you.

상황 8

U : 안녕하세요. 원문복사 신청 접수가 되었나 해서 전화드렸는데요.

L : 이름이 어떻게 되죠?

U : 홍길동입니다. 어제 아마 4시쯤에 신청을 했을 겁니다.

L : 홍길동이라 음 아! 여기 있군요. 이미 신청 접수된 상태이며, 자료소장 기관
　　으로 신청이 완료된 상태입니다.

U : 언제쯤 자료를 받을 수 있을까요?

L : 빠른 우편으로 신청을 하셨으니깐 아마도 내일이면 받을 수 있을 겁니다.
　　자료가 오면 곧바로 연락을 드리도록 하겠습니다.

U : 내일 4시까지 수업이 있어서요. 그 이후에 연락을 주세요.

L : 네. 알겠습니다.

Situation 8   Confirming Requests

U : Hello. I'm calling to confirm my document delivery request.

L : May I have your name, please?

U : Gil-dong Hong. I submitted a request around 4 p.m. yesterday.

L : OK. Let me see. Yes, I see your name. Your request has been completed with the lending institution.

U : When can I expect to receive my copies?

L : We'll probably get them tomorrow because you selected express mail. We'll contact you as soon as the copies arrive.

U : I have classes until 4 p.m. tomorrow. You can contact me anytime after that.

L : All right.

상황 9 　연락

L : 여보세요. 홍길동 학생이십니까?

U : 예, 접니다.

L : 신청하신 자료가 도착했는데요. 오늘 중으로 찾으러 오실 수 있나요?

U : 제가 지금 급한 일이 있어서 그런데, 제 친구를 대신 보내도 괜찮겠습니까?

L : 그러면 친구분이 신청자 본인을 확인할 수 있는 신분증을 가지고 오셔야
　　합니다.

U : 알겠습니다.

Situation 9 Notification

L : Hello. May I speak to Mr. Gil-dong Hong?

U : Yes, speaking.

L : This is Document Delivery Service at Hankook University. Your
   document has arrived. Would you be able to come and pick it up today?

U : Well, something urgent has come up. Could I have my friend pick it up
   for me?

L : Then please have your friend bring your ID card.

U : OK.

상황 10 　　서비스 자료 이상

L1: 안녕하세요? 제가 신청한 자료의 금액하고 발송 슬립에 적힌 금액이 다른데. 어떻게 된 건가요?

L2: 그래요? 한번 확인해 보도록 하겠습니다. 조금만 기다려 주시겠어요.
　　죄송합니다. 원문 복사한 페이지를 잘못 세어서 추가로 요금이 책정되었네요. 다시 한번 발송 슬립을 보내겠습니다.

L1: 그리고 4 페이지를 복사한 면이 상태가 안 좋아서 다시 복사해 주셨으면 좋겠는데요.

L2: 알겠습니다. 다른 페이지들은 괜찮은가요?

L1: 네. 다른 페이지는 이상이 없는 것 같습니다.

L2: 곧바로 복사를 해서 FAX로 보내드리도록 하겠습니다.

L1: 감사합니다.

Situation 10　Service Errors

L1 : Hello. The amount shown on the invoice for this service is different from my order. Can you explain this discrepancy?

L2 : Is that right? If you can hold for a second, I'll check to see what happened. We're sorry. We miscounted the number of pages. We'll send you a new invoice.

L1 : And another thing. Page 4 wasn't copied clearly, so could you send me a better copy?

L2 : All right. How are the rest of the pages?

L1 : They seem fine.

L2 : I'll copy page 4 right now and send it to you by fax.

L1 : Thank you.

상황 11 　자료 도착

U : 저 실례합니다! 원문 복사 신청한 것을 찾으러 왔는데요.

L : 이름이 어떻게 되죠?

U : 홍길동입니다. 지난 주 화요일에 신청을 했는데...

L : 여기 있군요. 원문복사 요금이 1,900원 나왔습니다.

U : 여기 2,000원 있습니다. 그리고 영수증을 좀 써주시겠습니까?

L : 잠시만요. 여기 잔돈 받으시고요. 영수증 있습니다.

U : 감사합니다. 그럼 수고하세요.

Situation 11 Document Arrivals

U : Excuse me, I'm here to pick up my order.

L : OK. What's your name, please?

U : Gil-dong Hong. I requested my copies last Tuesday.

L : Here they are. That'll be 1,900 won.

U : Here's 2000 won. I'd like to have a receipt, please.

L : OK. Here's your change and your receipt.

U : Thank you. Have a nice day.

상황 12 국회도서관 논문 출력

U : 안녕하세요. 보고 싶은 논문이 국회도서관에 있다는데 여기서 볼 수 있나요?

L : 그렇습니다. 국회도서관 자료는 지정된 PC에서만 열람할 수 있습니다. 한국 도서관에는 총 5대의 PC가 국회도서관 자료를 이용 가능합니다. 국회도서 지정PC에서는 원문열람, 저장, 인쇄가 가능합니다. 하지만 현재 모두 이용 중이라 원문복사 신청을 하시는 게 좋을 것 같습니다.

U : 그럼 지금 신청을 하도록 하겠습니다. 언제쯤 볼 수가 있을까요?

L : 잠시만 기다리면 되겠습니다. 검색을 해보고 소장 여부가 확인이 되면 곧바로 출력해서 드릴 수가 있거든요.

U : 그래요.

L : 아! 여기 있군요. 전부 200page인데 다 신청하시겠어요?

U : 앞부분은 필요 없으니까 4page부터 끝 페이지까지 출력해주시겠어요.

L : page당 50원씩 계산해서 197page니까 9,850원입니다.

U : 네 만 원 여기 있습니다.

L : 잔돈 150원입니다. 혹시 영수증 필요하세요?

U : 아뇨 필요 없습니다. 그럼 수고하세요.

Situation 12 · Printing National Assembly Library Dissertations

U : Hi. A dissertation I'm looking for is held by the National Assembly
   Library. Can I read the paper from here?

L : Yes, but only five PCs in the Hankook Library are connected to the
   National Assembly Library. It's possible to open a dissertation file, save,
   and print through those PCs. But all 5 PCs are being used right now, so I
   suggest using our document delivery service.

U : All right. Then I will place an order right now. When will it be ready?

L : Let me search first. If the full-text is available, I'll print it out for you now.

U : Thanks.

L : Yes, it's available. There are 200 pages in all. Do you want to order a
   copy of the full document?

U : I don't need the first few pages. Could you print from page 4 to the end?

L : It's 50 won per page, so the total comes out to 9,850 won for 197 pages.

U : Here's 10,000 won.

L : Here's your change, 150 won. Do you need a receipt?

U : No, thanks. Have a nice day.

상황 13 　단행본 전권 신청

L1 : 학생이 단행본 전권을 신청하였는데요. 서비스가 가능한지 모르겠어요.

L2 : 저희 도서관에서는 원칙적으론 단행본을 다 복사해드리지는 않습니다.

L1 : 서비스가 불가능하다는 말씀이신가요?

L2 : 예 저작권에 위반되기 때문에 단행본을 전권 복사해 드릴 수 없습니다.

L1 : 학생이 급하게 필요해서 그러는데 어떻게 안 될까요?

L2 : 죄송합니다. 도서관 규정상 어쩔 수가 없네요.

L1 : 잘 알겠습니다.

Situation 13　Ordering Photocopying Services

L1 : A student placed an order to copy a whole book. Is that allowed?

L2 : Entire books are not allowed to be copied in our library.

L1 : Are you saying that copy services are not available for copying an entire book?

L2 : Right. We can't copy a whole book because of copyright laws, but a user can place an order to copy some parts of the book.

L1 : Isn't there any way? This student needs this book urgently.

L2 : We're sorry. We have to follow the library regulations to abide by the law.

L1 : I understand.

상황 14　KERIS 사이트 이용

U : 저~ KERIS 사이트에서 저널을 찾아서 신청을 하고 싶은데요. 어떻게 해야 하는지 잘 모르겠어요.

L : 네! 일단 ww.riss.kr 에 접속을 해서 회원으로 등록을 하셔야 합니다.

U : 그러면 곧바로 문헌복사 서비스를 이용할 수 있게 되는 건가요?

L : 아닙니다. 이용자 인증 절차를 거쳐야 합니다. 소속 도서관에 이용자로 등록이 되어 있는지 확인한 후에 문헌복사 서비스를 이용할 수 있도록 이용자 인증을 확인하는 거죠.

U : 좀 복잡하군요.

L : 한번 해보시면 어렵지 않다는 것을 아실 겁니다.

U : 그러면 어떻게 인증을 받아야 하는 거죠?

L : 요즘에는 온라인으로 처리가 되기 때문에 학생이 특별히 할 일은 없습니다. 저희가 인증을 해드리면 신청이 완료되고 며칠 내에 원문을 받아보실 수 있습니다.

U : 알겠습니다. 일단 회원 가입을 하고 신청을 하겠습니다. 그리고 NII/CALIS 는 무엇인가요?

L : NII는 일본기관, CALIS는 중국기관과 협정을 체결하여 원문복사, 상호대차 서비스가 가능하도록 한 것입니다.

U : 그럼 국내에 없는 일본, 중국자료도 쉽게 볼 수 있는 건가요?

L : 예 쉽고 저렴하게 볼 수 있는 장점이 있습니다.

Situation 14 Using the KERIS Site

U : Hi. I'd like to request document delivery service for a journal article using the Korea Education and Research Information Service (KERIS) website. Could you show me how to use this site?

L : Sure. First, you need to connect to www.riss.kr and register as a user.

U : Can I then immediately use the copy service?

L : Not really. After you register as a user, we will have to verify whether you are registered as a library user. You can use the copy service only after your user status is confirmed.

U : It seems a bit complicated.

L : I think once you try it, you'll find that it's not so difficult.

U : Then how can I be verified as a user?

L : These days all verification is processed online, so you don't have to do anything. After we verify you as a library user, requests will be processed automatically and you can get a copy in a few days.

U : OK. I'll register at the KERIS website right away, and request a journal article. I have one more question. What's NII/CALIS?

L : National Information of Informatics (NII) is linked to Japanese libraries, and China Academic Library and Information System (CALIS) is linked to Chinese libraries. We signed agreements with Japanese and Chinese institutes for sharing resources through Interlibrary Loan and document delivery services.

U : Then could I receive a copy from Japan or China even if there's no copy in Korea?

L : Sure. It's also easier and cheaper than the other methods.

ㄴ : 안녕하세요. 한국대학교 도서관에서 원문복사 담당을 맡고 있는 김성균입니다.

ㄱ : 네! 안녕하세요. 원문복사 서비스 대행업체인 ABC입니다. 무엇을 도와 드릴까요?

ㄴ : 해외로 원문복사신청을 하고 싶어서요.

ㄱ : 네! 원하시는 자료들을 적으셔서 제 e-mail로 보내주시겠어요. 이메일 주소는 abc@abc.or.kr입니다.

ㄴ : 다시 한번 이메일 주소를 불러 주시겠어요?

ㄱ : 예. abc@abc.or.kr입니다.

ㄴ : 곧바로 메일을 보내도록 하겠습니다. 그러면 언제쯤 원문들을 받을 수 있을까요?

ㄱ : 먼저 서비스 가능한 자료인지 검색을 해보고요. 가능한 자료라면 해외로 복사 신청이 들어가고 나서 한 15일 정도면 받아 보실 수 있습니다.

ㄴ : 요금은 어떻게 책정이 되어 있나요?

ㄱ : 한 건당 $12달러로 되어 있습니다. 그날 환율에 따라 견적서 가격은 약간 차이가 있습니다.

ㄴ : 환율이 낮을 때 견적서 신청을 해야겠군요.

ㄱ : 그러시는 게 좋을 겁니다.

ㄴ : 그러면 대행사를 통해서 원문을 받게 되는 건가요?

ㄱ : 아뇨 직접 접수된 기관에서 일괄적으로 보내게 됩니다.

ㄴ : 알겠습니다. 신청한 원문이 도착하면 다시 연락을 하도록 하겠습니다.

Situation 15　International Document Delivery

L : Hello. This is Sungkyun Kim in charge of Document Delivery Service at Hankook University.

V : This is ABC, a document delivery service provider. What can we do for you?

L : I would like to place an international order for a document.

V : OK. Please send us an e-mail with the document information. Our email address is abc@abc.or.kr.

L : Can you repeat the address, please?

V : Yes. It's abc@abc.or.kr.

L : I'll send you an e-mail right now. When can I expect to receive the document?

V : First, we'll need to check the availability. If it is available, we'll place an order. After that, you should receive it within about 15 days.

L : What's the cost?

V : $12.50 per request. The price will vary slightly depending on the exchange rate on the day of the order.

L : I guess it would be best to place an order when the exchange rate is low, right?

V : Probably.

L : Will the document come directly from your agency?

V : No. They will send it to you directly.

L : I see. We'll contact you when our order arrives.

상황 16　　신청취소 문의

L : 여보세요. 홍길동 학생이지요? 도서관에 원문복사 신청한 자료가 도착했는데요.

U : 어쩌죠? 급해서 이미 다른 곳에서 자료를 구했는데요.

L : 미리 전화를 주시지 그러셨어요? 이미 신청을 해 버린 거라 요금을 지불하셔야 하거든요.

U : 꼭 요금을 지불해야 하나요?

L : 도서관에서 이미 타 기관에 요금을 지불한 상태라 그에 대한 요금을 지불하셔야 합니다.

U : 무슨 방법이 없을까요?

L : 예. 달리 방법이 없습니다.

U : 알겠습니다. 요금을 지불하도록 하겠습니다.

Situation 16 Order Cancellation Inquiries

L : Hello. Is this Mr. Gil-dong Hong? Your requested document has arrived.

U : I'm sorry but I needed the paper urgently, so I got it from another source.

L : Then you should have cancelled with us. We already placed your order.
I'm afraid you'll still have to pay for it.

U : Do I really need to pay?

L : Yes, unfortunately. We have already paid our vendor for it.

U : Is there a way out?

L : Sorry, but there's really no other way.

U : I understand. I guess I'll pay for it.

상황 17　　요금 문의

U : 원문복사 요금이 기관별로 다른 것 같네요. 좀 복잡하네요.

L : 예 좀 복잡하죠? 그러나 기관별로 약간씩의 차이가 있을 뿐입니다.

U : NDSL의 경우엔 한 건당 100원이 더 비싼 것 같아요.

L : 예 NDSL 사이트 이용료로 100원을 추가로 받고 있습니다.

U : KERIS 요금에 대해서 설명 좀 해주세요.

L : 보통 요금의 경우엔 기본요금이 700원이고 1page 복사비가 70원씩 계산이 됩니다. 빠른 우편은 기본 요금 1,000원에 복사비가 같은 요금을 적용해서 요금을 책정하고 있습니다.

U : 전자전송 신청도 가능하지요? 그럴 경우 요금이 어떻게 되나요?

L : 전자전송 신청은 가장 빠른 방법이긴 하지만 요금이 비싼데요, 페이지당 100원이며 수수료 100원이 별도 부과됩니다.

U : 아하! 그렇군요. 알겠습니다. 발송방법에 따라 요금 차이가 꽤 나는군요.

L : 아무래도 빠를수록 요금이 비싸게 되죠.

U : 이해가 되네요. 알겠습니다.

Interlibrary Loan • 상호대차

U : Hi. I'm confused about the different fees among document delivery service providers.

L : It is confusing, isn't it? However, the difference is only very slight.

U : Take NDSL, they seem to charge 100 won more per copy than the other providers.

L : You're right. NDSL does charge 100 won more.

U : How much does KERIS charge?

L : The base service charge is 700 won and each page costs an additional 70 won. For express mail, the base charge increases to 1,000 won.

U : Is electronic transfer service available? How much is it?

L : That service is available. Electronic transfer service is the fastest way, but it costs more. The fee is 100 won per page.

U : Oh. I see. So the fees vary significantly depending on delivery method?

L : The faster the service, the more expensive it is.

U : I understand. Thanks.

상황 18   원문복사 시스템에 문제가 발생한 상황

L : 원문복사 시스템에 문제가 생긴 것 같아요.

V : 어떤 부분에서 에러가 나는 가요?

L : 원문복사 서비스 통계를 뽑고 싶은데 출력물에서 자꾸 에러 화면이 뜨는 데요.

V : 그래요. 어떤 메시지가 뜨던가요

L : '런타임 오류'라는 메시지가 계속 뜨면서 시스템이 다운되어버리네요.

V : 시스템 환경 설정들이 제대로 되어 있는지 확인해 보시고요. 그래도 에러 메시지가 뜨면 그 화면을 캡쳐해서 제 e-mail 주소로 보내주시겠어요.

L : 환경 설정은 제대로 되어 있는데요. 에러 메시지 화면을 캡쳐해서 보내 보도록 하겠습니다.

V : 네 곧바로 처리해서 문제를 해결하도록 하겠습니다.

Interlibrary Loan • 상호대차

Situation 18 Document Delivery System Errors

L : There seems to be something wrong with the document delivery system.

V : What is wrong?

L : I want to print out statistical information on the copy service, but an error window pops up when I try to print.

V : Really? Can you tell me what the error message says?

L : The message 'Run-time error' keeps coming up and the system keeps going down.

V : You should check the system setting first. If the error message keeps showing up, could you capture the screen and e-mail it to me?

L : It looks like the setting is OK. I'll capture the error message screen and e-mail it to you.

V : We'll take a look and correct the problem as soon as possible.

상황 19 　♥ 외국학술지 지원센터

U : 원문복사를 저렴하게 이용하는 방법이 있을까요?

L : 네. 정부에서는 9개의 외국학술지 지원센터를 선정하여 운영하고 있습니다.

U : 외국학술지 지원센터요? 그게 뭐죠?

L : 정부에서 9개 대학을 선정하여 지원을 해주고, 그 9개 대학은 학술지를 구비하여 이용자 요청 시에는 무료로 제공합니다.

U : 7개 대학은 어떤 분야를 지원합니까?

L : 경북대ー정보통신, 강원대ー생명공학, 고려대ー인문학, 서울대ー자연과학, 연세대-임상의학, 부산대ー기술과학, 전북대ー농축산, 충남대ー행정경영학, 이화여대ー교육사회학 입니다.

U : 이용방법은 어떻게 되나요?

L : 일반 원문복사와 동일하게 이용할 수 있습니다. KERIS, NDSL, FRIC을 접속하여 학술지 검색 → 상세정보 클릭 → 복사/대출신청 클릭 → 제공도서관을 [무료]00대학교 외국학술지 지원센터를 선택하면 됩니다.

U : 어렵지 않군요. 감사합니다.

Situation 19   Foreign Research Information Center (FRIC)

U : Is there any cheaper way to request an article?

L : Yes. There are nine Foreign Research Information Centers managed by the government for specific fields.

U : Foreign Research Information Centers? What are they?

L : The government selects nine well-planned universities and supports them as a Foreign Research Information Center. The nine Foreign Research Information Centers hold many specialized journals and provide copies of them for free.

U : What are the nine universities and their subjects?

L : Kyungpook University collects Computer & Information Technology; Kangwon University. —Life Science; Korea University. —Humanities; Seoul National University. —Natural Science; Yonsei University. —Clinical Medicine; Pusan University. —Engineering Science; Chonbuk University. —Agriculture; Chungnam University. —Public Administration and Business Administration; Ewha Womans University. —Education and Sociology.

U : How can I use that service?

L : It's the same as Document Delivery Service. Connect to KERIS, NDSL, or FRIC and search the journal. From the detailed information for the journal, click 'Copy/Loan,' then choose the '[Free] 00 University Foreign Research Information Center'.

U : It does not seem that difficult. OK. Thanks.

상황 20　　PPV서비스 (Pay per View서비스)

U : 안녕하세요. 전 홍길동 교수라고 합니다. 보고 싶은 논문이 있는데요, 이걸
　　구해주실 수 있나요?

L : 네. 어떤 논문인지 말씀해주시겠습니까?

U : 자세한 정보는 제가 이메일로 보내드리겠습니다. PDF로 보고 싶은데 가능
　　할까요?

L : 예. 가능합니다. 도서관에서는 교수님을 대상으로 원하는 논문의 PDF를
　　제공하는 PPV서비스를 하고 있습니다.

U : 그게 뭐죠?

L : 필요한 논문을 출판사 홈페이지에서 직접 결재하여 PDF를 교수님께 전달
　　해드리는 것입니다. 보통 해외원문복사가 2주일 정도 걸리는 것에 반해
　　PPV는 1~2시간 안에 처리가 가능해서 만족도가 높습니다.

U : 그런 좋은 서비스가 있었나요! 비용은 어떻게 됩니까?

L : 비용은 도서관에서 무료로 제공하여 드립니다.

U : 알겠습니다. 친절한 설명 감사합니다. 앞으로 많이 이용하도록 하겠습니다.

Situation 20  Pay per View Service

U : Excuse me. I'm professor Gil-dong Hong. I am searching for a thesis that I really want to use. Can you help me?

L : Sure. Just tell me the citation information for the thesis.

U : I'll send you that by e-mail. I want to see that thesis in PDF format. Is that possible?

L : Sure. We offer a PpV (Pay per View) service that provides PDF files to professors for free for those journals that we don't have a license for.

U : Could you explain in more detail?

L : We check out the thesis directly from the publisher's website, and forward it to the professor. In general, foreign document delivery service takes 2 weeks, but this PpV service provides the articles within 2 hours. So professors are very satisfied with this service.

U : Really? I didn't know that. How much does it cost?

L : It's free. It's included in the library budget.

U : I see. Thank you for your explanation. I'll use the PpV service more often.

상황 21 　OCLC ILL 서비스 문의

U : 안녕하세요. 기계공학과 석사과정 홍길동인데 제가 찾는 자료가 국내에는 없는 것 같습니다.

L : 어떤 자료인가요?

U : 미국에서 발행된 학위논문입니다.

L : PQDT나 KERIS의 종합목록을 검색해 보았나요?

U : 예. 둘 다 검색해 보았는데 국내소장기관도 없고 PQDT를 통해서도 원문을 입수할 수 없습니다. 어떻게 해야 하는지요?

L : 그럼, OCLC ILL 서비스를 신청해 보는 것이 좋을 것 같습니다.

U : OCLC ILL 서비스가 무엇인가요?

L : ILL 이란 InterLibrary Loan의 약자로 도서관간 자료 상호대차 서비스를 의미하는데. 해외 도서관에 있는 자료의 복사 및 대출을 신청할 수 있는 서비스입니다.

U : 아, 그런 서비스가 있군요. 그런데 무료서비스인가요?

L : 대출비용은 무료인 경우도 있고 유료인 경우도 있지만, 기본적으로 우편요금과 이용 비용이 부과됩니다. 보통 미국의 사립대학교 도서관은 대출비용이 $20~25로 비싸고 공공도서관은 무료인 곳이 많습니다. 자세한 내용은 홈페이지의 이용안내 정보를 참고하세요.

U : 그럼, 이용안내 내용을 살펴본 후에 이 서비스를 신청하도록 하겠습니다.

L : 예, 그렇게 하십시오.

Situation 21 | OCLC ILL Service Inquiries

U : Hi. My name is Gil-dong Hong and I'm a master's student in Mechanical Engineering. It seems that the document I'm looking for is not available in Korea.

L : What is it?

U : It's a thesis published in the U.S.

L : Did you try PQDT or KERIS?

U : I did, but no one in Korea seems to have this paper. I couldn't get a hold of it through PQDT. What should I do?

L : Well, I think the best option would be to order it through the OCLC ILL service.

U : What is the OCLC ILL service?

L : ILL stands for InterLibrary Loan. Libraries can share documents through this service. You also can order a copy or be loaned a document from a foreign library.

U : Is that right? Is it free?

L : Some loans are free; others are not. But you would have to pay for shipping expenses. In most cases, private college libraries in the U.S. charge between 20 and 25 dollars for each loan and public libraries charge nothing. You can get more details on its homepage.

U : OK. I'll consult a service guide first and get back to you.

L : OK.

상황 22 　　신청한 OCLC ILL 자료 문의

U : 안녕하세요. 저는 홍길동인데 어제 OCLC ILL 서비스를 신청했습니다. 혹시 제 메일을 받아보셨는지요?

L : 예, 오늘 오전에 OCLC ILL 신청 메일을 받고 조금 전에 미국 소장기관에 신청 처리를 완료했습니다.

U : 그렇군요, 얼마나 기다리면 됩니까?

L : 자료에 따라 조금 다르지만 보통 2주~3주 정도 걸립니다.

U : 무료로 받아 볼 수 있을까요?

L : 미국 소장기관 중에서 대출요금(Lending charges)이 무료인 곳에 우선적으로 신청했는데 1차 신청기관에서 대출해 준다면 대출요금은 무료이고 우편요금과 IFM 비용만 부담하시면 됩니다. 만약 2차 신청기관에서 대출을 받게 되면 대출요금으로 10달러를 더 부담하셔야 할 것 같습니다.

U : 잘 알겠습니다. 급한 자료이니 최대한 빨리 연락 주시면 좋겠습니다.

L : 예, 알겠습니다. 자료가 도착하는 대로 바로 연락 드리겠습니다.

U : 감사합니다, 그럼, 수고하세요.

Interlibrary Loan • 상호대차

U : Hello. I'm Gil-dong Hong and I ordered my document through the OCLC ILL service. Have you received my e-mail?

L : Yes. We received your order this morning and sent it to a holding institute in the U.S. just a few minutes ago.

U : When can I expect to receive my document?

L : It depends on the resources, but it usually takes about 2 to 3 weeks.

U : Is it free?

L : We first request your document to primary institutions that can lend your document for free, and if they can, then it's free, although you would have to pay for the shipping and the ILL Fee Management (IFM) charge. If secondary holders lend your document, then you would have to pay a lending charge of $10 in addition to the mailing and basic service charge.

U : I understand. I need this document very urgently, so I would appreciate it if you contact me as soon as it arrives.

L : OK. We'll make sure to do that.

U : Thanks for all your help.

상황 23 　　　신청 취소

L : (전화) 여보세요, 한국도서관 ILL센터입니다. 홍길동씨 계신가요?

U : 예, 제가 홍길동인데 무슨 일인가요?

L : 어제 OCLC ILL로 미국 인디애나 대학교 (Indiana Univ.) 학위논문을 신청
하셨지요?

U : 예, 맞습니다. 그런데 뭐가 잘못되었나요?

L : 아니요, 인디애나 대학교에 ILL을 신청하기 전에 신청자에게 확인할 것이
있어서 전화드렸습니다.

U : 무슨 일인가요?

L : 인디애나 대학교는 해외로 대출해 주는 자료에 대해 대출요금으로 $25를
부과합니다. 자료 반송 우편요금과 서비스 비용까지 합하면 약 $40 정도 될
텐데 그래도 신청하시겠습니까?

U : 그렇게 비용이 많이 드나요? 너무 비싸네요. 무료인줄 알고 신청한 건데요

L : 이 자료는 인디애나 대학교에만 소장되어 있기 때문에 이 방법밖에는 없는
데요. 어떻게 처리할까요?

U : 죄송하지만 취소해 주실 수 있나요?

L : 예, 그럼, 취소 처리하겠습니다.

U : 고맙습니다.

Interlibrary Loan • 상호대차

Situation 23 Canceling OCLC ILL Orders

L : (Telephone call) Hello. This is a manager at the Interlibrary Loan center from the Hankook Library. May I speak to Mr. Gil-dong Hong?

U : Yes. This is he.

L : I understand that you ordered a thesis from Indiana University through OCLC ILL yesterday.

U : Yes. I did. Is there a problem?

L : No. We just need to check some information before we place an order.

U : What can I help you with?

L : Indiana University charges an international lending fee of 25 dollars. Combined with the mailing and service charges, the total comes out to about 40 dollars. Do you still want to order the thesis?

U : Does it cost that much? It seems pretty high. I thought it was free.

L : Indiana University is the only place that holds this document. What do you want us to do?

U : I'm sorry, but is it still possible to cancel the order?

L : Yes. Then, we'll cancel it.

U : Thank you.

상황 24　♥ 자료 도착 통보

L : (전화) 여보세요, 한국대학교 중앙도서관 원문복사서비스 담당자입니다.
　　홍길동씨 계신가요?

U : 예, 제가 홍길인데 무슨 일인가요?

L : 3주전에 OCLC ILL로 신청한 학위논문이 오늘 도착했습니다

U : 그래요? 어떻게 받아 볼 수 있는지요?

L : 도서관 4층 참고열람실 원문복사서비스 코너로 오시면 됩니다.

U : 예, 잘 알겠습니다. 오늘은 수업이 있어서 내일 오후 3시쯤에 가보겠습
　　니다.

L : 가급적 빨리 오셨으면 좋겠습니다. 자료가 예정보다 늦게 도착하여 반납
　　기일이 촉박하거든요.

U : 아, 그렇습니까? 그럼, 오늘 오후 5시에 가도 될까요?

L : 예, 그럼 오늘 5시에 오는 것으로 알고 있겠습니다.

U : 예, 그 때 뵙겠습니다.

Situation 24 Notifying OCLC ILL Document Arrivals

L : (Phone Call) Hello. I'm a librarian at the Document Delivery Service of the Main Library. May I speak to Mr. Gil-dong Hong?

U : Yes. This is he. What can I do for you?

L : The paper that you ordered 3 weeks ago through OCLC ILL arrived today.

U : Great! Where can I pick it up?

L : Come to the Document Delivery Service corner in the reference room on the 4th floor of the library.

U : OK. But today I have classes, so I'll have to stop by around 3 p.m. tomorrow.

L : The sooner the better, because the document arrived later than expected, and there will be a tight return schedule.

U : Really? Then, I'll stop by today around 5 p.m.?

L : Yes. Then we'll see you around 5 p.m.

U : I'll be there.

상황 25 ♥ 자료 열람

U : 안녕하세요. 홍길동인데 OCLC ILL로 신청한 자료를 찾으러 왔습니다.

L : 예, 자료는 여기 있습니다. 열람하시기 전에 이용자 준수 확약서를 먼저 제출하셔야 합니다.

U : 이용자 준수 확약서라니요? 그것을 꼭 제출해야 하나요?

L : 예, 그렇습니다. OCLC ILL은 해외 기관으로부터 자료를 직접 대출하여 이용하는 것이기 때문에 우리 소장자료를 대출해서 이용하는 것보다 까다롭습니다.

U : 예, 알겠습니다. 여기 제가 서명한 확약서를 제출합니다. 그런데 집에 가져가서 볼 수 없나요? 도서관 내에서만 열람하라고 되어 있네요.

L : 예, 자료의 훼손이나 분실을 방지하기 위해 그런 것이니 이해해 주시기 바랍니다.

U : 자료를 열람하기 너무 불편하네요. 그런데 일부분 복사는 가능합니까?

L : 예, 일부분 복사는 가능합니다. 열람실 내에 복사실이 있으니 그곳에서 필요한 부분만 주의해서 복사해 주시기 바랍니다.

U : 오늘 다 못 보면 어떻게 하나요?

L : 열람시간 마감 전까지 보신 후 일단 반납하시고 내일 다시 오셔서 이용해 주세요. 반납기한이 15일 정도 남아 있으니 최대 5일정도 열람이 가능합니다. 5일 후에는 자료는 반납해야 합니다.

U : 잘 알겠습니다.

Situation 25 Using OCLC ILL Documents

U : Hello. My name is Gil-dong Hong and I'm here to pick up a paper that I ordered through OCLC ILL.

L : Here it is. Before you use it, you have to sign a user agreement first.

U : A user agreement? Do I really need to submit something like that?

L : Yes. OCLC ILL is quite cautious because they borrow documents from foreign countries.

U : I understand. Here is the agreement with my signature. But would it be possible to take the paper home, even though it says that I am only allowed to use it in the library?

L : I'm afraid not. It's to prevent damage or loss. I hope you understand.

U : It's very difficult to read it here. Can I at least copy some portions of it?

L : Yes, you can. Go to the copy corner in the reading room and copy the parts you need. Please handle it with care.

U : What if I can't use it all by today?

L : Well, you still need to return it today and come back tomorrow. It is due in 15 days, so you have at most 5 more days to use it. After that, we will have to send it back.

U : OK.

상황 26   IFM 정산

U : 이 자료를 다 보았습니다. 오늘 반납하겠습니다.

L : 예, 그럼 비용 정산을 해드리겠습니다. 이 자료는 IFM으로 정산하면 되는 자료이니 대출비용 $15와 IFM 비용 $1.85는 우리 도서관 외화통장에 직접 무통장 입금하시면 되고 자료 반납 항공 우편요금은 원화로 지불하시면 됩니다. 이 정도 무게라면 우편요금이 약 15,000원 정도 들 것 같습니다.

U : 그런데 IFM이 무엇인가요?

L : IFM은 OCLC ILL Fee Management Service로 대출요금을 대여기관에 직접 송금하는 것이 아니라 OCLC에서 일정 기간별로 일괄 정산해 주는 서비스입니다. 이런 경우, 수표 환전이나 송금 수수료가 들지 않기 때문에 이용자 입장에서는 비용이 보다 저렴합니다. 저희 외화통장에 달러로 입금해 주시면 모았다가 분기별로 저희가 OCLC 한국지사로 직접 송금 처리합니다.

U : 아, 그렇군요. 그럼 외화통장번호를 알려 주시면 입금하겠습니다.

L : 예, 한빛은행 125-XXX-XX .. 입니다. 우편요금은 지금 함께 우체국에 가서 반납처리를 하면서 직접 지불하시면 좋겠는데요.

U : 지금은 그럴 시간이 없는데요. 잠시 후에 수업이 있거든요.

L : 그럼 일단 20,000원을 주시면 자료를 제가 먼저 반송하고 항공우편 영수증과 남은 잔액을 드리도록 하겠습니다. 홍길동씨는 외화통장에 $16.80를 입금하시고 입금 영수증을 저에게 주시면 됩니다.

U : 감사합니다. 그럼 내일 입금하고 다시 오도록 하겠습니다.

L : 예, 그렇게 하세요.

Situation 26   ILL Fee Management (IFM) Payment

U : I'm finished with this document. I'd like to return it.

L : All right, let me figure your total. This document is an IFM document, so you need to deposit $15 for the loan and $1.85 for the IFM fees to our foreign exchange account. You may pay for the shipping in won. The shipping costs about 15,000 won.

U : By the way, what is IFM?

L : IFM stands for OCLC ILL Fee Management Service. We don't need to send fees directly to the lender. Instead, this service computes the total fee for a certain period. This helps users to cut costs because there is no check conversion or money transfer fee. When you deposit your payment into our foreign exchange account, we will hold the amount for a certain period of time and send it to the Korean branch of the OCLC periodically.

U : I see. Can you tell me your foreign exchange account number?

L : Yes. Hanvit Bank 125-XXX-XX ... You can pay for shipping at the post office when you process your return.

U : Well, I really don't have time right now. I have to go to class.

L : If you give me 20,000 won, I'll return the document for you and give you a mailing receipt and your change back. All you need to do is deposit $16.80 and give us the deposit receipt.

U : I really appreciate your help. I'll deposit the money tomorrow.

L : That will be fine.

상황 27　복사비용 무료

U : 제가 받은 자료는 Article 복사본인데 이것도 반납해야 합니까?

L : 아닙니다. 이 자료는 반납하실 필요가 없습니다.

U : 비용 지불을 해야 하나요?

L : 이 자료는 무료로 제공받은 것이라 대출 비용이 없고 자료를 반납하지 않아도 되기 때문에 항공 우편요금도 없습니다.

U : 이렇게 구하기 힘든 자료를 무료로 제공해 주시니 놀라운데요. 정말 고맙습니다. 저에게 큰 도움이 되었습니다.

L : 아니, 뭘요. 도움이 되었다니 저도 기쁩니다.

Situation 27 Free Loan Service

U : I received a copy of an article. Do I need to return the copy?

L : No, you don't..

U : Do I have to pay for it then?

L : You don't need to pay for the loan because this document is free of charge, and you don't need to pay the shipping charges either because you don't need to return this.

U : Great. I can't believe that it is free to obtain such a hard-to-find document. Thanks a lot. You've been a great help.

L : You're welcome. We're glad we could help you out.

Library Facilities

시 설

● ● ●

한양대학교 학술정보관

4 시설 / Library Facilities

L1 : 안녕하세요. 한국대학교 도서관, 송혜림입니다. 무엇을 도와드릴까요?

U : 안녕하세요. USC의 동양학 담당사서 Stewart Green입니다. 한국대 도서관을 방문하고 싶은데, 어떻게 하면 될까요?

L1 : 그럼, 방문 업무를 담당하는 김한양 씨에게 전화를 연결해드리겠습니다. 잠깐만 기다려주세요.

U : 감사합니다.

L2 : 안녕하세요. 정보지원팀, 김한양 입니다. 무엇을 도와드릴까요?

U : 안녕하세요. USC의 동양학 담당사서 Stewart Green입니다. 한국대 도서관을 방문하고 싶어서 연락 드렸습니다.

L2 : 아, 그러세요? 방문하시려는 목적이 뭔가요?

U : USC의 한국학 자료를 보강해야 하는데, 한국의 대학 도서관에는 어떤 자료들이 구비되어 있는지 조사를 좀 하려고요.

L2 : 아~ 그러시군요, 언제쯤 방문할 계획이신가요?

U : 5월 1일 수요일 오전이 좋겠는데, 괜찮으신가요?

L2 : 네, 수요일 오전 10시가 좋겠네요. 모두 몇 분이 오실 예정인가요?

U : 저와 동양학 관련 사서 한 명을 포함해서 총 2명입니다.

L2 : 네, 그럼 5월 1일 오전 10시, 도서관 1층 사무실로 방문해주시면 됩니다.

U : 감사합니다. 그때 뵙겠습니다.

Situation 1 Arranging a Visit

L1 : Hello, this is Hey-Rim Song at the Hankook University Library. What can I do for you?

U : Hello, this is Stewart Green, an East Asian Studies librarian in at the University of Southern California. Could you please tell me how I can visit your library?

L1 : Mr. Hanyang Kim takes care of visits. If you wait a moment. I'll put you through to Mr. Kim.

U : Thank you.

L2 : Hello, this is Hanyang Kim at the Library Support Team. May I help you?

U : Hello, this is Stewart Green, an East Asian Studies librarian at the University of Southern California. I would like to visit your library.

L2 : May I ask the purpose of your visit?

U : I am surveying resources and materials to expand the Korean studies collection at USC.

L2 : When are you planning to visit our library?

U : How about the morning of Wednesday, May 1? Is that all right?

L2 : Yes, 10 a.m. would be fine. How many people are planning to come?

U : Just two including myself. Another East Asian Studies librarian from USC will visit with me.

L2 : Then, can we meet at the main office on the first floor at 10 a.m. on May 1?

U : OK. See you then.

상황 2   위치 안내

L1 : (전화벨이 울린다) 안녕하세요. 한국대학교 도서관, 송혜림입니다.

U : 안녕하세요. 오늘 방문하기로 약속한 Stewart Green입니다. 김한양 씨 연결 부탁드립니다.

L1 : 지금 통화중입니다. 잠시 기다리시겠습니까 아니면 메시지를 남겨드릴까요?

U : 기다리겠습니다.

L2 : (잠시 후) 여보세요. 김한양입니다. 기다리게 해서 죄송합니다.

U : 아닙니다. 지금 학교 안으로 들어왔는데 도서관이 어디에 있나요?

L2 : 도서관은 사범대학 건물 바로 옆에 있습니다. 주차는 지하 주차장을 이용하시면 됩니다.

U : 아! 사범대 옆에 6층짜리 회색건물이 보이는데, 도서관이 맞나요?

L2 : 네, 맞습니다. 주차하신 후에 1층 사무실로 오시면 됩니다.

U : 알겠습니다. 잠시 후에 뵙겠습니다.

Situation 2 Direction Guides

L1 : (Bell rings) Hello. This is Hey-Rim Song at the Hankook University
Library. What can I do for you?

U : Hello, This is Stewart Green. I have an appointment with Mr. Kim. May I
speak to Mr. Hanyang Kim?

L1 : Please hold on a second. (In a minute) Hello, his line is busy. Would you
like to wait a moment, or leave a message?

U : I will wait for him.

L2 : (After a moment) Hello. This is Hanyang Kim. What can I do for you?

U : I'm on campus right now. How can I get to the library?

L2 : The library is next to the College of Education. You may use the parking
lot in the basement of the library.

U : I see a gray six-story building next to the College of Education. Is it the
library?

L2 : Yes, it is. Please come in to the main office on the first floor after parking
your car.

U : All right. See you soon.

상황 3   첫 만남

L1 : 실례합니다. Stewart Green씨, 맞나요?

U : 네. 김한양 씨인가요?

L1 : 네, 제가 김한양입니다. 반갑습니다.

U : 만나서 반갑습니다. 이렇게 시간 내주셔서 감사합니다.

L1 : 별 말씀을요. 저희 도서관에 오신 걸 환영합니다. 관장님께서 기다리고 계십니다.

(관장실로 들어가 인사를 나눈다)

L1 : 관장님, USC에서 오신 Stewart Green 씨입니다.

L2 : 반갑습니다. 저희 도서관에 오신 걸 환영합니다. 박지성입니다.
앉으시지요.

L1 : Stewart Green씨는 USC에서 동양학을 담당하고 계시고 한국학 자료 보강을 위해 한국에 오셨습니다.

L2 : 그러시군요, 부담 갖지 마시고 필요한 부분은 얼마든지 문의주세요. 최대한 도와드리겠습니다.

U : 대단히 감사합니다.

Situation 3  First Meeting

L1 : Excuse me, but are you Mr. Stewart Green?

U : Yes, I am. You must be Mrs. Kim.

L1 : Yes. Nice to meet you.

U : Nice to meet you, too. Thank you for your time.

L1 : My pleasure. Welcome to the Hankook University Library. The director is
waiting for you.

(They go to meet the director)

L1 : Sir, this is Stewart Green from USC.

L2 : Nice to meet you, Mr. Green. I am Ji-Sung Park. Welcome to the
Hankook University Library. Have a seat, please.

L1 : Mr. Green is in charge of East Asian materials at USC Library. He is
visiting Korea for the Korean Studies Collection.

L2 : Oh, that's wonderful. Please feel free to ask me any question.

U : Thank you so much.

상황 4 　　▶ 도서관 역사 소개

U : 도서관이 새 건물처럼 보이네요! 지은 지 얼마나 되었나요?

L : 1998년 개교 59주년에 문을 열었으니까 13년 정도 되었습니다. 한국대학교
　　의 세 번째 도서관이기도 하죠.

U : 그럼 이전에 두 개의 도서관이 더 있었다는 얘기네요?

L : 그렇습니다. 첫 번째 도서관은 1948년에 설치되었고, 두 번째 도서관은
　　1959년에 종합대학으로 승격되면서 신축한 중앙도서관이었습니다. 현재
　　이 두 건물은 다른 용도로 사용되고 있습니다.

U : 도서관 건물이 여러 번 바뀌었군요.

L : 네, 도서관은 대학의 연구활동을 지원하기 위한 가장 기본적인 시설인데다
　　가 그 중요성이 매우 크기 때문이죠.

U : 새로운 도서관이 필요한 이유는 무엇이었나요?

L : 시설, 규모, 서비스 측면에서 대학의 위상이 성장하고 발전하게 되면 과거
　　의 도서관으로는 감당할 수 없는 부분이 발생하기 때문에 좀 더 나은 서비
　　스를 제공하기 위한 투자라고 볼 수 있습니다. 실제로 이 도서관은 1998년
　　에 신축되면서 그 해 건축문화대상을 수상할 정도로 많은 노력을 기울인
　　도서관입니다.

U : 대단하군요!

Situation 4 History of the Library

U : This building seems very new. When was it built?

L : It opened in 1998 to celebrate the 59th anniversary of the founding of Hankook University. This is Hankook University's third library building.

U : So the university had two library buildings prior to this one?

L : Yes. The first one was founded in 1948, and the second in 1959. The second library building was built when Hankook University was expanded. Those two buildings are being used for other purposes now.

U : It seems that the main library building has been changed several times.

L : Sure. The library is not only the essential facility for assisting research, but also a core of academics.

U : Why did you need a new library?

L : It was a new investment for better services. In order to meet increased expectations commensurate with Hankook's improved academic reputation, it was imperative to enlarge the scale of the library accordingly. Actually, this building was recognized with an architecture award in 1998.

U : That's wonderful!

상황 5   ▶ 규모 및 체제

(관장 인사를 마친 후 Stewart Green은 사서의 안내로 도서관을 둘러본다.)

L : 저희 도서관은 지상 6층, 지하 3층으로 구성되어 있습니다.
    연면적 20,500m² 에 열람좌석은 4,000석입니다.

U : 장서 규모는 얼마나 됩니까?

L : 200만 권 정도입니다.

U : 도서관은 이 건물 하나 뿐인가요?

L : 아니오. 음악, 법학, 의학분야는 분관이 따로 있습니다. 그 외에도 자연과
    학과 산업과학 분야의 저널은 해당 대학건물에 각각 소장하고 있습니다.

U : 그럼 각 학문분야별로 도서관을 운영하고 계시군요?

L : 그렇습니다. 과거에는 자료형태별로 자료실로 운영했지만 현재는 학문분
    야별로 운영하고 있습니다. 예를 들어 과학 관련자료는 2층, 인문학 관련자
    료는 5층에 있는 것처럼 말이죠.

U : 이용자들의 반응은 어떻던가요?

L : 사실 처음엔 조금 혼란스러워했지만 지금은 오히려 효율적이라는 반응입
    니다.

Situation 5　　Library Size and Layout

(After having met the director, Mr. Stewart Green tours the library)

L : This library is a nine-story building with three stories below and six above the ground. The floor space is about 20,500 m² with a seating capacity of 4,000.

U : How many books do you have?

L : There are about 2,000,000 books in this library.

U : Is this the only library on campus?

L : No. There are branch libraries for the College of Music, the Law School, and the Medical School. In addition, the Industrial Science Library and the Natural Science Library carry journals and reference books.

U : It sounds like you have separate subject libraries.

L : Yes. Our collections used to be organized and managed by material type. But now they are organized by subjects. For instance, the resources for natural sciences are on the second floor and resources for humanities are on the fifth floor.

U : Do your users like it?

L : Actually, they were confused with the new system at the beginning, but now they think the new system is more effective.

상황 6   이용시간

U : 도서관은 몇 시까지 이용할 수 있나요?

L : 도서관 자료실 이용시간은 평일은 오전 9시부터 오후 10시까지, 주말은 오전 9시부터 낮 12시까지 입니다.

U : 자유열람실 이용시간도 자료실과 똑같은가요?

L : 자유열람실은 연중 휴일 없이 하루24시간 개방하고 있습니다.

U : 아무래도 야간에는 이용자가 적겠네요.

L : 네, 그렇기 때문에 밤 11시 이후에는 자유열람실 1개 실만 운영하고 있습니다.

Situation 6 Hours of Operation

U : What hours are you open?

L : Hours of operation are from 9 a.m. to 10 p.m. on weekdays and 9 a.m. to 12 p.m. on weekends.

U : Do you open study rooms at the same time?

L : As for study rooms, we are open for 24 hours, everyday.

U : Are there fewer users during the night?

L : Yes, so we run only one study room after 11 p.m.

상황 7 전시실과 게이트

L : 이곳은 전시실입니다.

U : 도서관에서 전시실은 어떤 용도로 사용하시나요?

L : 도서관에서 전시회를 열기도 하구요, 학교의 동아리와 학과의 요구가 있을 시에 대여를 해주기도 합니다. 주로 회화나 사진, 공예품 같은 것을 전시하고 있습니다.

U : 그런데 전시실이 출입 게이트 바깥쪽에 위치해 있네요!

L : 그렇습니다. 저희 도서관은 출입관리를 위해 전교생이 RF Card를 사용하고 있기 때문에, 외부인이 전시실을 방문할 경우를 대비해서 출입 게이트 바깥에 설치했습니다.

U : 아! 그렇겠네요.

Situation 7 Exhibition Room and Gate System

L : This is the Exhibition Room.

U : An exhibition room? What is this room used for?

L : The library uses this room for its own exhibition events. Also, people request to use this room for club activities or academic meetings from different departments. Usually, we have exhibitions of fine arts, photographs, or handicrafts.

U : This room is outside of the Gate System.

L : Yes, it is. Everyone has to have an RF Card in order to pass the Gate System. However, since the exhibition room is open to the public as well as to library patrons, it is located outside of the Gate System.

U : Oh, I see.

상황 8   Information Commons

U : 여기는 흥미로운 공간이네요. 다양한 코너가 있고 사람도 많네요.

L : "Information Commons"라고 하는데요, 다양한 정보자원을 편리하게 이용할 수 있는 공간입니다

U : 그래요? 학생들에게 인기가 좋겠어요.

L : 그렇습니다. 이곳은 학술정보 검색코너, 협업작업코너, 학술정보교육실 등으로 구성되어있고, 과제수행에 필요한 SW는 물론 노트북도 지원하고 있어 학생들이 활발히 이용하고 있습니다.

U : 이곳을 이용할 때 학생증이 필요한가요?

L : 네, 각 코너이용은 좌석 발급기를 이용하시면 되고, 각종 기기 대여 관련해서는 안내데스크에 있는 사서에게 문의하시면 됩니다.

Situation 8 Information Commons

U : What an interesting place here. There are various sections and many people, too.

L : You are in the 'Information Commons'. Users can easily access library resources on this floor.

U : Oh, students seem to love it.

L : Yes, they do. The Information Commons consists of several sections such as the Digital Library Search Area, Collaborative Computing Booths and the Library Instruction Room. Also, a service desk provides the necessary software and a laptop loan service.

U : Do we need our student ID card?

L : Yes. Please use the seat allocator for each section, and contact a librarian for the loan service.

상황 9　자유열람실

L : 이곳은 자유열람실입니다.

U : 도서관에 이런 열람실이 모두 몇 개가 있죠?

L : 총 6개가 있는데, 지하 1, 2층에 각 3개씩 있습니다. 이용하실 때는 여기있는 좌석발급기에서 좌석을 배정받아 이용하면 되고, 홈페이지에서 실시간 좌석현황을 확인할 수 있습니다.

U : 이용시간은 어떻게 되죠?

L : 아침 6시부터 밤 12까지 개실하고, 이 중 한 열람실은 24시간 개실하고 있습니다.

U : 열람실 관리는 어떻게 하시나요?

L : 청소와 시설관리 용역사무소가 상주하고 있고 도서관 근로장학생들이 각 열람실의 관리를 담당하고 있습니다.

U : 열람실을 24시간 개실하고 있는데, 열람실 좌석의 독점문제는 어떻게 해결하고 계신가요?

L : 야간담당 직원을 한 명 배치하여 감독하고 있고 근로장학생들의 활동이 매우 적극적이라 별 문제가 없습니다.

Situation 9  Study Rooms

L : These are study rooms.

U : How many study rooms do you have?

L : There are six. Three of them are in the first basement-level and the others in the second. Use this seat allocator to get your seat number. Then, you can check the seat occupancy on the library website.

U : What are the hours?

L : One of the rooms is open 24 hours a day. Other rooms are open from 6 a.m. to midnight.

U : Who takes care of the study rooms?

L : Cleaning and facilities are outsourced and student assistants oversee each room.

U : How do you prevent students from monopolizing seats in the study rooms? Some students might put their books there without studying at all.

L : The night staff and student assistants ensure that those problems do not occur.

상황 10　　　환기 및 온도조절

U : 도서관 내의 환기는 어떻게 하고 계십니까?

L : 층마다 2대씩 설치되어 있는 공조기를 통해 관리하고 있습니다.

U : 공조기가 어떤 장치인가요?

L : 공조기는 공기를 순환시키고 탁한 공기를 필터로 걸러내서 계속해서 신선한 공기를 공급하는 장치를 말합니다.

U : 그런데 공조기가 냉방기능도 갖추고 있는 건가요?

L : 천장의 공조기는 흡기구 또는 배기구의 역할을 하지만 코일에 뜨거운 물이나 찬물을 공급하기 때문에 공기가 이를 통과해서 냉난방의 기능도 할 수 있습니다.

U : 그럼 온도조절은 공조기를 통해서만 하고 계신가요?

L : 그렇지는 않습니다. 여름이나 겨울에는 벽쪽에 있는 냉난방기와 공조기를 통해 적절한 냉난방을 하고 봄 가을에는 공조기만으로도 적정 온도가 유지됩니다.

U : 적정 온도는 몇 도를 기준으로 하시나요?

L : 계절과 사용 인원에 따라 다릅니다. 모든 열람실에는 온도계가 있어서 기계실 직원이 수시로 체크하고 학생들의 의견을 반영하여 조절하고 있습니다.

Situation 10 Ventilation, Cooling and Heating System

U : How do you ventilate the library?

L : Each floor has two diffusers on the ceiling.

U : What are diffusers?

L : Diffusers ventilate air and filter the air to provide fresh air at all times.

U : I see. By the way, do they work as a cooling system as well?

L : That's exactly right. The diffusers operate not only as an inflator or a deflator, but also as a cooler or heater using coils with hot or cold water.

U : Are the diffusers the only system that controls temperature?

L : No. During summer and winter both the diffusers and the cooling and heating systems work to control the temperature. During spring and fall, it is sufficient with only the diffusers.

U : What is the target temperature?

L : It depends on the weather and how crowded the library is. Usually, a technician controls the temperature and makes changes based on students' requests.

상황 11 　　사물함

U : 하루 도서관 출입인원은 몇 명이나 되죠?

L : 글쎄요. 정확한 출입인원은 알 수가 없지만, 출입관리기에 표시되는 출입 횟수는 하루 약 3만 번입니다.

U : 이용자가 많은데 도서관에 도난사고가 발생한적도 있나요?

L : 물론 있습니다. 그러나 분실물이 발생했을 경우를 대비해 분실함을 운영하고 있고, 도난사고 방지는 물론 이용자편의를 위해서 약 2,200개의 사물함을 운영하고 있습니다.

U : 와! 그렇게 많이 필요한가요?

L : 각 단과대별로 사물함이 따로 있지만 도서관에 설치되어 있으면 무거운 사전이나 참고서 등 개인 소지품을 넣어 둘 수 있어서 공부하는 학생들에게는 매우 편리하기 때문입니다.

U : 여기 관리는 누가 하고 있나요?

L : 근로장학생들이 관리하고 있습니다.

U : 사물함 배정은 어떻게 하세요?

L : 가급적이면 많은 인원이 이용할 수 있도록 2달에 한 번씩 추첨을 통해 배정하고 있습니다.

Situation 11 Lockers

U : What's the average number of library users a day?

L : Well, according to the Gate System numbers, we have more than 30,000 visits a day. However, I don't exactly know the actual number of visitors.

U : Since the library has a lot of visitors, there must be many cases of theft.

L : Inevitably, yes. For lost personal belongings, we have a Lost and Found counter. In addition, we provide more than 2,200 lockers in order to prevent the loss of personal belongings and theft.

U : Wow! Do you really need so many lockers?

L : Even though every college has its own lockers, the library still provides lockers, so students don't have to carry heavy dictionaries and textbooks all the time.

U : Who takes care of the lockers?

L : Student workers do.

U : How do they distribute the lockers?

L : By drawing lots every other month. It's the fairest method of distributing them.

상황 12　　주제사서 업무

U : 홈페이지에 소개된 주제사서제에 대해서 설명해주실 수 있나요?

L : 네, 주제사서제는 주제정보실의 각 사서가 특정 학문분야를 나눠 전담하고 그 분야의 학부, 대학원에 대한 One stop 서비스를 제공하는 것을 말합니다.

U : 주제사서가 제공하는 서비스는 구체적으로 어떤 것들인가요?

L : 주제사서별로 담당한 주제분야의 자료 선정, 열람업무, 참고봉사 및 온라인 서비스와 이용자 교육 등이 있습니다.

U : 그 모든 업무를 사서 한 분이 담당하시는 건가요?

L : 본인의 주제분야 서비스는 혼자 담당하고, 그 외 주제사서팀간의 공통업무는 서로 분담하고 있습니다. 팀별로 분담하고 있는 업무에는 ILL, 중소기업 지원, 중고교사 지원, 통계 등이 있습니다.

U : 과거의 서비스와 비교해서 어떤 점이 달라졌나요?

L : 일단은 사서 한 사람당 업무영역이 보다 광범위해졌고 다양한 업무를 하게 되었다는 점입니다. 도서관은 끊임없이 변화하고 있고 이용자의 정보요구 패턴도 다양해지고 있으므로 매체에 국한되지 않는 참고서비스의 중요성은 점점 더 커지고 있습니다. 따라서 주제사서들은 끊임없는 자기개발을 통해 이용자와 함께 성장하고 있습니다.

U : 업무 부담은 더 커진 것 아닌가요?

L : 물론 과거보다는 다양한 일을 하다 보니 더 커졌다고 볼 수 있지만 이를 통해 개인적인 역량 또한 커졌다고 봅니다.

Situation 12 Subject Librarians

U : I am interested in the Subject Librarians, which you posted about on the website.

L : The Subject Librarian provides one stop service for students. Each librarian in the Subject Information Center takes charge of one specific field and assists students who need help in that field.

U : What kind of services do they provide?

L : First of all, they select resources for their specialized fields. They also manage circulation, consult with the students, provide online services, and offer bibliographic instructions.

U : I can't believe that a librarian can do all of those things.

L : They are responsible for a variety of tasks within their subject expertise. There are, of course, some common tasks which Subject Librarian Teams share. Each team is in charge of certain tasks such as ILL, statistics, assisting minor enterprises, and helping secondary school teachers.

U : What is the difference between the old system and the new one?

L : Most of all, a librarian now has to take care of wider fields, and manage a variety of tasks. Libraries are constantly changing these days. As the number of library users increases, they ask for different kinds of information. Therefore, a librarian who is in charge of the subject field develops into a more specialized professional. As a result, reference services involves being increasingly involved in the research process.

U : The burden to the tasks must have increased.

L : As the amount of tasks has increased, so the capabilities of librarians have improved as well.

상황 13 　🗨 과학기술실

U : 과학기술실의 위치와 자료배치를 알고 싶습니다.

L : 과학기술실은 도서관 2층에 있구요. 입구에서 오른쪽에 공학분야자료, 왼쪽에 컴퓨터와 자연과학 분야 자료들이 있습니다.

U : 과학기술실에는 어떤 자료들이 소장되어 있죠?

L : 이곳에서는 DDC분류번호의 001.6, 003-006, 500, 600(650제외)에 해당하는 단행본, 정기간행물, 학위논문 자료를 소장하고 있습니다.

U : "담헌문고"는 무슨 자료실인가요?

L : "담헌" 이성우박사가 기증한 자료를 모아놓은 개인문고입니다. 개인문고자료는 대출은 제한되고 관내에서 열람과 복사만 가능합니다. 안내데스크에 자료를 신청하시면 열람하실 수 있습니다.

U : 과학기술실에서 제공하는 '중소기업 정보지원서비스'라는 것은 어떤 서비스죠?

L : 그것은 우리대학교의 산학연계 프로그램의 하나로 제공하는 서비스입니다. 중소기업에게 도서관 자료와 서비스를 제공하고 있는데요, 이로써 중소기업의 연구활동을 촉진하고 대외경쟁력을 제고할 수 있도록 하고 있습니다. 서비스를 신청한 회사에는 특별열람증을 발급하고 있어서 본교 학생과 동일하게 도서관을 이용할 수 있습니다. 도서도 20권까지 30일 동안 대출할 수 있습니다.

Situation 13 Natural Sciences & Technology Room

U : I want to look around the Technology & Natural Sciences Room.

L : It is located on the second floor. The resources for Technology are on the right side of the room. The resources for computer science and natural sciences are on the left side.

U : What types of materials are in this room?

L : We have books, periodicals and dissertations that are classified by DDC as 001.6, 003-006, 500, 600 (besides 650).

U : Could you tell me what Damhon Mun-go is?

L : Those are the materials that were donated by Damhon, Dr. Sung-Woo Lee. They cannot be checked out, but you can read them in the reading room or you may copy a part of them. You can use the books if you ask a librarian.

U : What is the Assisting Minor Enterprises Services?

L : It is a collaborating program between the university and the business community. The university provides companies with information and services. It originated from a philosophy of nurturing research in minor enterprises, and enforces their capability to be strong companies. If a company applies for this program, the library will issue a special ID card. With the card, they can use the library as other students do. They can check out 20 books for 30 days, for example.

상황 14 · 사회과학실

U : 사회과학실에 대해 간단히 소개해 주시겠습니까?

L : 사회과학에 관련한 단행본, 연속간행물, 논문 등을 소장하고 있고, DDC 분류상 650대에 해당하는 경영관련 분야까지 서비스하고 있습니다.

U : 사회과학의 소주제들을 각각 담당하고 계신 분이 따로 있습니까?

L : 그렇습니다. 크게 상경학분야와 교육학, 일반사회학으로 나누어 각각 주제 담당사서가 맡고 있고, 340대의 법학자료는 법학자료실에서 따로 서비스하고 있습니다.

U : 다른 자료실과는 다른 형태의 자료들이 있는데, 어떤 자료들인가요?

L : 이곳에서는 일반적인 자료 외에 관보, 사보, 유학자료, 앨범, 통계청 자료, 국내 각 대학의 요람 자료를 별도의 서가에 비치하여 서비스하고 있습니다.

Situation 14 Social Sciences Room

U : Would you please inform me about this subject room?

L : This room has books, periodicals and dissertations on social sciences. It also includes business materials classified '650' by the Dewey Decimal classification (DDC) system.

U : Are there subject librarians for the social sciences?

L : Yes, there are. There are librarians in the disciplines of economics & business, education and general social science. The law library houses the legal resources.

U : It seems that the types of resources in this room are different from those in the other rooms. What are these resources?

L : This room also houses official gazettes, magazines, studying-abroad resources, graduate albums, statistics from the Department of Statistics of Korea and catalogs from other universities.

상황 15 　 인문과학실

U : 이 자료실에는 인문과학자료만 소장하고 있나요?

L : 네. 2000년 8월부터 주제분야별로 자료실을 운영하고 있거든요. 여기에는 인문과학분야 관련자료만 소장하고 있습니다.

U : 인문과학이면 어떤 학문을 포함하는 건가요?

L : DDC분류상의 100, 200, 400, 800, 900대 자료, 즉 철학, 종교, 언어, 문학, 역사, 지리 분야의 국내서, 국외서 및 참고도서와 같은 단행본, 연속간행물, 학위논문, 지도를 소장하고 있습니다.

U : 멀티미디어 매체나 비도서 매체도 이곳에 소장되어 있나요?

L : 인문과학실에 소장된 비도서는 지도뿐이에요. 지도 외의 비도서나 멀티미디어 자료는 모두 Information Commons에서 관리합니다.

U : 이곳 인문과학실은 주로 어느 학과를 대상으로 서비스하시죠?

L : 사학과, 철학과, 국어국문학과, 중어중문학과, 독어독문학과, 영어영문학과, 국어교육학과, 영어교육학과 등입니다. 그렇다고 다른 학과나 학부가 서비스 대상에서 제외된다는 뜻은 아니죠.

U : 사서는 몇 분이나 근무하시나요?

L : 인문학 분야 2명, 어문학 분야 2명, 총 4명입니다.

Situation 15 Humanities Room

U : Does this room only have the humanities collection?

L : Yes, it does. Since August 2000, we have managed the collections by subjects. All humanities resources are collected in this room.

U : Could you specify in more detail?

L : This room houses materials on philosophy, religion, languages, literature, history and geography. They are classified as 100, 200, 400, 800 and 900 by the DDC system. It also has books, periodicals, dissertations and maps in those fields.

U : Does this room have other multimedia and non-print materials?

L : Not really. Maps are the only non-print resources that we keep here. Others are in the Information Commons.

U : Who uses the collection mostly?

L : Students who major in history, philosophy, linguistics, literature and education. However, it doesn't mean that this room is limited to those humanities students only. It is open to non-humanities majors as well.

U : How many librarians work here?

L : There are four librarians—two in the humanities and two in linguistics and language.

상황 16 ▶ 편의시설

U : 학생 편의시설은 어떤 것이 있습니까?

L : 지하 1층과 3층에 휴게실이 1개씩 있고 자판기와 식수대, 대형 TV, 키오스크, 현금출금기 등이 설치되어 있습니다.

U : 키오스크가 무엇인가요?

L : 도서관을 처음 이용하는 이용자들을 위해 규정, 분류표, 검색, 대출 반납 및 층별 자료 배치 안내 등에 관한 내용을 누구나 쉽게 이용할 수 있도록 간단한 화면 터치만으로 이용할 수 있는 안내장치입니다.

U : 장애인을 위한 시설로는 어떤 것이 있습니까?

L : 각 열람실마다 일정석의 장애인 전용좌석이 배치되어 있고 경사로와 각 자료실의 장애인 출입구 등은 기본적으로 갖춰져 있습니다. 현재 장애학우를 위한 열람실이 곧 설치될 예정입니다.

U : 혹시 매점이 있나요?

L : 매점은 건물 내에는 없고 도서관 앞 광장 왼쪽에 편의점이 있습니다.

Library Facilities ● 시설

Situation 16 Student Facilities

U : Are they any leisure or rest facilities for students in the library?

L : There are two resting lounges. One is in the basement and the other on the third floor. The lounge provides vending machines, water fountains, TVs, the Library Kiosk, and ATMs.

U : What is a Library Kiosk?

L : It helps new patrons by providing information on library regulations, classification tables, search options, check-in and check-out of library materials and a guide for each floor of the library. It is very convenient because users can easily follow each option just by touching buttons on the screen.

U : What facilities are there for physically handicapped people?

L : Each reading room has special desks for the disabled. Also, we provide a wheelchair ramp. We are going to build a special study room for disabled people soon.

U : Is there a cafeteria in the library?

L : You can find one in front of the library.

상황 17　　분관

U : 검색하다 보면 소장처가 중앙도서관이 아닌 곳도 있던데요.

L : 맞습니다. 우리 도서관은 현재 일부 단과대학별로 학술저널 자료실을 운영
하고 있고, 음악, 법학, 의학도서관 등 3개의 분관이 있습니다. 분관은 해당
전공의 이용자를 대상으로 서비스를 제공하는데요. 단행본, 저널, 학위논
문 등 모든 자료를 이용할 수 있어 주제 전문형 서비스라고 할 수 있죠.

U : 그래서 중앙도서관에서 그 분야의 책들을 찾아볼 수 없었던 거군요.

L : 그렇습니다. 우리 대학은 13개 단과대학의 34개 학부가 있는 종합대학이므
로 앞으로도 분관 형태의 자료실을 활성화해 나갈 것입니다.

U : 분관이나 분실을 설치하는 기준이 있나요?

L : 의학, 법학, 음악은 학문분야와 자료형태에서 차별성이 있기 때문에 별도
의 분관을 이용하도록 하였습니다. 산업과학과 자연과학은 대학원생 이상
의 고급 이용자들이 학술저널을 자주 이용하기 때문에 각 단과대에 저널자
료 중심의 분실을 둔 것입니다.

U : 분관과 분실의 이용률은 어떤가요?

L : 의학, 법학, 음악분관 이용이 다른 분실보다 상대적으로 이용률이 더 많은
편입니다.

Situation 17 Branch Libraries

U : I can see that some materials are not in the main library.

L : That's correct. We have branch libraries that mainly contain academic journals on specific subjects. There are three branch libraries : the Music Library, the Law Library, and the Medical Library. They are designed for users whose majors are in these areas. In these libraries, students and faculty can use monographic publications, periodicals and dissertations related to their subjects.

U : That explains why I can't find some books at the main library.

L : Hankook University is one of the biggest universities in Korea. It has thirteen colleges and thirty-four departments. We will establish more branch libraries in the future.

U : What criteria make up a branch library?

L : Since medicine, law and music are quite different from other fields in the nature of their subject matter and resources, it is convenient that each subject branch library houses all types of materials on its subject. In addition, graduate students in technology and the natural sciences heavily use academic journals. Thus, we set up journal rooms in the technology and natural sciences schools.

U : Do students use branch libraries frequently?

L : The materials in the Medicine, Law and Music Libraries are used more often than others.

상황 18   영어 이외의 언어 사용자 방문

L : 안녕하세요, 무엇을 도와 드릴까요

U : 법학도서관을 견학하려고 방문했습니다.

L : 그러세요. 제가 안내해 드리겠습니다.

U : 방문객 대부분이 일본인인데 일본어로 안내해 주실 수 있습니까?

L : 제가 일본어가 능숙하지 않은데요, 잠깐 기다려주시면 일본어로 안내할 수
    있는 사서분을 소개해 드리겠습니다.

U : 고맙습니다.

L : (잠시 후) 죄송합니다. 하필 일본어를 하시는 분이 출장 중이시네요.

U : 할 수 없군요. 영어로라도 좀 부탁 드리겠습니다.

Situation 18 Non-English Speaking Foreign Visitors

L : Hello. How may I help you?

U : I want to arrange for a group to visit the Law Library.

L : OK. I can assist you.

U : Most of the visitors are Japanese. Are you able to guide them in Japanese?

L : I'm sorry, but I am not able to guide them in Japanese. I will find
    someone who can guide them in Japanese. One moment, please.

U : Thank you.

L : (A few seconds later) I'm so sorry, but the librarian who speaks Japanese
    is not here today.

U : That's too bad. Can you give a tour in English, then?

상황 19 멀티미디어센터

U : 영화자료는 어디에서 찾아볼 수 있을까요?

L : 네, 도서관 2층으로 가시면 멀티미디어센터가 있는데, 그곳에 영화나 음악 같은 멀티미디어 자료 열람 코너가 마련되어있습니다. 영화를 직접 감상하시려면 학생증을 맡기시고 미디어 감상실을 이용하시면 됩니다.

U : 영화제작 동아리 친구들과 다 같이 모여서 감상할 수도 있나요?

L : 그럼요, 미디어 감상실은 20명까지 수용할 수 있거든요.

U : 혹시 영상을 편집할 수 있는 시설도 있나요?

L : 네, 멀티미디어센터는 자료열람에서 촬영, 제작시설까지 지원하고 있습니다. 영상스튜디오와 미디어제작실을 이용해보시면 좋겠네요.

U : 정말 좋네요. 자주 들러야겠어요.

Situation 19   Multimedia Center

U : Where can I find film resources?

L : You should go to the multimedia center on the 2nd floor. The library's audio and video collections are located there. For VOD/DVD, you need to submit your ID card at the service desk.

U : Is it possible to watch movies together with my moviemaking team?

L : Sure, we have a DVD room with a 20-seat capacity.

U : Are there any video editing facilities in the library?

L : Yes, video editing is available at the multimedia editing station. The library provides video collections and also facilities for video imaging and editing in the multimedia center.

U : That's great. I'll come by again.

상황 20   배웅

U : 벌써 시간이 많이 지났네요, 너무 많은 시간을 빼앗지 않았나 모르겠습니다.

L : 별말씀을요. 도움이 되셨나 모르겠습니다. 한국의 도서관은 미국과 비교하면 많은 차이가 있을겁니다.

U : 규모나 투자면에서는 차이가 있겠지만 질적으로는 유사한 것 같습니다. 이번에 한국 도서관에 대해 알게 되어서 앞으로 업무에 많은 도움이 될 것 같습니다.

L : 도움이 되셨다니 다행입니다. 이것은 저희가 준비한 기념품입니다.

U : 정말 감사합니다.

Situation 20  Farewell

U : I've stayed here for a long time. I'm afraid I took too much of your time.

L : Don't worry about it. I hope I've been helpful. The libraries in Korea are quite different from the libraries in the States.

U : When it comes to scale and the amount invested, they are different. But they are similar inside. I was able to learn about the Korean library system and this will help my work a lot.

L : It's been my pleasure to help you today. Here is a souvenir from the Hankook University Library.

U : Thank you so much.

상황 21　근로장학생 신청

U : 도서관에서 근로장학생을 하고 싶어서 찾아왔습니다.

L : 현재는 모든 인원이 찼거든요, 홈페이지의 대기자 명단에 이름을 등록해주시겠어요.

U : 아! 그런가요? 그런데 근로장학생은 주로 어떤 일이 하게 되죠?

L : 반납된 도서나 학생들이 열람한 자료를 제자리에 다시 배열하는 일을 주로 하게 되구요. 사서들의 업무를 보조하는 일도 합니다.

U : 장학금 지급은 어떤 식으로 되나요?

L : 월급제이고 일한 만큼 시급으로 계산이 되요. 시간당 6,000원이고 매달 25일에 통장으로 입금될 거에요.

U : 실은 제가 휴학 중이거든요. 휴학생도 신청 할 수 있나요?

L : 가능하죠. 그런데 휴학생의 경우에는 풀타임 근무자만 신청받고 있어요. 급여는 월 70만원입니다.

U : 잘 알겠습니다.

Situation 21 Applying for Part-Time Jobs at the Library

U : I'd like to apply for a part-time job at the library.

L : I'm sorry, there aren't any positions currently available. Why don't you sign up on the waiting list on our website?

U : Oh, I can do it online? By the way, what are some of the duties of the library assistant?

L : Shelving books on the stacks and assisting librarians are the main duties.

U : What are the salary conditions?

L : You will be paid once a month. It's 6,000 won per hour, and the library will deposit the money into your bank account on the 25th of each month.

U : Actually, I'm on leave and not registered this semester. Am I still eligible?

L : Yes, you are eligible. However, in your case, you should work full-time at a salary of 700,000 won per month.

U : I see. Thank you. Bye.

상황 22 　사회봉사

U : 안녕하세요. 이번에 도서관 사회봉사를 신청한 학생입니다. 여쭤볼게 있는데요.

L : 네, 말씀해보세요.

U : 매주 월요일 3시간씩 봉사활동을 하는 것으로 되어있는데, 장소가 어딘지 궁금해서요.

L : 이름이 어떻게 되세요?

U : 전자전기공학부 2학년 홍길동입니다.

L : 학생이 배정된 부서는 자료정리 부서네요. 1층 정보지원팀 사무실로 찾아가시면 됩니다.

U : 어떤 일을 하게 되나요?

L : 담당 사서분이 자세히 안내해 주실 텐데요, 간단히 말해서 구입 또는 기증된 자료에 바코드와 라벨을 부착하는 일을 하게 될 겁니다.

U : 제가 근무요일을 변경할 수가 있나요?

L : 원칙적으로 불가하다고 알고 있지만, 담당사서와 의논해 보세요. 저쪽 끝에 앉아 계시는 분입니다. 지금 만나보시겠어요?

U : 네. 감사합니다.

Situation 22   Volunteer Services

U : Hello. I applied for volunteer service in the library. May I ask some questions?

L : Yes, sure.

U : I was assigned to work for three hours every Monday. Where should I work?

L : What's your name?

U : I'm Gil-dong Hong, a sophomore in the Department of Electronic Engineering.

L : You will work at the Cataloging Department. Go to the Library Support Team on the 1st floor, and they will let you know what to do.

U : What am I supposed to do?

L : For a quick overview, you will attach labels and barcodes on new and donated books.

U : May I change my schedule?

L : I'm afraid you can't. But you may consult with your supervisor. He is over there. Why don't you introduce yourself?

U : Thank you.

U : 안녕하세요. 문헌정보학과 홍길동입니다. 오늘부터 도서관 실습을 하게 되었습니다. 잘 부탁드립니다.

L : 만나서 반가워요, 실습기간이 언제까지인가요?

U : 오늘부터 한달 동안입니다.

L : 여기 교육 스케줄 표가 있습니다. 먼저 사서장님과 면담한 후에 각실의 사서 선생님들과 인사하는 시간을 갖도록 하겠습니다.

U : 예 알겠습니다.

L : 교육 스케줄에 따라서 오늘과 내일은 수서 부서에서 실습이 있을거에요. 그 이후에는 정리, 대출, 상호대차, 전산 등에 대한 교육이 차례로 있어요. 인사가 끝나는 대로 1층 정보지원팀 사무실로 내려오면 담당선생님이 기다리고 있을 것입니다.

U : 알겠습니다. 고맙습니다.

Situation 23　Student Interns

U : Hello. I'm Gil-dong Hong from the Department of Library and Information Science. I will begin my work as an intern starting today. I'm pleased to meet you.

L : Glad to meet you, too. How long will you be working here?

U : I am planning to work for a month.

L : Here's the work schedule. First of all, introduce yourself to the head librarian, and say hello to the other librarians.

U : Thank you.

L : There will be an orientation for two days in the Acquisitions Department. After that, you will learn how to arrange documents, deal with interlibrary loans and other computer skills. Come to the Library Support Team on the first floor after greeting other librarians. Your supervisor will be waiting.

U : I understand. Thank you.

상황 24 　 그룹스터디룸

U : 예전에 비해서 도서관에 그룹스터디룸이 많아졌네요.

L : 요즘 대학교에는 조별과제나 그룹스터디가 예전보다 활발해졌거든요. 그래서 도서관에 스터디룸을 확충하게 되었습니다.

U : 미리 예약을 하고 사용해야 하나요?

L : 네, 도서관 홈페이지에서 예약하시면 됩니다. 실별로 수용인원과 이용가능 시간을 실시간으로 확인할 수 있습니다.

U : 그룹스터디룸에 화이트보드는 설치되어 있죠?

L : 그럼요 보드마카 펜과 지우개는 안내데스크에서 대여하시면 됩니다.

U : 그룹스터디룸은 좌석이 얼마나 되나요?

L : 6인실에서 20인실까지 다양합니다. 20인실에는 빔프로젝터와 스크린도 설치되어 있습니다.

Situation 24   Group Study Rooms

U : There are more Group Study Rooms in the library than before.

L : Because of the increasing number of group projects and group studies, we have expanded the study rooms in the library.

U : Do I have to make a reservation?

L : Yes. You can reserve a study room on our website. Also, you can check the seating capacity and the available time for each room in real time there.

U : Are Group Study Rooms equipped with whiteboards?

L : Yes. And the library provides you with a marker and whiteboard erasers at the service desk.

U : How many seats are there in a Group Study Room?

L : The rooms seat between 6 and 20 people. Also, the room for 20 people has a projector and a screen.

상황 25 ♥ 국제회의실

U : 안녕하세요, 문헌정보학과 사무실입니다. 올해 학술대회를 도서관에 있는 국제회의실에서 진행할 계획이어서 대여신청을 하려고 합니다.

L : 그러세요, 학술대회가 언제 예정되어있나요?

U : 올해 가을 10월 15일입니다.

L : 네 현재 일정이 비어있어 예약이 가능합니다. 국제회의실은 250명 정도 수용 가능한데 충분하신가요?

U : 그 정도면 충분합니다. 마이크와 프로젝트 등은 준비해주실 수 있죠?

L : 그럼요. 단, 국제회의실 예약은 공문으로 신청하셔야 합니다.

U : 네. 고맙습니다.

Situation 25 International Conference Hall

U : Hello. This is the Department of Library and Information Science. I'd like to reserve the International Conference Hall of your library to hold a conference this year.

L : Hello, when will the conference be held?

U : It'll be on October 15th.

L : Okay. The schedule for that day is empty, so it is available. The International Conference Hall can seat up to two hundred fifty. Is that enough?

U : That will do. Do you provide equipment such as microphones and a projector?

L : Sure. But, you have to officially reserve the hall.

U : Okay. Thank you.

상황 26 북카페

U : 안녕하세요 북카페에 있는 책을 대출할 수 있나요?

L : 죄송하지만 북카페 도서는 북카페 안에서만 이용할 수 있습니다. 다른 자료실에도 같은 책이 있으니까 그 책을 대출해주시겠어요?

U : 아 그렇군요. 북카페 도서는 읽고 싶은 책이 많네요. 직원분들이 직접 선정하시는 건가요?

L : 네 도서관 사서분이 매월 주제를 정해서 인기도서와 우수도서를 선정합니다. 관심있는 주제가 있으면 저희에게 신청해주셔도 됩니다.

U : 그래도 되요? 사실 잠깐 시간 내어 읽기 좋은 신문 같은 간행물도 비치해주시면 좋을 것 같아요.

L : 좋은 의견이네요. 다음 달부터 그렇게 하겠습니다.

Situation 26  Book Cafe

U : Hello. Can I borrow books shelved in the Book Cafe?

L : I'm sorry. The books in the Book Cafe are only available inside the
library. We have the same books in other rooms and you can check out
those books.

U : Oh, okay. There are many books I'd like to read in this Book Cafe. Does
the library staff select all the books in person?

L : Librarians select best-selling books and outstanding books monthly. If
you have some fields in which you're interested, you could request it to
the librarians.

U : Is it okay? Actually, I'd like to read some magazines and newspapers in
the Book Cafe.

L : That's a good idea. We'll consider that suggestion.

Acquisition

수 서

● ● ●

연세대학교 중앙도서관

5 수서 / Acquisition

U : 안녕하세요? 자료구입을 신청하고 싶은데 어떻게 하면 될까요?

L : 네, 혹시 신청하려는 자료가 이미 도서관에 소장되어 있는지는 검색해 보셨나요?

U : 아니요.

L : 그럼 먼저 도서관 목록을 검색하셔서 소장여부를 확인하시고요. 해당 자료가 도서관에 소장되어 있지 않으면 '자료구입 신청' 메뉴에 들어가서 간단한 서지사항을 입력하시면 신청이 끝나게 됩니다.

U : 자료구입을 신청하면 언제쯤 이용할 수 있나요?

L : 책에 따라 다릅니다만, 신간의 경우 국내서는 보통 1~2주, 국외서는 4~6주 정도가 소요됩니다.

U : 네, 알려 주셔서 감사합니다.

Acquisition • 수서

U : Hi. I'd like to request a book purchase. Could you advise me on the procedures I should follow?

L : Have you searched our library catalog to see whether our library has the book?

U : No, I haven't.

L : Then before submitting a purchase request, please check our library catalog to make sure the library doesn't already own it. Once you have confirmed that it is not available here, go to the 'Purchase Request' menu on the library website and fill out the brief bibliographic information of the book on the purchase request form.

U : How long does it take to receive the book?

L : It depends, but in the case of a newly-published book, it usually takes about two weeks for a domestic book and 4 to 6 weeks for a foreign book.

U : I see. Thank you for your help.

상황 2 　💬 저널 구독신청

U : 안녕하세요? 문헌정보학과 김연세 교수입니다. 해외 저널 구독을 신청하고 싶은데, 어떻게 하면 될까요?

L : 네, 신청할 저널의 서지사항을 알려주시겠어요? 만약에 해당 저널이 전자 저널로도 구독이 가능하다면 인쇄저널과 전자저널 중 어떤 형태로 구독하 길 원하시나요?

U : 전자저널로 구독했으면 합니다.

L : 네, 그럼 가능하다면 전자저널로 주문하겠습니다.

U : 지금 신청하는 저널은 언제부터 이용할 수 있나요?

L : 올 해의 저널 구독신청 기간은 이미 지났기 때문에, 지금 신청하는 저널은 내년부터 구독할 수 있습니다.

U : 논문 작성에 꼭 필요한 저널이라 빨리 이용할 수 있으면 좋겠는데 다른 방 법은 없을까요?

L : 이 저널은 최근 1년 분을 제외하고는 AAA 데이터베이스에서 원문을 이용 할 수 있네요.

U : 아, 그래요? 어떻게 이용하면 될까요?

L : 도서관 홈페이지의 통합검색이나 전자저널 항목에서 해당 저널을 검색하 여 이용하거나, 직접 AAA 홈페이지에 접속하여 이용할 수도 있습니다.

U : 네, 잘 알겠습니다. 감사합니다.

Situation 2　Recommend a Journal Subscription

U : Hello, I am Yonsei Kim, a professor of the school of Library and Information Science. I would like to recommend a journal for subscription.

L : Could you tell me the bibliographic information of the journal? If the journal is available both in print and online, in which format would you prefer to subscribe?

U : I prefer subscribing to the online journal.

L : Okay, then. I will order the online journal, if possible.

U : When will the journal be available at the library?

L : Since the journal subscription order period for this year has already ended, the journal you request will be available beginning next year.

U : I need to read the journal as soon as possible. Could you suggest any alternatives?

L : Let me check. You may use this journal online using the AAA database, except for the full-text of the last 12 months.

U : That is great. Then how can I access the journal in the AAA database?

L : You can access the journal either from the library catalog or from the e-journal list on the library website. You can also directly access the AAA website.

U : I see. Thanks a lot.

상황 3　💬 학술DB 추천

U : 안녕하세요, 경영대학 김연세 교수입니다. 학술DB AAA의 구독을 신청하고 싶습니다. 경영학관련 연구자들에게 유용한 자료입니다.

L : 네, 교수님, 좋은 자료 추천해 주셔서 감사합니다. 학술DB AAA에 대해서 검토해 본 후 진행상황을 알려드리도록 하겠습니다.

U : 구독 여부는 어떻게 결정되나요?

L : 학술DB 선정기준에 따라 결정하게 됩니다. 수록 콘텐츠 내용과 구독조건, 예산, 시범 서비스 기간 중 이용통계, 컨소시엄 구성 여부 등을 검토합니다. 관련 학과의 펀드 지원이 있는지도 확인해봐야 하구요.

U : 네, 그렇군요. 그럼, 일단 시범 서비스를 받아보는 게 좋을 것 같습니다.

L : 시범 서비스 신청 후 서비스가 세팅 되면 홈페이지를 통해 공지하고 교수님께도 알려드리도록 하겠습니다.

U : 감사합니다. 구독할 수 있었으면 좋겠네요.

Situation 3

U : Hello. My name is Yonsei Kim. I am a professor of the Business School.
I'd like to recommend a subscription to the AAA database. It's a very
useful database for scholars of business administration.

L : Thank you for your suggestion. We will review the AAA database, and
will let you know our decision.

U : How will the decision be made?

L : Decisions regarding new database subscriptions are made according to
the selection criteria. We will review the contents of the database,
conditions of subscription, library budget and usage during the trial
period. We will check if there are any funds available from the related
department as well.

U : I see. Then I'd better ask for a trial service for the database.

L : All right. I will let you know when the trial service is open. I will also
post a notification about the new database trial on the library website.

U : Thank you. I hope it works out.

상황 4 　🍃 신청 중인 자료에 대한 문의

U : 안녕하세요? 저는 대기과학과 교수 김연세입니다. 제가 구입 신청한 책이 도서관에 들어왔는지 알고 싶어서요. 검색해 보니 주문중이라고 나오는군요.

L : 네, 주문중인 자료는 아직 도서관에 들어오지 않은 책입니다. 책 제목을 알려 주시면 처리상황을 알려 드리겠습니다.

U : 서명은 *Elements of Dynamic Oceanography* 이고요, 저자는 'D. Tolmazin' 입니다.

L : 네, 지금 시스템에서 처리사항을 확인하고 있으니 잠시만 기다려 주세요. 문의하신 책은 4월 16일자로 해외로 주문되었습니다. 대행사 쪽에 확인해 보니 현재 운송중이라고 하네요. 대략 2주 정도 후면 도서관에 입수될 것 같습니다.

U : 도서관에 들어오는 대로 빨리 이용하고 싶은데요.

L : 책이 도착되어 입수처리가 되면 신청자에게 문자메시지와 이메일로 통보가 가게 됩니다. 도서관 홈페이지의 'My Page' 메뉴에서 교수님 휴대폰 번호와 이메일 주소가 정확히 입력되어 있는지 다시 한 번 확인해 주십시오. 도착 통보를 받으신 후 우선정리를 신청하시면 책을 빨리 이용하실 수 있습니다.

U : 네. 고맙습니다. 휴대폰 번호와 이메일 주소가 정확한 지 확인해 보겠습니다. 수고하세요

Situation 4   Inquiring about Books on Order

U : Hello. I am Yonsei Kim, a professor of Atmospheric Sciences. I would like to know whether the book I requested for purchase has been received. I checked (with) the library catalog and found the item status is On-order.

L : Well, if the processing status is labeled as 'On-order', it means that it hasn't been received yet. Could you give me the title? I'll check its processing status.

U : The title is *Elements of Dynamic Oceanography* by D. Tolmazin.

L : OK. Wait a moment. I will check the system. The book was ordered on April 16. According to our agency's website, it's now being shipped. It will take about 2 more weeks to arrive at the library.

U : I would like to use it as soon as it arrives.

L : Once the book is received by the library, an e-mail notification and SMS will be sent to the requester. Please check your 'My Page' information at the library website to make sure your cell phone number and e-mail address are correct. After receiving notification, please request 'Urgent Processing' to use the book as early as possible.

U : Thanks a lot. I'll make sure my e-mail address and cell phone number are correct at the library website.

상황 5　　자료 선정

L1: 국외 자료는 누가 선정하고 있습니까?

L2: 국외단행본은 교수와 학생, 연구자 등의 이용자 신청과 주제사서의 선정에 의해 구입하고 있습니다. 연속간행물은 주로 학과의 신청에 의해 구독하고 있습니다.

L1: 주제사서가 선정하는 도서의 비율은 어느 정도나 됩니까?

L2: 60% 정도의 비율이 되는 걸로 파악되고 있습니다.

L1: 그럼 각 주제사서에게 예산을 배정해 주나요?

L2: 그런 셈입니다. 회계 연도 초에 주제사서 선정 분의 예산을 배정하여, 각자 정해진 예산범위에서 선정하도록 하고 있습니다. 주로 단행본 의존도가 높은 인문, 사회 분야의 도서 선정이 많이 이루어지고 있습니다.

L1: 자료 선정의 연간 특별한 시기가 있습니까?

L2: 예산범위 내에서 주제사서가 수시로 선정하고 있습니다.

L1: 장서 구성에 어떠한 변화가 있을 수 있을까요?

L2: 장기적인 계획을 가지고 해당 주제분야의 핵심 장서 구성을 다져가고 있습니다.

Situation 5   Selecting Foreign Books

L1 : Who is in charge of selecting foreign books?

L2 : Foreign books are purchased either at the request of faculty members or by the selection of subject librarians. Subscription of foreign periodicals is decided by the faculty members of each department.

L1 : What percentage of books is selected by subject librarians?

L2 : About 60% of total books.

L1 : Then do you allocate a budget to each subject librarian?

L2 : Yes, we do. We allocate a budget to each subject librarian at the beginning of the fiscal year. Books in the fields of humanities and social sciences are selected by subject librarians. Those fields have a high dependency on books.

L1 : Is there a specific time period for selecting books?

L2 : Not really. Selection is made throughout the year as long as the budget allows.

L1 : Does selecting books by subject librarians make any difference in terms of collection development?

L2 : The library can build core collections in each subject field according to a long-range plan.

상황 6 　　신규 거래

L : 저는 한국대학교 도서관 수서담당 사서 김연세입니다. 귀사의 악보를 구입하고자 합니다.

P : 네, 저희 회사와는 거래가 처음이신가요?

L : 그렇습니다. 귀사는 본교 음악대학의 나작곡 교수를 통해 알게 되었습니다.

P : 그러시군요. 우선 주문서를 보내 주시겠어요?

L : 주문서는 귀사의 이메일로 이미 보냈습니다.

P : 아! 주문서가 도착해 있네요. 그런데 현재 우리에게 재고가 없는 자료가 좀 있는데요. 이를 제외한 자료는 곧 보내드릴 수 있습니다.

L : 그럼 가지고 계신 자료만 우선 보내 주시고, 나머지 자료도 입수하는 대로 보내주시기 바랍니다.

P : 네, 그러지요. 오늘 인보이스를 보내 드리겠습니다. 지불이 확인되는 대로 자료를 항공편으로 보내 드리죠.

L : 감사합니다. 인보이스가 도착하면 바로 지불하도록 하겠습니다.

P : 주문에 감사 드립니다.

Acquisition • 수서

Situation 6  New Vendors

L : Hi. This is Yonsei Kim. I work at the acquisitions department of Hankook University Library. We would like to purchase musical scores from your company.

P : Is this your first time doing business with our company?

L : Yes. Chak-kok Nah, Professor of Music at our university, has recommended your company.

P : I see. Could you send an order slip first?

L : I have already sent it by e-mail.

P : Ah! I found your order form. I think some of the scores you ordered are out of stock now. But, I can send the scores in stock first.

L : Then, please send us the available scores first and send the rest of our orders as soon as possible.

P : Sure. I'll send an invoice to you. When the bill is paid, we'll ship the scores via airmail.

L : Thank you. I will pay the bill as soon as the invoice arrives.

P : Thank you for your order.

상황 7 　 시범 서비스 신청

L : 안녕하세요, 한국대학교 도서관 김연세입니다. 귀사의 학술DB AAA의 구독을 검토하고 있습니다. AAA의 콘텐츠, 플랫폼 검토를 위해 시범 서비스를 신청하고 싶습니다.

V : 네, 신청해 주셔서 감사합니다. 두 달 동안 무료로 이용하실 수 있고 한 번 더 연장이 가능합니다. 신청서를 보내드릴 테니 FTE 규모, IP 주소, 신청자 정보 등을 기입하셔서 보내주시기 바랍니다.

L : 서비스 방법은 어떻게 되나요?

V : 기관 IP내에서 별도의 로그인 없이 모든 원문정보를 이용하실 수 있습니다. 시범 서비스 기간 동안은 프락시 서버 사용은 하실 수 없습니다.

L : 네 잘 알겠습니다. 시범 서비스 기간 동안 이용통계도 제공하시는지요?

V : 네 제공하고 있습니다. 학술DB AAA에 대한 설명자료와 플랫폼 이용방법 등을 이메일로 보내드리도록 하겠습니다. 이용자들에게 많은 홍보 부탁 드립니다.

L : 신청서 작성해서 보내드리겠습니다. 친절한 지원 감사 드립니다.

Situation 7 — Requesting Database Trial Service

L : Hi. My name is Yonsei Kim from Hankook University Library. Our library is considering subscribing to the AAA database from your company. I would like to request a trial service of the database to review its contents and platform.

V : Thank you for your request. We can offer a 2-month trial service. You may extend your trial period one more time, if you want. I'll send an application form. Please fill in the columns such as FTE, IP addresses, and library information, and send it back to us.

L : Could you tell me more about your trial service?

V : You may use the full-text of the database from any IP addresses of your institution without logging in. However, during the trial service period, the use of a proxy server is prohibited.

L : I see. Do you provide usage statistics during the trial service period?

V : Yes, we do. I will send a brochure for the AAA database and a users' guide to the database platform to your e-mail. We will appreciate if you could promote our database to your users.

L : Thank you for your support. I will send an application.

상황 8   가격 조건 협상

L : 귀 연구소에서 발간한 자료를 구입하고 싶습니다. 일반 서적상을 통해 구할 수 없는 자료인 것 같습니다. 그런데 저희 도서관은 대학 도서관인데, 혹 교육기관에 대한 가격 할인 혜택이 있습니까?

R : 저희 연구소 회원인 경우 20% 정도 할인하여 판매합니다.

L : 저희 대학 수학과 방정식 교수님이 그 곳 회원이며 편집위원으로 활동하고 있다고 들었습니다.

R : 구입하려는 책이 얼마나 되나요?

L : 약 50책 정도 됩니다.

R : 그럼 20% 정도 할인하여 자료와 인보이스를 보내겠습니다.

L : 감사합니다. 인보이스가 도착하는 대로 지불하겠습니다.

R : 주문해 주셔서 감사합니다. 신속히 납품하도록 하겠습니다.

Situation 8  Negotiating Prices

L : We would like to purchase some materials from your institute. They are not available from any bookstores. I work for a university library. Do you offer any special discounts for educational institutions?

R : We only offer a 20 percent discount to the members of our institute.

L : Chong-sik Pang, a professor of Mathematics at our university, is a member of your institute. He also works there as an editor from time to time.

R : How many books do you plan to purchase?

L : About fifty.

R : Then I will send you the materials and the invoice with the 20% discounted price.

L : Thank you. I'll pay the bill as soon as the invoice arrives.

R : Thank you for your order. We will deliver them promptly.

상황 9 · 긴급 주문

V : 오늘 총 5책의 주문서를 이메일로 보냈습니다. 저희 대학 교수님이 급히 필요로 하는 자료라 최대한 빨리 자료와 인보이스를 보내 주시면 고맙겠습니다.

L : 주문서가 도착했네요. 그런데 5책 중 3책은 재고가 있습니다만, 나머지 두 책은 출판사에 연락해서 구해야 하므로 시일이 좀 걸릴 것 같네요.

V : 급하지만 어쩔 수 없네요. 그럼 우선 재고가 있는 3책을 먼저 DHL로 보내 주세요. DHL비용은 저희가 부담할 테니 인보이스에 포함시켜 주시고, 나머지 두 책도 구하는 대로 같은 방법으로 보내주세요.

L : 알겠습니다.

V : 언제쯤 자료를 받을 수 있을까요?

L : DHL로 보내더라도 1주일 정도는 걸립니다. 아마 다음 주 초에 받으실 수 있을 겁니다.

V : 고맙습니다. 최대한 신속히 처리해 주실 것을 다시 한 번 부탁 드립니다.

Situation 9   Rush Orders

V : I sent an urgent order for five titles via e-mail. I would appreciate it if you send the books and invoice as soon as possible. A professor from our university needs them urgently.

L : We've got your order form. However, we only have three of the titles in stock. As for the other two, we need to place an order to the publisher, which will take a few days.

V : They are urgently needed materials, but I guess we have no choice. Please send us the three books in stock first by DHL. We will pay the delivery charge. Please add it to the invoice. Please send the other two in the same manner when you get them.

L : OK.

V : How soon can we get the books?

L : It takes about a week even if sent by DHL. You will probably receive them early next week.

V : Thank you. Please be as prompt as you can.

상황 10 　주문 취소

L : 4월 26일에 보낸 주문서번호 WS11-0426의 주문번호 ONW11-01234를 주문 취소하고 싶습니다. 저희 도서관에 있는 책인데 제가 실수로 주문하였네요. 죄송하지만 지금이라도 주문을 취소할 수 있을까요?

V : 이미 출판사에 주문이 나갔는지 확인해 봐야 할 것 같네요. 잠깐만 기다려 주세요.

L : 네.

V : 다행입니다. 아직 출판사로 주문이 나가지가 않았네요. 원하시는 대로 주문 취소해 드리겠습니다. 주문번호 ONW11-01234 맞으시죠?

L : 네. 감사합니다.

Acquisition • 수서

 Situation 10  Canceling Orders

L : I would like to cancel Item No. ONW11-01234 from the order form WS11-0426 issued on April 26. I ordered the book again by mistake, not knowing our library had already acquired it. I'm sorry but, would it be possible to cancel the order now?

V : Please wait a minute while I check the order records to see if it has been already ordered from the publisher.

L : Thanks.

V : Fortunately, it has not yet been ordered from the publisher. I will delete the item from the list. Item No. ONW11-01234, correct?

L : That's correct. Thank you for your help.

상황 11　📎 도서상태 NOP 에 대한 문의

L : 안녕하세요. 지난달에 보내 주신 주문 리포트에 'NOP'가 있었는데 그게 무슨 뜻인가요?

V : 그건 'Not Our publication'의 약어로, 출판사에서 자기 회사에서 출판한 자료가 아닐 경우 그렇게 표시합니다.

L : 아! 그렇군요. 그런데 이상하네요. 분명히 그 출판사에서 나온 자료로 알고 있었는데요.

V : 우리도 그렇게 알고 출판사로 주문했었거든요.

L : 그럼 구입을 하지 못하게 되는 건가요? ISBN으로 다시 한번 찾아보면 안될까요?

V : 판권이 넘어갔는지도 모르겠네요. 좀 더 알아보겠습니다.

L : 대단히 감사합니다. 꼭 필요한 자료이거든요.

Situation 11 Inquiring about the Book Status NOP

L : Hello. The word NOP is written on the order form you sent me last month. What does that mean?

V : It is an acronym for 'Not Our Publication'. We use this term when a book is not published by the publisher that the user indicated on the form.

L : Oh, I see. That's strange. I was sure it was published by Springer.

V : We also thought so, and so we made an order to Springer.

L : So is this item not possible to obtain? Can you search the book by its ISBN again?

V : Maybe the copyright has been handed over to another publisher. I'll check it again.

L : I appreciate it. This is a very important book to me.

상황 12 　　　입수 확인-누락 및 파본

L : 오늘 귀사에서 보낸 10상자의 자료를 잘 받았습니다. 그런데 인보이스에서 1책이 빠졌고, 잘못 제본된 도서도 있네요.

V : 어떤 자료인가요?

L : 누락된 도서의 제목은 *Vendors and Library Acquisitions*이고 주문번호 ONW11-000004321입니다. 잘못 제본된 도서는 Inventing the Future이구요.

V : 다시 한 번 확인해 보시겠습니까? 패킹시 저희가 다 맞춰서 보냈는데요.

L : 여러 번 확인해 보았지만 분명히 없었습니다.

V : 그럼 저희가 실수했나 봅니다. 곧 다시 보내 드리겠습니다.

L : 잘못 제본된 도서는 새 것으로 교체해 주시겠지요?

V : 네, 물론이지요.

L : 반송료는 어떻게 해야 하나요?

V : 저희가 부담할 테니 착불로 보내주시면 됩니다.

L : 감사합니다.

Situation 12　Omitted or Damaged Items

L : We received ten boxes of books from your company, but one book is omitted from the invoice. I also found another book which is poorly bound.

V : Which ones are they?

L : The omitted one is *Vendors and Library Acquisitions*, Item No. ONW11000004321, and the poorly-bound one is Inventing the Future.

V : Could you check for the missing item again? We checked all the items when shipping.

L : I have already checked for the missing item several times, but couldn't find it.

V : Then we probably made a mistake. We'll send it to you soon.

L : Could you exchange the poorly-bound book with a new one?

V : Sure.

L : What about the delivery charge?

V : We'll bear the expense this time.

L : Thanks a lot.

상황 13 　입수 확인-주문서와 다른 도서 입수

L : 며칠 전에 받은 도서 중 *Positioning : The Battle for* …는 저희가 주문한 책이 아닙니다. 저자는 같은데 서명이 좀 다르네요.

V : 그래요? 그 책의 IBSN이 뭐죠?

L : '1560241217'인데요

V : 저희가 출판사에 주문사항을 입력할 때 실수로 ISBN을 잘못 입력했네요. 죄송합니다.

L : 그럼 원래 저희가 주문한 도서를 최대한 빨리 보내 주십시오. 잘못 입수된 그 도서는 나중에 반송해 드려도 될까요?

V : 반송하실 필요 없습니다. 저희 실수로 번거롭게 해 드렸으니 도서관에 기증하는 것으로 하겠습니다.

L : 네, 감사합니다.

V : 앞으로도 무슨 문제가 있으면 제게 연락 주십시오.

Acquisition • 수서

L : Among the materials we received a few days ago, the book *Positioning : The Battle for* ⋯ is not the one that we ordered. We ordered a book by the same author, but the title is different.

V : Is that right? What is the ISBN of the book?

L : It is 1560241217.

V : We made a mistake when we ordered from the publisher. We input the wrong ISBN. I am sorry.

L : Then please send us the book we ordered as soon as possible. Can we return the wrong title later?

V : You don't need to return it. Since we troubled you with our mistake, we will donate that book to your library.

L : Thank you.

V : You're welcome. Please contact me at any time if you have a problem.

상황 14 　가격 확인-오리지널 인보이스 요청

L : 안녕하세요? 한국대학교 도서관 김연세인데요, Smith양과 통화할 수 있을
　　까요?

V : 아, 홍 선생님, 안녕하셨어요? 저 Smith 입니다.

L : 네, 안녕하세요? 다름이 아니라 인보이스 WS20110722-1 에서 56번의 도서
　　가격이 정확한 지 확인 부탁을 드리려고요.

V : 네…, 56.50달러네요

L : 제가 주문할 때 조사한 가격은 46.25달러였는데 차이가 많이 나네요.

V : 그럼, 저희가 출판사로부터 받은 인보이스를 확인해 보겠습니다. 잠시만
　　기다리세요. 아! 여기 있네요. 주문번호가 56번이라고 하셨죠? 그 금액이
　　맞네요.

L : 그래요? 그 사이 가격이 올라서 그런가요? 제가 Amazon에서 검색했을 때
　　는 46.25달러로 나와있었거든요.

V : 저희는 출판사에서 받은 인보이스 금액을 정확히 청구하고 있습니다. 보통
　　Amazon 데이터베이스는 수시로 갱신하지 않기 때문에 출판사에서 가격이
　　오르더라도 가격 조정이 안된 경우가 있어 간혹 이런 일로 문의해 오는 거
　　래처가 있습니다.

L : 아, 그렇군요.

V : 저희가 출판사로부터 받은 오리지널 인보이스를 메일로 보내 드릴까요?

L : 그렇게 해 주시면 감사하겠습니다.

Situation 14 — Checking Prices—Asking for the Original Invoice

L : Hello. My name is Yonsei Kim from Hankook University Library. May I speak to Ms. Smith?

V : Hi, Mr. Hong. This is she. How are you?

L : I'm good. I have a favor to ask. Could you verify that the price of Item No. 56 in Invoice WS20110722-1 is correct?

V : Let me see. It's $56.20.

L : When I was checking the price, it was $46.25. There is a considerable gap between those two prices.

V : Let me check the invoice from the publisher. Please wait a moment. Ah! Here it is. Item No. 56? $56.50 is right.

L : Is it? Has the price gone up since then? When I was searching the price from Amazon, it was $46.25.

V : We charge exactly the same amount as shown in the publisher's invoice. Usually, the Amazon database is not updated in a timely manner, so we often encounter this kind of problem.

L : Oh, I see.

V : Do you want me to send you the original invoice from the publisher by e-mail?

L : I would appreciate it if you would do that..

상황 15　　클레임

L : 주문서번호 WS11-0722-LAW의 주문도서 중 아직 도서관에 납품되지 않은 도서가 여러 권 있습니다. 작년에 주문했는데 1년이 되도록 미착도서가 많네요. 왜 그런지 주문처리 상황을 조사해서 알려 주시겠어요?

V : 저희 회사 주문 기록에 의하면, 아직 납품되지 않은 도서는 현재 출판사에 재고가 없거나 절판된 도서들입니다. 저희가 주문 리포트를 보낸 것 같은데 못 받으셨습니까?

L : 아니, 못 받았는데요. 절판된 도서가 언제쯤 재 발행되는지 알 수 있나요?

V : 출판사에 물어보고 알려 드리겠습니다.

L : 고맙습니다.

Acquisition • 수서

Situation 15 Claims

L : Several books from Order Form WS11-0722-LAW have not been delivered yet. We ordered them last year. Could you check the status of the order?

V : According to our order records, the books were not delivered because they were either out of stock or out of print. Didn't you get the order report we've sent?

L : No, we didn't. Do you know when the out-of-print books will be reprinted?

V : I will let you know after checking with the publisher.

L : Thank you.

상황 16　💬 전신환 송금

L : 오늘 도서 대금을 귀사에 전신환으로 송금하려고 합니다. 거래 은행과 계좌번호를 알려 주시겠어요?

V : 잠깐만요. 불러 드리겠습니다. 메모 준비되셨어요?

L : 네, 말씀하세요.

V : 씨티은행, 계좌번호는 012-3746입니다. 그런데 송금 금액은 얼마인가요?

L : 미화 5,500달러입니다. 인보이스 번호 'RI012345'에 대한 금액입니다. 3~4일 후에 입금 확인해 보세요.

V : 네, 확인하는 대로 연락 드리겠습니다.

L : 그런데, 도서 대금을 신용카드로 결재할 수는 없나요?

V : 카드 결재도 가능합니다.

Acquisition • 수서

Situation 16　Electronic Remittances

L : We are going to pay the bill by wire transfer. Could you give me your
　　bank account number, please?

V : Just a moment, please. Are you ready to write it down?

L : Yes. Go ahead.

V : It's Citi Bank. The account number is 012-3746. How much are you going
　　to send?

L : US$5,500 for Invoice No. RI012345. Please check within three or four
　　days to see whether it has been received.

V : OK, I will. I will let you know upon receipt.

L : By the way, is it possible to pay the bill by credit card?

V : Of course.

상황 17　♥ 송금 확인-인보이스 자료 미수령

V : 인보이스 번호 SR01410이 아직까지 지불되지 않았습니다. 미지불 인보이스에 대한 문서를 보냈는데 못 받으셨습니까?

L : 받긴 했는데, 저도 이상하게 생각하고 있었습니다. 그 인보이스를 받은 적이 없거든요. 물론 해당 자료도 받지 못했구요.

V : 작년 말에 발행한 것인데, 받지 못하셨다니 이상하네요.

L : 현재까지 귀사로부터 받은 인보이스는 모두 지불했습니다. 일단 그 인보이스의 복사본을 팩스나 이메일로 보내 주시겠어요?

V : 그러죠. 그런데 자료도 받지 못하셨다면서요?

L : 우선 인보이스를 보고 혹시 기증도서로 처리된 건 아니지 확인해 보겠습니다.

V : 네, 그럼 인보이스 복사본을 보내 드리겠습니다.

Situation 17  Missing Invoices

V : Invoice No. SR01410 has not been paid yet. We sent a statement for the unpaid invoice. Have you received it?

L : Yes, I have. I was thinking it was strange because I had never received either the invoice or the materials.

V : We sent them last year. We're sorry you did not receive them.

L : We have paid all the invoices from your company. Would you send a copy of the invoice to us by fax or e-mail?

V : Yes, I will. So you didn't get the materials either?

L : No, we didn't. We are going to check if we processed them as gifts.

V : How kind of you! I'll send a copy of the invoice soon.

L : Don't worry about it. I'll call you.

상황 18　송금 확인-수표 재 발행 요청

L : 지난 번 말씀하신 미지불 인보이스 건은 이미 작년 말에 지불한 것으로 되어 있습니다. 그 쪽에서 누가 수표를 수령하였는지 확인해 보시겠어요?

V : 이미 은행에 알아봤는데요, 해당 돈이 은행에 남아 있답니다. 그런데 우리가 그 돈을 수령하려면 수표 원본이 있어야 하거든요. 미안하지만 수표를 재 발행하여 보내 주시기 바랍니다.

L : 알겠습니다. 그런데 수표를 재 발행하려면 우리도 거래 은행에 요청해야 하므로 시간이 좀 걸릴지도 모르겠습니다.

V : 괜찮습니다. 번거롭게 해 드려 대단히 죄송합니다.

Situation 18   Reissuing Checks

L : It says here that the unpaid invoice you mentioned before was paid last
year. Do you know who received our check?

V : I've already checked with the bank and they said your check has not
been paid yet. We need the original check in order to cash it. I'm sorry
but, could you reissue the check and send it to us?

L : OK. Unfortunately, it might take some time because we have to ask the
bank to reissue the check.

V : That's OK. Sorry to trouble you.

상황 19 　　인보이스를 받지 못한 경우

L : 두 달 전쯤에 귀사로부터 주문한 도서를 수령하였습니다. 그런데 아직 인보이스가 도착하지 않아 지불 처리를 못하고 있습니다.

V : 인보이스는 항공편으로 따로 발송했습니다. 며칠만 더 기다려 보시겠어요?

L : 잘 알겠습니다. 그런데 보통 지불기간이 90일 아닌가요?

V : 그렇긴 합니다만, 걱정하지 마세요. 나중에 인보이스가 도착하는 대로 지불하시면 됩니다.

L : 이번 달 말까지 인보이스를 받지 못하면 다시 연락하겠습니다.

V : 네, 제게 다시 연락 주시기 바랍니다.

Situation 19 Invoices Not Received

L : We received the books that we ordered from your company about two months ago. However, the invoice has not arrived yet, so we could not pay the bill.

V : We sent the invoice separately via airmail. Could you wait a few more days?

L : OK, but don't we have to pay the bill within 90 days?

V : Yes, but don't worry about it. You can pay it after you receive the invoice.

L : I'll call you again if we do not receive the invoice by the end of this month.

V : Yes, please do so.

상황 20 　　환불

L : 아! 이걸 어쩌죠? 문제가 생겼습니다.

V : 무슨 문제인데요?

L : 제가 실수로 같은 인보이스를 이중으로 지불한 것 같습니다.

V : 인보이스 번호가 몇 번이죠? 언제 지불하였나요?

L : 작년에 지불했는데, 인보이스 번호는 393737 입니다. 확인해 주시겠어요?

V : 저희 회사 회계 파트에 알아봐야 하므로 지금 당장은 확인이 곤란합니다.

L : 작년 12월에 지불한 것을 금년 1월에 재차 지불하였습니다. 환불이 가능한
　　가요?

V : 이중으로 수령한 것이 확실하다면 당연히 환불 가능합니다.

L : 그럼 확인해서 알려 주시기 바랍니다.

V : 네, 알겠습니다.

Acquisition • 수서

Situation 20 　Refunds

L : Ah! What shall I do? I have a problem, Ms. Smith.

V : What's the matter?

L : I made a mistake by paying the same invoice twice.

V : What is the invoice number and when did you pay it?

L : I paid it last year and the number is 393737. Can you check it for me?

V : I have to ask our Accounting Department, so I am afraid I cannot tell you right now.

L : I paid the invoice in December and then again in January. Can I get a refund?

V : Of course, you will be reimbursed if it is confirmed that you've paid it twice.

L : Please let me know.

V : I'll call you

상황 21 저널 견적 요청

L : 안녕하세요? 한국대학교 도서관 저널 담당 김연세입니다. 이번에 신규로 구독하려는 저널 15종에 대해 견적을 요청합니다.

V : 인쇄저널에 대한 견적만 보내 드리면 되겠습니까?

L : 저널 A, B, C는 전자저널을 포함하여 견적을 내 주시기 바랍니다.

V : 언제까지 보내 드리면 될까요?

L : 9월 30일까지 보내 주세요.

V : 예, 그러지요. 다른 문의사항은 없으신지요?

L : 없습니다.

V : 감사합니다. 좋은 하루 되세요.

Situation 21  Asking for Quotes on Periodicals

L : Hello, this is Yonsei Kim of Hankook University Central Library. I would
like to request price quotes for subscribing to 15 new journals.

V : Do you want an estimate for printed journals?

L : Yes. Could you also include the price for the electronic version for A, B
and C?

V : How soon do you need it?

L : By September 30, please.

V : OK. I'll take care of it. Do you have any other questions?

L : No, I don't.

V : Thank you. Have a nice day.

상황 22 　 구독 갱신 및 주문 확정

V : 안녕하세요? ABC 한국지사 김철수입니다. 방금 구독갱신 저널 리스트를 메일로 보내 드렸습니다.

L : 아, 그러세요. 확인해 보고 연락 드리겠습니다.

V : 언제 정도면 주문이 확정될까요?

L : 주문에 변동사항이 좀 있을 것 같습니다. 7종을 취소하고 12종을 추가할 예정입니다.

V : 혹시 알고 계실지 모르겠지만 9월까지 주문 완료하면 조기 갱신 할인혜택이 있습니다.

L : 아 그렇습니까? 얼마나 할인이 되나요?

V : 8월까지 갱신주문을 완료하면 전체 구독료의 3%, 9월까지는 1% 할인됩니다. 계약금액이 크니 할인 금액도 꽤 됩니다.

L : 알겠습니다. 검토해 보겠습니다.

V : 그리고 JETS 서비스도 한 번 신청해 보시지요?

L : JETS 서비스를 이용하면 어떤 이점이 있나요? 비용이 더 들지 않나요?

V : JETS 서비스는 여러 지역의 출판물들을 모아 입수기록을 한 후 일정한 주기로 선적하여 보내주는 door-to-door 서비스로 결호에 대해서는 즉시 클레임 처리를 해 주며, 모든 자료는 패킹 리스트와 함께 배달되기 때문에 안전합니다. 또한 미국 국내가격이 적용되기 때문에 비용 면에서도 경제적입니다. 좋은 조건으로 제안 드리니 검토해 주시기 바랍니다.

L : 네, 검토 후에 연락 드리겠습니다.

Acquisition • 수서

V : Hello. This is Chol-su Kim from ABC Korea. I have just e-mailed you the journal renewal list.

L : Have you? Let me call you back after I check.

V : When do you think the order will be decided?

L : We expect there will be some changes in the order. We are planning to cancel seven journals and add twelve new ones.

V : If you order by September, you can get an early bird discount.

L : Really? How much is the discount?

V : If you order no later than August, you will get an extra 3% discount, and a 1% discount if by September. Since the whole sum is quite large, it's a good offer.

L : I see. I will consider it.

V : Would you like to subscribe to the Journal Expediting & Technical Services (JETS)?

L : What is the benefit of JETS? Does it cost extra?

V : JETS is a door-to-door service to collect publications from several locations, create acquisition records and ship them regularly. It promptly claims missing issues and is reliable because all the materials are delivered with packing lists. Moreover, the less expensive U.S. domestic price is applied. This is an exclusive offer, so please consider it.

L : OK. Let me get back to you after I look it over.

상황 23　♥ 인보이스 오류

L : 안녕하세요? 한국대 도서관 김연세입니다. 인보이스에서 이상한 점이 있어 확인하고자 합니다.

V : 아, 그러세요. 어느 인보이스에서 어떤 문제가 생겼나요?

L : 인보이스 번호12345에서 타이틀 *ABC*'는 저희 도서관에서 주문 한 것이 아닙니다. 또 타이틀 *XYZ*'는 누락되었습니다.

V : 확인해 보겠습니다. 잠시만 기다려 주세요.

L : 그리고 저희가 최근에 전자저널 형태로 구독 변경하였는데 모두 인쇄저널로 인보이스가 발행되었습니다. 저희가 보낸 주문서를 확인해 보시기 바랍니다.

V : 죄송합니다. 확인 후 인보이스를 다시 보내드리겠습니다.

Situation 23  Invoice Errors

L : Hello. This is Yonsei Kim of Hankook University Library. There
seem to be some errors on the invoice you sent to our library.

V : Oh, is that so? Could you tell me the invoice number?

L : The invoice number is 12345. We did not order the title *ABC* and also the
title *XYZ* has been omitted.

V : Let me check. Just a moment, please.

L : In addition, recently we've changed our journal subscription format to
online, but the invoice was still issued for print journals. Please check our
order form again.

V : Sorry for the inconvenience. I will check and send a new invoice soon.

상황 24 　입수 확인

L : 안녕하세요? 한국대학교 도서관 김연세입니다. 지난 4월 28일자로 받은 저
　　널 중에서 패킹리스트와 다른 저널들이 있습니다.

V : 아, 그러세요? 어떤 저널들인지요?

L : 우리 도서관에서 구독하지 않는 저널도 있고, 리스트에는 없는 저널도 있
　　습니다.

V : 우선 죄송합니다. 구독분이 아닌 저널에 대해서는 번거롭겠지만 반송하여
　　주시고, 리스트에 없는 저널은 그대로 입수 처리하시기 바랍니다.

L : 그렇게 하지요

V : 죄송합니다. 다시는 이런 실수가 생기지 않도록 주의하겠습니다.

Situation 24 Confirming Acquisitions

L : Hello. This is Yonsei Kim of Hankook University Library. I found some mistakes in the journal package received on April 28.

V : Did you? Could you tell me what they are?

L : I found one journal that we didn't subscribe to and there was another journal not found on the packing list.

V : I'm sorry. Please send us back the journal you don't subscribe to and keep the one not on the list.

L : OK. I will.

V : Sorry for the inconvenience. We'll make sure that these mistakes will never happen again.

상황 25　♥ Online 저널 등록 확인

L : 안녕하세요. 한국대학교 도서관 저널담당 사서 김연세입니다. 이번 해에
　　Online Only 조건으로 신규로 구독하는 저널의 원문이용이 안 되고 있습니
　　다. 무엇이 문제인지요?

V : 그렇습니까? 저널명이 무엇인지요? Print로 구독하던 것을 Online으로 변
　　경하신 것인가요?

L : 저널명은 〈AAA〉입니다. 올해 신규로 구독 하는 저널입니다.

V : 아, 이 저널은 아직 시스템 등록 처리가 안되어 원문이 안 열리고 있습니다.
　　연초라 등록 담당 부서에서 일이 밀려서 늦어지고 있습니다. 귀 도서관에
　　서 최대한 빨리 원문이용이 가능하도록 담당 부서에 요청하겠습니다.

L : 이용자가 논문작성을 위하여 급하게 이용하기를 원하는 저널이니 빠른 처
　　리를 부탁 드립니다. 시스템 등록을 위해 우리 학교의 IP 주소를 알려 드리
　　겠습니다. 등록이 완료되면 바로 연락 주시기 바랍니다.

V : 알겠습니다. 이 저널의 등록이 늦어진 점 죄송하게 생각합니다.

Situation 25 Confirming Online Journal Registration

L : Hello. I'm Yonsei Kim. I'm in charge of journal subscriptions at Hankook University Library. One of the journals that we are subscribing to from your company seems to have a problem regarding access to its full-text. We started subscribing to the online journal this year with the understanding that we could access the full-text. What could be the problem?

V : I'm sorry to hear that. May I have the journal title? Have you recently changed your subscription from print to online?

L : No. We started subscribing to the journal just this year. The title is ⟨AAA⟩.

V : Well, this journal has not been registered in our system. That's why you cannot access the full-text. We are sorry for the delayed processing. I will ask our systems department to expedite processing.

L : One of our patrons needs the journal urgently for his thesis, so please do so as quickly as possible. I will let you know our IP addresses for your system registration. Please let me know when you are done with the registration.

V : I will. I'm sorry again for the delay.

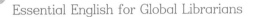

상황 26　저널 클레임

L : 안녕하세요? 한국대학교 도서관 김연세입니다. 귀 학회에서 발행되는 학회지 23권 2호가 아직 입수되지 않았습니다.

V : 학회비는 납부하셨나요?

L : 예, 4월 12일자로 송금했습니다.

V : 확인해 보고 보내 드리도록 하겠습니다. 주소를 알려 주시겠습니까?

L : 주소는 서울시 서대문구 한국로 50입니다. 빠른 시일 내에 자료를 받았으면 좋겠습니다.

V : 예, 빨리 처리하도록 하겠습니다.

Acquisition • 수서

Situation 26 Journal Claim

L : Hello. This is Yonsei Kim of Hankook University Library. Issue 2 of volume 23 of the journal your institute publishes has not been received yet.

V : Did you pay the membership fee?

L : Yes, I remitted it on April 12th.

V : Then I will check our account again and send the issue to you. May I have your address?

L : It is 50 Hankook-ro, Seodaemun-gu, Seoul. I would like to receive it as soon as possible.

V : Sure, I will take care of it right away.

상황 27 저널 클레임에 대한 회신

V : 안녕하세요? ABC社의 홍길동입니다. 일전에 보내주신 클레임에 대한 회신
을 메일로 보냈습니다.

L : 잠시만 기다려 주시겠습니까? 확인해 보겠습니다.

V : 그런데, 이번 클레임 건 중에 *XYZ* 타이틀은 본사에서는 이미 발송한 것으
로 되어 있는데, 다시 한 번 확인해 주시겠습니까?

L : 도서관에서는 받지 못했는데, 우편사고가 발생한 건 아닌지요. 이런 경우
어떻게 처리하면 좋을까요?

V : 도서관에서 다시 한 번 점검하여 주시고, 그래도 없다면 다시 클레임 처리
하겠습니다.

L : 예, 알겠습니다. 저희 쪽에서도 다시 한번 체크해 보도록 하겠습니다.

Situation 27 Replying to Claims

V : Hello. This is Gil-dong Hong from ABC. I sent an e-mail regarding the claim you sent to us.

L : Would you wait for a minute? I'll check.

V : The title *XYZ* has already been sent from the main office. Could you check for it again?

L : I have checked it again, but we haven't received it. I'm afraid that there might be something wrong with the delivery. What should I do in this case?

V : Why don't you check for the title once again? If you still don't find it, we will claim it again.

L : OK, I see. We will check again and I will call you back.

상황 28 임시 증간호

L : 안녕하세요? 한국대학교 도서관 김연세입니다. *판례시보* 1769호가 입수되지 않았습니다.

V : 예, 1769호는 임시 증간호입니다. 임시 증간호는 정기구독 비용에 포함되지 않고 별도로 판매하는 것입니다. 구매하시겠습니까?

L : 우선 견적서를 보내 주시지요.

V : 그러지요. 팩스 번호를 좀 알 수 있을까요?

L : 예, 팩스 번호는 82-2-123-4567 입니다.

V : 곧 보내 드리도록 하겠습니다. 감사합니다.

Situation 28   Special Issues

L : Hello. This is Yonsei Kim of Hankook University Library. It seems that
    Law Reports No. 1769 has not been received yet.

V : No. 1769 is a special issue which is not included in the subscription.
    Would you like to purchase it?

L : Then, could you send us an estimate first?

V : OK. May I have your fax number?

L : Sure, the number is 82-2-123-4567.

V : I will send it soon. Thank you.

상황 29　♥ 회원 가입-학회

V : 안녕하세요? 한국대학교 도서관이죠? 여기는 역사학회인데요, 저희가 공문을 보내 드렸는데 받으셨습니까?

L : 네, 받았습니다. 역사학회에서 발행하는 간행물에는 어떤 것들이 있나요?

V : 한 달에 한 번씩 발행되는 *역사학회지*'가 있습니다.

L : 지금 단체회원으로 가입하면 이번 달부터 자료를 받아 볼 수 있을까요?

V : 네, 물론입니다. 원하시면 창간호부터 제본된 자료도 받아 보실 수 있습니다.

L : 그러면 회원 가입 신청서를 이메일로 보내 주세요

V : 네. 저희 학회에 가입하여 주셔서 감사합니다. 자료는 매달 초에 보내 드리고 청구서는 따로 공문으로 보내 드리겠습니다.

L : 감사합니다. 그럼 수고하세요.

Situation 29 Membership in Institutes or Associations

V : Hello? Is this Hankook University Library? This is the Association of Korean History. Have you received an official letter we sent to you?

L : Yes, we have. Could you tell me what kind of periodicals your association publishes?

V : We publish *Yoksa Hakhoeji* monthly.

L : If we become a member of your association, can we receive the transactions starting from this month?

V : Yes, of course. You can also have bound volumes of all back issues from the first issue, if you want.

L : Then could you send a membership application form by e-mail?

V : Sure. Thank you for joining our association. We usually send a transaction at the beginning of the month and send invoices separately by mail.

L : Thank you. Have a good day.

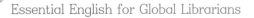

상황 30 　크레디트

L : 안녕하세요? 한국대학교 도서관 김연세입니다. 저희 도서관에서 구독하던
　　저널 ABC가 발행 중단되었다는 편지를 받았습니다.
V : 예. 그렇습니다. 나머지 구독료를 어떻게 처리할까요? 환불해 드릴까요?
L : 아니오, 환불보다는 크레디트 처리해 주세요.
V : 그렇게 처리하도록 하겠습니다.
L : 그리고 현재까지의 거래 기록도 보내 주시겠습니까?
V : 예, 그렇게 하겠습니다.

Situation 30   Account Credit

L : Hello. This is Yonsei Kim of Hankook University Library. We are subscribing to the journal ABC and we received a notice that the publication of the journal has ceased.

V : I'm afraid so. What would you like us to do with your remaining subscription fee? Shall we refund it?

L : We'd prefer to receive it as account credit.

V : OK, I will do so.

L : And could you send a current account statement?

V : OK, I will.

V : 안녕하세요? 해외 학술 데이터베이스를 판매하고 서비스하는 ABC社의 문
영진입니다.

L : 아, 그러세요. 무슨 일로 오셨나요?

V : 이번에 새로 나온 DB를 소개해 드리고자 방문하였습니다. 영미 문학 작품
의 원문을 그대로 수록한 DB인 'English Online'이라는 제품인데요, 영문학
을 연구하는 사람들에게 아주 유용한 DB입니다.

L : 우리 도서관에서는 영미문학 DB AAA을 이미 구독하고 있습니다만,
소개해주신 DB의 특징은 무엇입니까?

V : 저희 DB의 특징은 …입니다. (DB 상세 설명 계속)

L : 구독회원 기관수는 어느 정도 됩니까?

V : 국내에만 10개 기관 회원이 있고 개인 서비스로 가입하신 이용자도 많이
있습니다.

L : 모바일 웹 서비스도 가능한가요?

V : 네 가능합니다. 모바일 웹페이지가 있습니다.

L : 테스트용 ID/PW가 있으면 알려주시기 바랍니다.

V : 예, 바로 보내드리겠습니다. 그리고 궁금한 사항이 있으시면 언제든지 연
락 주시기 바랍니다.

Situation 31 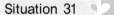 Introducing New Materials

V : Hello. I am Young-jin Moon from ABC. Our company sells overseas academic databases and provides related services.

L : Hi, how are you? What can I do for you?

V : I came here to introduce a new database to you. English Online is a database that offers original full-text of English and American literature. It is very helpful to those who study English literature.

L : We've already been subscribing to the AAA database in the field of English and American literature, but could you explain the features of your database?

V : Our database has strong points in···
(The introduction of database continues.)

L : How many customers do you have?

V : 10 institutional customers and many more private customers in Korea.

L : Do you offer a mobile web service?

V : Yes, we do have a mobile webpage.

L : Would you like to provide us with a trial ID and password so we can check it out for ourselves?

V : Sure. Do not hesitate to contact me if you have any questions.

상황 32 　　📣 학술DB 견적 요청

ㄴ : 안녕하세요, 그 동안 시범서비스로 이용하던 학술DB AAA와 계약을 하려고 합니다. AAA의 구독 조건에 대해 알려주시기 바랍니다.

V : IP로 등록하시거나 ID/PW 방식으로 이용하실 수 있는 두 가지 옵션이 있습니다. IP 방식에서는 동시 이용자수 제한 없이 이용하실 수 있고, FTE 규모에 따라 4가지로 나뉘는데 귀 대학은 FTE 15,000 이상인 A 그룹에 해당합니다.

ㄴ : 교외에서 이용할 수 있는지요? 우리 기관에서는 프락시 서버를 사용하고 있습니다.

V : 프락시 서버 사용도 가능합니다. 원하시면 교외 접속용 ID/PW를 발급받아서 사용할 수도 있습니다.

ㄴ : Backfile을 제공하는지요?

V : 구독 기간 동안의 raw data를 CD-ROM 형태로 제공하고 있습니다.

ㄴ : 이용통계에 대한 정보도 제공하나요?

V : 관리자 계정을 통해 COUNTER 통계정보를 온라인으로 조회할 수 있습니다.

ㄴ : License는 본사와 직접 계약하게 되는 건지요?

V : 네, 그렇습니다. 계약은 본사와 직접 하시고 한국지사에서는 서비스 지원과 교육을 도와드리고 있습니다.

ㄴ : 메타서치와 링킹서비스를 사용할 수 있나요?

V : 네, 사용하실 수 있습니다. 링킹 서버의 주소를 알려주시면 세팅해 드리고 있습니다.

ㄴ : 네, 잘 알겠습니다. A그룹 IP 등록 옵션, 기간은 시범 서비스가 끝나는 다음 달 1일부터 1년으로 계약하고 싶습니다. 계약서와 견적서를 이메일로 보내주시기 바랍니다.

V : 주문해주셔서 감사합니다. 서비스에 불편이 없도록 시스템 설정을 준비하도록 하겠습니다.

ㄴ : 감사합니다.

Situation 32　Asking for the Estimate

L : Hi. We've been using AAA database on a trial basis. Now we'd like to make an official contract. Could you tell me the terms and conditions for the subscription?

V : You have two options for subscribing to the AAA database. You may either register IP addresses or access it through ID and password. If you choose to register IP addresses, you may access the database regardless of the number of simultaneous users. We classify institutions according to the FTE scale and your institution is classified as group A which has over 15,000 FTE numbers.

L : Do you allow off-campus access? We use proxy servers.

V : You may use proxy servers, or you can also access the database by logging in with ID and password.

L : Do you provide backfiles?

V : We provide CD-ROMs containing raw data of the subscription period.

L : What about the statistics for usage analysis?

V : If you log in to administrator accounts, you can check the COUNTER statistics online.

L : Are we supposed to have a license contract directly with the main office?

V : Yes, you are. You will make a contract with the head office and the branch office in Korea will give support in service and training.

L : Are we able to use meta search and linking service as well?

V : Sure. Let us know the linking server address of your institution and we will set up a linking service

L : I see. We'd like to make a 1 year contract beginning next month. Please send us the contract and subscription estimates by e-mail.

V : Thank you for subscribing to our database. We will do our best to provide support for you.

L : Thank you.

상황 33 ☞ 학술DB 이용 문의

L : 안녕하세요. 한국대학교 도서관 학술DB 담당 사서 김연세입니다. 우리 도서관에서 귀사의 학술DB AAA를 신규로 구독하게 되었는데, DB 이용에 대해 몇 가지 문의 드리려고 합니다.

V : 네, 구독해 주셔서 감사합니다. 궁금하신 점은 언제든지 문의하시기 바랍니다.

L : 통계 데이터는 어떻게 확인할 수 있나요?

V : 통계 데이터는 관리자 계정에서 확인할 수 있습니다

L : 관리자 계정에서는 통계 데이터 외에 어떤 정보를 확인할 수 있나요?

V : 관리자 계정에서는 통계 데이터 외에도 프락시 서버나 기관 IP 등록 정보 등을 확인하시거나 변경하실 수 있습니다. 학술DB 신규 업데이트 정보는 관리자 계정에 등록된 e-mail로 정기적으로 보내드리고 있습니다.

L : Backfile CD-ROM은 어떻게 이용할 수 있나요. 별도의 프로그램이 있어야 이용할 수 있나요?

V : 네 그렇습니다. 홈페이지에서 프로그램을 다운로드 받으실 수 있습니다. CD-ROM은 1년에 한번 보내드리고 있습니다.

L : 학술DB 서버 점검 기간이 있나요?

V : 네, 있습니다. 점검 기간은 미리 공지해 드리고 있는데 1년에 1~2회, 4시간 정도 소요됩니다.

L : 친절한 답변 감사합니다.

Situation 33 Inquiring about Database Subscription

L : Hi. My name is Yonsei Kim, the librarian in charge of database subscription at Hankook University Library. Our library will begin subscribing to database AAA, so I would like to make sure of several things.

V : Thank you for your subscription. Please feel free to ask.

L : How can I check the usage statistics?

V : You may check the usage statistics via the administrator's account.

L : What else can I check from the administrator's account?

V : You can also register or change proxy servers or institutional IP addresses. We regularly send updated information on the database to the e-mail address registered at the administrator's account.

L : How can I use backfile CD-ROMs? Do I need a certain program?

V : Yes, but you can download the necessary programs from our website. We send CD-ROMs once a year.

L : How often do you check the server? Is there a special period for server inspection?

V : Yes, there is. We usually announce the server inspection period beforehand. We inspect our server, once or twice a year and it usually takes about 4 hours.

L : Thank you for your helpful answer.

상황 34 전자저널 등록

L : 귀 출판사에서 발행하는 저널 *Development*를 온라인으로 이용하고 싶습니다.

V : 인쇄저널을 구독하고 있나요?

L : 예, 그렇습니다.

V : 그렇다면, 인쇄저널 구독료의 20%만 추가 지불하시면 온라인 저널도 함께 이용하실 수 있습니다.

L : 그럼 올해는 20% 추가 지불로 인쇄저널과 온라인 저널을 병행해서 구독하고 내년도에 구독 갱신할 때에는 Online only로 주문하면 되겠군요.

V : 그렇습니다. 전자저널 추가 구독료에 대한 인보이스와 라이센스 협약서 보내드리겠습니다. 구독료는 송금해 주시고 협약서는 검토 후 이견이 없으시면 서명하여 팩스로 보내주시면 됩니다. 그리고 출판사 홈페이지에서 온라인 등록을 해 주셔야 합니다.

L : 등록과 동시에 바로 이용할 수 있나요?

V : 보통 라이센스 협약서를 받는 대로 바로 서비스를 오픈 하고 확인 메일을 보내드립니다.

L : 네, 알겠습니다.

V : 이용 중에 문제가 발생하면 언제든지 연락 주시기 바랍니다.

Situation 34 Registering E-Journals

L : We would like to subscribe to your company's journal *Development* in the online format.

V : Are you currently subscribing to the print one?

L : Yes, we are.

V : In that case, you may use the online journal by paying an extra 20% of the print journal subscription fee.

L : Then, we will pay 20% of the print journal subscription fee this year for the additional use of the online format. We will change our journal subscription format to online next year.

V : OK. I will send an invoice for the additional fee with a license agreement. Please review the license agreement and have it signed and send it back to us with the payment. You will also need to register online on our website.

L : Can we access the online journal as soon as I register?

V : We usually send a confirmation mail when we receive a license agreement and then commence service.

L : Thank you for your help.

V : Sure. If you have any problem, please contact me at any time.

상황 35 　　접속 장애

L : 귀 출판사의 저널 *Development*를 전자저널로 이용하고 있습니다. 그런데, 며칠 전부터 접속이 안되고 있습니다.

V : 어떻게 안되고 있습니까?

L : 원문을 열려고 하면 아이디/비밀번호를 요구합니다.

V : 혹시 프록시 서버를 운영하고 있습니까?

L : 아니요, 프록시 서버를 사용하지 않습니다.

V : 잠시 기다려 주세요. IP가 올바르게 등록되었는지 확인해 보겠습니다. 저희 서버 상에는 이상이 없습니다만, 여러 가지로 원인을 찾아 보도록 하겠습니다.

L : 네, 감사합니다. 빠른 복구를 기다리겠습니다.

Situation 35 Access Errors

L : We are subscribing to the journal *Development* published by your company online. But we have had some problems accessing it for the last couple of days.

V : Could you specify the problem?

L : Whenever I try to view the full-text, it requires ID and password.

V : Do you have a proxy server?

L : No, we don't use a proxy server.

V : Please wait a minute while I check if your IP is registered correctly. I can't find any problems with our server at this moment, but I will try to find out possible causes.

L : Thanks. It would be great if we could use it soon.

상황 36　♥ 수증

L : 안녕하십니까? 한국대 도서관 김연세입니다.

D : 저는 1995년에 한국대 국문과를 졸업한 김수미라고 합니다. 제가 소장하고 있는 책을 기증하려고 연락 드렸습니다.

L : 책을 기증하신다고요? 감사합니다. 책의 양은 어느 정도입니까?

D : 대략 200권 정도 됩니다만, 한 번 방문하셔서 직접 보시면 좋겠습니다.

L : 언제 방문하면 좋을까요?

D : 7월 30일 오후 5시는 어떻습니까?

L : 예, 좋습니다. 주소를 알려주시겠어요?

D : 여기는 서대문구 신촌동 134번지 입니다.

L : 그럼 7월 30일에 방문 드리도록 하겠습니다. 그럼, 그 날 뵙겠습니다.

Situation 36 Receiving Gifts

L : Hello? This is Yonsei Kim from the Acquisitions Department of the Hankook University Library.

D : Hi, this is Sumi Kim. I graduated from Hankook University in 1995, majoring in Korean Literature. I would like to donate my books to your library.

L : Thank you for your intention to donate. How many books are you planning to give?

D : About 200 books. Why don't you visit me and take a look at them?

L : Sure. When is a convenient day for you?

D : How about July 30th at 5pm.?

L : That's fine for me. Could you tell me your address?

D : It is 134 Shinchon-dong, Seodaemun-gu.

L : Then I will visit you on July 30th. See you then.

상황 37　　기증 의뢰-단행본

L : 안녕하십니까? 한국대학교 도서관 김연세입니다. 귀 기관에서 발행한 연보에 대해 문의하려고 연락 드렸습니다.

D : 아, 그러세요? 말씀하세요.

L : 그 책을 구입할 수 있을까요?

D : 죄송하지만 그 책은 비매품입니다.

L : 그럼 혹시 기증받을 수는 있을까요?

D : 예, 드리도록 하겠습니다. 몇 부나 필요하신가요?

L : 2부를 기증해 주시면 좋겠습니다. 위치를 알려주시면 직접 가지러 가도록 하겠습니다.

D : 저희 사무실은 신촌동 프라자 건물 내에 위치하고 있습니다.

L : 언제 방문하면 되겠습니까?

D : 8월 11일은 어떨까요?

L : 네, 그럼 8월 11일 오전 10시에 찾아 뵙도록 하겠습니다. 기증해 주셔서 감사합니다.

Situation 37　Requesting Donations – Books

L : Hello? This is Yonsei Kim from Hankook University Library. May I ask a question about the yearbook you publish?

D : Sure. Go ahead.

L : Is the yearbook for sale or not?

D : It's not for sale.

L : Then, is it possible to donate the yearbook to our library?

D : Sure. How many copies do you want me to give?

L : I would appreciate it if you could donate two copies. Could you tell me your address so that I can go to get them?

D : My office is in the Plaza Building, Shinchon-dong.

L : When do you want me to visit?

D : How about August 11th?

L : OK. I will visit your office at 10 a.m. on August 11th. Thank you for your donation.

상황 38 　♪ 감사패 증정

L : 저희 도서관에 자료를 기증하여 주셔서 감사 드립니다. 감사의 표시로 총 장님 명의의 감사패를 드리려고 합니다.

D : 감사합니다. 감사패를 받게 되다니 영광입니다.

L : 저희 도서관을 방문해 주실 수 있을까요?

D : 제가 요즘 바빠서 시간을 낼 수가 없는데, 우편으로 보내 주실 수 있을까요?

L : 네, 그러지요. 주소를 말씀해 주시겠습니까?

D : 제 주소는 서울 서대문구 신촌동 134입니다.

L : 네, 그럼 감사패를 댁으로 보내 드리도록 하겠습니다.

D : 감사합니다.

Situation 38 Presenting an Appreciation Plaque

L : Thank you for your donation to our library. As a token of our gratitude, we would like to present you with an appreciation plaque in the name of our university president.

D : Thank you so much. I'm honored to receive an appreciation plaque.

L : Could you visit our library?

D : I'm sorry but I don't have time these days. Could you send it to me by mail?

L : Sure. May I have your address?

D : It is 134 Shinchon-dong, Seodaemun-gu, Seoul.

L : I will send the appreciation plaque to you, then.

D : Thank you.

상황 39 · 자료 교환

L1 : 안녕하세요? 한국대학교 도서관 김연세라고 합니다. 귀교와 저희 한국대학 교가 학술교류협정을 체결한 것으로 알고 있습니다만, 혹시 내용을 알고 계십니까?

L2 : 네, 들었습니다.

L1 : 우선 양 교의 간행물을 상호 교환하면 어떨까 해서 연락 드렸습니다.

L2 : 예, 좋습니다. 그럼 양 교 간행물에 대해 리스트를 교환하고, 서로 빠진 부 분에 대해 보충하도록 합시다.

L1 : 네, 그렇게 하지요, 그리고 향후 발간되는 학교 간행물에 대해서는 우선적 으로 상호 교환하도록 하지요. 저희 대학 간행물 20종을 5월말까지 발송하 도록 하겠습니다.

L2 : 감사합니다. 저희 쪽에서도 빠른 시일 내에 발송하도록 하겠습니다.

Acquisition • 수서

L1 : Hello? This is Yonsei Kim from Hankook University Library. Have you been informed that our university made an agreement with your university on academic exchanges?

L2 : Yes, I was informed of it.

L1 : To begin with, how about exchanging university publications with each other?

L2 : That's a good idea. Let's exchange the lists of publications first and fill in the missing issues.

L1 : OK. Let's start exchanging university publications from now on. We will send twenty publications to you by the end of May.

L2 : Thank you. We will also send ours soon.

상황 40　　등록번호의 체계

L1 : 안녕하세요? ABC의 홍길동입니다. 자료를 등록하는 방법에 대해 문의해도 되겠습니까?

L2 : 예, 물론입니다.

L1 : 등록번호는 어떻게 부여하나요? 모든 자료를 입수순으로 부여합니까?

L2 : 아닙니다. 등록번호는 8자리로 구성되어 있는데 첫 번째 자리의 수는 자료 구분을 표시하는 식별기호입니다. 등록번호의 첫 번째 자리의 수가 1은 동양서, 2는 서양서, 3은 비도서, 5는 연속간행물을 뜻하고 나머지 7자리는 입수순으로 매겨지는 일련번호입니다.

L1 : 그럼 등록번호만 보면 어떤 자료인지 알 수 있겠군요?

L2 : 네, 그렇습니다.

Situation 40  Assigning Registration Numbers

L1 : Hello. This is Gil-dong Hong from ABC. May I ask you some questions about registering new items?

L2 : Sure. Go ahead.

L1 : How do you give registration numbers to items? Do you register all items in the sequence of acquisition?

L2 : No. A registration number has eight digits. The first digit indicates the category of the item. For example, we use 1 for eastern books, 2 for western books, 3 for non-print materials and 5 for periodicals. The last seven digits are given sequentially as they come.

L1 : So, we can easily recognize what kind of item it is by reading its registration number.

L2 : Yes, that's correct.

상황 41 　　 자료 제적

L1 : 안녕하세요. 한국대학교 도서관인데요, 자료의 제적에 대해 문의 드리려고 연락 드렸습니다. 주로 어떤 책을 제적 처리 하시나요?

L2 : 네, 저희는 이용자가 분실한 자료와 장서점검 결과 3년 이상 소재불명인 자료 등 저희 도서관 자료제적에 관한 내규에 따라 제적 대상자료를 정하고 있습니다.

L1 : 제적한 자료는 등록 원부에서도 완전히 삭제하시나요?

L2 : 네, 그렇습니다. 제적대상 자료의 목록을 작성하여 총장의 승인을 얻은 후에 등록 원부에서 완전히 삭제합니다.

L1 : 제적하는 자료가 얼마나 됩니까?

L2 : 일년에 약 300책 정도 됩니다.

L1 : 네, 알려 주셔서 감사합니다. 저희 업무에 많이 참고가 되었습니다.

Situation 41 Discarding Materials

L1 : Hello. This is Hankook University Library. I have a question about discarding library materials. What kind of items do you discard?

L2 : We select items to discard according to our library book discarding policy. For example, we discard lost items and items declared missing for more than three years.

L1 : Do you also delete item records from the register?

L2 : Yes, we do. We make a list of the items to discard and delete them from the register upon the approval of the president.

L1 : How many items do you discard every year?

L2 : About 300 volumes a year.

L1 : Thank you for your information. It was very helpful to us.

상황 42　　상담하기

V : 저는 영국의 John Smith社에서 온 A. Gertis 입니다.

L : 네, 기다리고 있었습니다. 제가 국외도서 구입 담당자 김연세입니다. 만나서 반갑습니다.

V : 저도 반갑습니다. 제 명함입니다.

L : 감사합니다. 한국에는 처음이십니까?

V : 아니 세 번째입니다만, 귀 도서관은 처음 방문입니다. 캠퍼스가 아름답습니다.

L : 네, 그렇죠?

V : 저희 회사와 서비스 및 거래 조건 등에 대해 소개 드릴까 합니다. (설명생략)

L : 잘 들었습니다. 귀사의 거래 조건 등을 신중히 검토하여 구입시 참조하도록 하겠습니다.

V : 시간 내 주셔서 감사합니다. 귀 도서관을 저희 고객으로 모시게 되길 바랍니다.

L : 네, 나중에 다시 뵙겠습니다. 안녕히 가세요.

Acquisition • 수서

Situation 42 Business Meetings

V : Hello. I'm A. Gertis, a sales manager from John Smith, England.

L : I have been waiting for you. I am Yonsei Kim, in charge of foreign books. Nice to meet you.

V : Nice to meet you, too. Here is my business card.

L : Thanks. Is this your first time to Korea?

V : No, this is my third time, but the first to your library. The campus is very beautiful.

L : Yes, isn't it?

V : May I introduce our company and its services, business terms and conditions to you? (The explanation is skipped.)

L : Thank you for the introduction. I will examine your terms and conditions of business and consider them when purchasing.

V : Thank you for your time. I hope we'll have a chance to do business with your library.

L : I hope so too. See you then. Bye.

상황 43 　수서업무 전반에 대한 소개-직원 구성 및 예산 규모

L1 : 현재 수서업무는 몇 분이 하고 있나요?

L2 : 팀장 1명을 포함하여 총6명이 담당하고 있습니다.

L1 : 국외자료 수서는 몇 사람이 하는지요?

L2 : 단행본 1명, 연속간행물 1명, 모두 2명입니다.

L1 : 귀 도서관의 연간 도서 구입 예산이 얼마나 되는지 물어도 될까요?

L2 : 대략 500만불 정도 됩니다.

L1 : 그 중 국외자료의 비중은 얼마나 되나요?

L2 : 국외자료 구입비는 단행본, 연속간행물 합해서 전체 예산의 60% 이상 됩니다.

Situation 43 Introduction to Acquisitions—Organization and Budget

L1 : How many staff members are working in Acquisitions?

L2 : There are six librarians, including a section chief.

L1 : How many are in charge of foreign materials?

L2 : Two. One is in charge of books, and the other periodicals.

L1 : Could you tell me your annual budget for purchasing library materials?

L2 : It's about 5 million dollars.

L1 : What's the portion for foreign books?

L2 : Including both books and periodicals, more than 60% of the total purchasing budget is allocated for foreign materials.

상황 44 　　국외자료 구입

L1 : 작년 도서관에서 구입한 국외 단행본 책 수는 얼마나 되는지요?

L2 : 대략 10,000여 책 됩니다.

L1 : 모두 국내업체로부터 구입하였나요? 아니면 국외 대행사에서도 구입하셨나요?

L2 : 거의 80-90%는 국내업체에서 구입하였고, 일부 계속 주문 및 국내에서 구입하기 어려운 도서를 국외업체로부터 구입하였습니다.

L1 : 국내업체라면 어디와 거래하고 있나요?

L2 : ABC, XYZ 등 5~6개 업체입니다.

Situation 44　Purchasing Foreign Books

L1 : How many foreign books did your library purchase last year?

L2 : About 10,000 volumes.

L1 : Did you purchase all of them from domestic vendors? Or from overseas vendors as well?

L2 : We purchased about 80 to 90 percent of foreign books from domestic vendors. However, some of our standing order books and books that are difficult to obtain from domestic vendors were purchased from overseas vendors.

L1 : Which domestic vendors do you have business with?

L2 : Five to six vendors such as ABC, XYZ and so on.

상황 45 　거래업체 서비스 평가

V : 주로 국내업체에서 국외자료를 구입한다고 들었습니다. 업체 서비스에 대해서는 만족하고 있습니까?

L : 대체적으로 만족하는 편입니다. 국내업체도 국외업체 못지 않게 업무처리를 잘 합니다. 또한 가격도 저렴한 편입니다. 정가에서 할인을 받고 있거든요. 그리고 언어장벽도 없어서 일 처리하는데도 편리하구요.

V : 네, 그렇군요. 저희 회사와도 거래해 보시면 어떨까요? 저희 회사는 꽤 오래된 신용 있는 회사입니다. 모든 도서 주문을 정확하게 처리하고 최대한 신속히 공급할 수 있습니다.

L : 가격조건은 어떻습니까? 귀사에서는 도서 할인이 가능합니까?

V : 저희 회사에서는 연간 10만 불 이상 구매하는 고객에 대해서는 정가에서 5% 정도를 할인하여 공급합니다. 이 경우 우편요금도 면제해 줍니다.

L : 제시한 거래 조건 및 서비스에 대해 검토해 보겠습니다.

V : 시간 내 주셔서 감사합니다. 저희와 거래할 수 있게 되길 바랍니다.

Situation 45 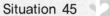 Evaluating Vendor Services

V : I heard that you purchase most of your foreign books from domestic vendors. Are you satisfied with their services?

L : I am generally satisfied with the services of domestic vendors. They run their businesses as well as overseas vendors do. In addition, the prices they offer are quite reasonable and they also give us occasional discounts. Moreover, we don't have any difficulties in communication, so they are very convenient to work with.

V : Oh, I see. What do you think of doing business with our company? Our company has a strong reputation with a long history. We can supply your orders promptly.

L : What about terms of prices? Can you give us some discounts?

V : Our company gives five percent off to clients purchasing more than $100,000 a year, with no delivery charge.

L : Then I will examine the terms of business you offered.

V : Thank you for your time. I hope we'll have a chance to provide our services to you.

Cataloging

정 리

성균관대학교 학술정보관

6 정리 / Cataloging

L1 : 이 북트럭의 자료는 희망도서입니다. 다른 자료보다 우선적으로 정리해 주십시요.

L2 : 물론이지요. 희망도서는 우리 정리파트에서도 우선적으로 하고 있습니다. 빨리 처리하도록 하겠습니다.

L1 : 이 인계대장에 인수확인 서명 좀 해 주세요.

L2 : 모두 몇 권이지요?

L1 : 국내서 80권, 서양서 12권입니다.

L2 : 잠깐만요... 맞군요. 정리계 인수대장에도 기재해야 하니 조금만 기다려 주세요.

Situation 1 Receiving Books

L1 : The users requested these books. Please process them first.

L2 : We process requested books as a high priority. We'll take care of them as soon as possible.

L1 : Please sign the transfers-sent book list here.

L2 : How many books are there in all?

L1 : 80 domestic books and 12 foreign books.

L2 : Hold on⋯ Yes, I see that's correct. Please wait one second. We have to record them in the transfers-sent book list.

상황 2 분류 협의

L1: 이 책은 도대체 어느 쪽으로 분류해야 하는지 정말 판단하기 힘듭니다. 한 번 봐 주시겠어요?

L2: (다 살핀 후) 제 생각엔 전자상거래에 관련된 것 같은데요. 우리 학교에서는 전자상거래를 마케팅쪽인 658.84로 분류하니까 그 쪽에 넣으면 되지 않을까요?

L1: 요즘은 학문의 주제가 복합적이어서 분류하기 점점 힘들어 집니다. 선생님께서는 이런 경우 어떻게 하시나요?

L2: 분류하기 힘든 자료들이 있습니다. 그럴 때는 분류하기가 쉬운 책들을 먼저 작업하고 나서, 복잡한 책들은 시간을 좀 더 가지고 고민해 보거나 다른 분들과도 상의해서 분류합니다.

L1: 그거 괜찮은 방법이네요. 저도 한번 그렇게 해 봐야겠습니다.

Cataloging • 정리

Situation 2 Classification Standards

L1 : I'm having a really difficult time classifying this book. Please take a look.

L2 : (After examining) Let's see⋯ I think it's related to electronic commerce. At our school, we put books related to electronic commerce together with marketing in 658.84, so I would think this book belongs there.

L1 : Nowadays, the subjects are increasingly complicated, so it's getting harder to classify books. How do you handle such cases?

L2 : When I have challenging materials, I process the easy ones first and try to take time with more difficult ones, often consulting other librarians.

L1 : That's a good idea. I'll try that next time.

상황 3 　　정리업무의 흐름

L1 : 정리업무의 흐름을 설명해 주십시요.

L2 : 수서계에서 도서인수를 하면 복본조사부터 합니다. 복본일 경우 복본처리를 하고 신규도서일 경우에는 분류와 목록작업을 거쳐 서지DB가 완성되면 KERIS 종합목록에 업로드를 합니다. 도서 장비작업을 하고 각 실별로 자료인계를 합니다.

L1 : KERIS 종합목록이라는 것이 무엇입니까?

L2 : KERIS 종합목록은 전국 대학도서관에서 공동으로 목록을 작성, 목록데이터를 통합하여 제공하는 시스템입니다. 이 시스템을 통하여 전국 대학도서관이 소장하고 있는 모든 자료의 서지 데이터와 소재를 확인할 수 있습니다.

L1 : 그 시스템에서 우리가 얻을 수 있는 것이 무엇인가요?

L2 : 각 대학 도서관이 작성한 편목 데이터를 활용할 수 있고 또한 분류도 참조할 수 있겠죠

L1 : 완성된 서지 데이터를 KERIS에 어떠한 방식으로 업로드합니까?

L2 : 실시간 업로드 방식과 배치 업로드 방식이 있는데 저희는 실시간 업로드 방식을 주로 사용하고 있습니다.

Cataloging • 정리

Situation 3   Introducing Technical Processing Workflow

L1 : Can you explain the technical processing workflow?

L2 : When we receive a book from the acquisitions department, we first check whether the book is a duplicate. If the book is an added copy, then we register it as a copy. If the book is new, then we catalog it on the local bibliographic database. Then we upload it onto the Korea Education and Research Information Service (KERIS) Union Catalog. After putting on a spine label, we send the book to its location.

L1 : What's the KERIS Union Catalog?

L2 : It's a shared union catalog, created, maintained, and used by all university libraries in Korea. We can use this database to find out which library in the country holds which books.

L1 : How does the KERIS benefit us?

L2 : We can use cataloging records created by other universities, including the classification information.

L1 : Then how do you upload a cataloging record into KERIS?

L2 : There are batch upload and real-time upload options, and we usually use the real-time upload option.

상황 4　　KERIS 공동목록 시스템교육

L1 : KERIS 공동목록 시스템 교육을 체계적으로 받고 싶은데 교육프로그램이 있나요?

L2 : KERIS에서 1년에 3~4회 정도 교육일정을 잡고 있는 걸로 알고 있습니다.

L1 : 어디에서 그 교육에 관한 구체적인 정보를 얻을 수 있을까요?

L2 : KERIS 홈페이지에 공고가 되어 있습니다. 우리학교는 회원교이기 때문에 신청기간에 접수하면 교육에 참가할 수 있습니다. 교육인원을 항상 20명 정도로 제한하기 때문에 미리미리 신청해야 합니다.

Situation 4 KERIS Union Cataloging System Training

L1 : I would like to learn about the KERIS Union Cataloging System thoroughly. Are there any programs available?

L2 : As far as I know, KERIS offers training sessions 3 to 4 times a year.

L1 : Where can I get some more information?

L2 : Information is posted on the KERIS homepage. Our university is a member, so if you register during the registration period, you can get training. A class is limited to 20 people, so I suggest you register early.

상황 5 　분류 체계

L1 : 귀 도서관에서는 어떤 분류표를 사용하고 계십니까?

L2 : 우리 도서관에서는 DDC를 기준으로 분류하고 있습니다.

L1 : 동양서도 DDC를 기준으로 하십니까?

L2 : 그렇습니다.

L1 : DDC는 서구 중심인데 문학, 역사 등 한국이나 동양 부분을 좀 더 세분할 필요가 있을 때는 어떻게 하십니까? 혹시 부가적으로 다른 분류표를 참고하지는 않습니까?

L2 : 예, 다른 분류표도 참고합니다.

L1 : 무엇을 참고하십니까?

L2 : 국회도서관의 '동양관계세분전개표'를 적용합니다.

L1 : 주로 어느 주제분야에 사용합니까?

L2 : 언어, 문학, 역사, 동양철학, 불교 분야에 적용합니다.

Situation 5 Classification System

L1 : Which classification system does your library use?

L2 : We use DDC.

L1 : Do you classify eastern books by DDC also?

L2 : Yes.

L1 : As you know, DDC was developed for western books. Then, what about Korean and other eastern books on literature and history? Do you have any supplemental classification system for these subjects?

L2 : Yes, we do.

L1 : What do you use?

L2 : The 'Eastern Book Subclassification Table' developed by the National Assembly Library.

L1 : For which subjects do you use that table?

L2 : Language, literature, history, eastern philosophy and Buddhism.

상황 6 · DDC 적용

L1: DDC는 현재 몇 판을 적용하고 계십니까?

L2: 저희 도서관은 16판과 22판을 혼용하여 적용하고 있습니다.

L1: 혼용하는 이유는 무엇입니까?

L2: 기존에 사용하던 판만으로는 공학 분야처럼 학문의 변화 속도가 빠른 분야의 자료를 모두 수용하기 어렵기 때문입니다. 우리 도서관은 현재 경영학과 컴퓨터학만 22판을 적용하고 있으나 조만간에 전 주제에 22판을 적용할 계획입니다.

L1: 그렇다면 전 주제에 DDC 22판을 그대로 사용할 계획이십니까?

L2: 아닙니다. 동양학 분야는 지금처럼 '동양관계 세분전개표'를 적용할 것입니다.

Situation 6　DDC

L1 : Which version of the DDC do you currently use?

L2 : We use both versions 16 and 22.

L1 : Why do you use both?

L2 : The old schedule is not updated enough to cover fast-changing subjects such as engineering. So we currently apply version 22 only to books on management and computers, but eventually we will use it for other subjects.

L1 : Then are you planning to use DDC 22 for all subjects?

L2 : No. We will still use the 'Eastern Book Subclassification Table' for some subjects, as we do now.

상황 7 저자기호표

L1 : 저자기호표는 어떤 것을 사용하십니까?

L2 : 동양서는 이춘희 편 '동양저자기호표'를 사용하고, 서양서는 C. A. Cutterd 의 'Cutter-Sanborn Three-Figure Author Table'를 사용하고 있습니다.

L1 : 그 외에 사용하고 있는 다른 저자기호표가 있습니까?

L2 : 대학간행물에 한해 '대학간행물 특수저자기호표'를 사용하고 있습니다.

L1 : 모든 대학간행물에 그 저자기호표를 적용하십니까?

L2 : 아닙니다. 대학출판부 판매용으로 출판하는 단행본류를 제외한 요람, 연구 보고서, 연구소 저널, 연보 등에만 적용합니다.

Situation 7　Author Table

L1 : Which Author Table do you use?

L2 : Choon-Hee Lee's 'Eastern Author Table' for eastern books, and C. A.
Cutter's 'Cutter-Sanborn Three-Figure Author Table' for western books.

L1 : Do you use any other Author Tables?

L2 : There is the Special Author Table for University Publications.

L1 : Do you use this table for all university publications?

L2 : No. We use this table only for university catalogs, research reports,
journals, yearbooks and so on, excluding books published by the
university press for sale.

상황 8   자료목록체계

L1 : 어떤 종류의 MARC 형식을 적용하고 계십니까?

L2 : 동양서는 KORMARC를 서양서는 MARC21를 적용하고 있습니다.

L1 : 단행본과 연속간행물에 같은 KORMARC을 적용합니까?

L2 : 네, 2005년에 국립중앙도서관에서 통합서지용 KORMARC을 발표하였고 우
리는 모든 유형의 자료에 그것을 적용하고 있습니다.

L1 : 서지레코드 작성시 기술규칙은 무엇을 적용하고 계십니까?

L2 : 동양서는 KCR4, 서양서는 AACR2를 적용하고 있습니다.

Situation 8 Cataloging Standards

L1 : What kind of Machine Readable Cataloging (MARC) format do you use?

L2 : We use Korean Machine Readable Cataloging (KORMARC) for eastern books and MARC21 for western books.

L1 : Do you use the same system for both books and serials?

L2 : Yes. The Integrated KORMARC for bibliographic format was promulgated by the National Library of Korea in 2005, so we use it for both.

L1 : Which cataloging rules do you use?

L2 : We apply Korean Cataloging Rules 4th edition (KCR4) to eastern books and Anglo-American Cataloging Rules 2nd edition (AACR2) to western books.

상황 9   💬 청구기호 체계

L1 : 청구기호는 어떻게 구성되어 있습니까?

L2 : 청구기호는 별치기호, 분류기호, 저자기호, 발행연도, 권호사항, 복본기호 등으로 구성되어 있습니다.

L1 : 별치기호는 어떻게 사용하고 있습니까?

L2 : 연속간행물 "P", 참고도서 "R", 귀중본 "貴", 희귀본 "稀", 특수자료 "E", 석사학위논문 "TM", 박사학위논문 "TD"를 사용하고 있습니다.

L1 : 개인문고는 어떤 자료를 의미합니까?

L2 : 기증자의 이름을 붙여 별치하는 자료입니다.

L1 : 저자기호를 부여함에 있어서 부가되는 기호가 따로 있습니까?

L2 : 예 있습니다. 비평서에는 피비평자 기호다음에 "Y"를 부가하고, 번역서의 경우 번역어 영문 첫자의 대문자를 부가합니다.

Situation 9  Call Number System

L1 : What does a call number consist of?

L2 : A call number consists of a location code, classification number, author number, year, volume/issue information and copy number.

L1 : What are the location codes?

L2 : "P" for periodicals, "R" for references, "貴" for precious copy, "稀" for rare books, "E" for special documents, "TM" for master theses, "TD" for doctoral dissertations.

L1 : What are personal collections?

L2 : They are separate collections named after their donors.

L1 : Does the author number include any additional information?

L2 : Yes. For criticism, a "Y" is added after the author number being critiqued. For translated editions, the first alphabet of the Romanized title of a translated book is added.

상황 10 💬 업무용 서지 DB

L1 : 어떤 종류의 서지 데이터베이스를 이용하고 있습니까?

L2 : 현재, KERIS 종합목록과 OCLC Connexion, LC 목록을 사용하고 있습니다.

L1 : 어떤 방법으로 이용하고 있습니까?

L2 : 전용 프로그램을 설치하여 서지 데이터의 검색 및 다운로딩을 한 다음, 자관 목록 프로그램에 반입하여 입력합니다. 그리고 KERIS 공동목록에 업로딩하여 타 도서관이 쉽게 이용할 수 있도록 합니다.

L1 : 모든 자료를 다 카피 카타로깅 합니까?

L2 : 아닙니다. 카피 카타로깅을 종종 하지만 원목도 상당수 합니다. 즉, 동양서는 자관에서 직접 입력하고 있으며, 서양서의 경우도 검색되지 않는 자료는 직접 입력하고 있습니다.

Situation 10   Bibliographic Utilities

L1 : Which bibliographic utilities do you use?

L2 : We currently use the KERIS Union Catalog, OCLC Connexion and the LC Catalog.

L1 : How do you use them?

L2 : Using the web or software installed locally, we search and download a record into our local system for cataloging. Then we upload the record to the KERIS Union Catalog to share it with other libraries.

L1 : Do you copy-catalog for all materials?

L2 : No, we often do copy-cataloging, but in many cases, we have to do original cataloging. In other words, we directly input the bibliographic record for all eastern books as well as western books that are not currently cataloged.

상황 11 · 학위논문 분류 및 정리

L1 : 학위논문은 주제가 특수하여 분류하기가 까다로운데 어떻게 분류하십니까?

L2 : 학위논문의 분류는 일반 단행본과 다르게 하고 있습니다. 학위논문에 따로 별치기호를 주고, '학위논문 학과 코드'로 분류한 다음, 논문 작성자 이름의 가나다 순으로 배열하여 이용시킵니다.

L1 : 그렇게 하는 이유는 무엇입니까?

L2 : 아시다시피 학위논문은 주제가 세분되어 있는데다가, 자료의 두께도 얇아 서 일반 단행본과 같은 수준으로 분류번호를 매기면 자료를 정리하거나 찾 기가 어렵기 때문입니다.

L1 : 최근 학위논문의 원문 데이터베이스를 구축하는 대학이 많은데, 이곳에서 도 구축하고 있습니까?

L2 : 예, 구축하고 있습니다.

Situation 11　Cataloging Theses

L1 : Theses and dissertations are difficult to classify because the subjects are often very specific. How do you classify them?

L2 : We classify them in a different way than we do books. We assign separate location codes for theses and dissertations. Shelving in the thesis room is organized based on department codes, and then alphabetically by the authors' names in Korean.

L1 : Why do you do that?

L2 : Theses are so thin that it is difficult to arrange and locate them by the classification number.

L1 : Lately some universities are developing a full-text database for their theses. How about your university?

L2 : We are as well.

상황 12 딸림자료 정리

L1 : 딸림자료는 어떤 방법으로 정리하고 있습니까?

L2 : 딸림자료는 주 자료의 부록으로 입력하고 있습니다.

L1 : CD-ROM 같은 자료도 마찬가지로 정리합니까?

L2 : CD-ROM이 단품으로 나온 경우에는 비도서 자료로 정리하지만, 부록으로 나온 경우에는 딸림자료로 처리하고 있습니다.

L1 : 딸림자료 CD-ROM은 어떻게 이용시키시나요?

L2 : 각 주제자료실에 소장하여 주 자료와 함께 대출하여 이용할 수 있도록 하고 있습니다.

L1 : 그러면 각 주제실에서 딸림자료 CD-ROM은 어떻게 관리합니까?

L2 : 비도서 서가에 등록번호순으로 배열하고, 자료실에서 별도로 대출 반납을 관리합니다.

Situation 12 Cataloging Accompanying Materials

L1: How are you organizing accompanying materials?

L2: We input them as appendices of the main document.

L1: CD-ROMs, too?

L2: We catalog stand-alone CD-ROMs as non-book materials, but if it is an accompanying material, we handle it like other materials.

L1: How are the accompanying materials circulated?

L2: They are kept in the subject rooms, and can be circulated with the parent materials.

L1: How are the accompanying CD-ROMs maintained in the subject libraries?

L2: They are shelved according to their registration numbers in the non-book materials section and circulated separately.

상황 13 ❯ 정리업무 회의

L1 : 목록담당자들 사이에 회의가 있습니까?

L2 : 예, 있습니다.

L1 : 얼마나 자주 모이십니까?

L2 : 팀별로는 주 1회, 다른 캠퍼스 도서관의 사서들과는 월 1회 정기 회의가 있습니다. 본관에는 여러 주제자료실에 각각 정리업무 사서가 있고, 멀리 떨어져 있는 과학도서관에도 정리업무 사서가 있으므로 업무의 일관성과 통일성을 유지하기 위하여 분류 및 MARC 관련 협의를 수시로 하고 있습니다.

L1 : 정기 회의 외에 일상적인 협의는 어떤 방법으로 이루어집니까?

L2 : 수시로 전화나 이메일을 통해 협의하고, 모두 공유해야 할 경우는 그룹웨어를 통하여 알립니다.

Situation 13 Technical Processing Team Meetings

L1 : Do catalogers have meetings?

L2 : Yes.

L1 : How often do they meet?

L2 : Each library team meets once a week and all catalogers meet once a month. Our cataloging librarians work in various subject libraries, and the Main Library and Science Library are far apart. In order to maintain consistency and uniformity in applying cataloging standards, they need to meet regularly.

L1 : How do they communicate with each other outside of regular meetings?

L2 : By phone or e-mail. They use a grouplist to distribute information to everyone.

상황 14 ❥ 우선 정리 요청

L1 : 특별히 우선적으로 정리하는 자료가 있습니까?

L2 : 희망도서를 우선적으로 정리하고 있습니다.

L1 : 희망도서가 정리 완료되면 이용자에게 알려 줍니까?

L2 : 물론입니다. 이메일 통지뿐만 아니라 SMS 서비스를 통하여 휴대폰으로 문자로 요청한 자료가 대출 가능함을 알려 줍니다. 그리고 구입 희망자에게 1주일의 우선 대출권한을 부여해 줍니다.

L1 : 이용자가 정리중인 자료를 대출하고자 할 때는 어떻게 합니까?

L2 : 현재 검색화면에서 '우선 정리 요청' 아이콘을 클릭하여 신청하면 우선적으로 신속하게 정리하여 제공해 줍니다.

Situation 14   Request for Rush Processing

L1 : Are there any special materials that need to be processed as a priority?

L2 : Books requested by patrons are processed first.

L1 : Once they are processed, do you notify the user?

L2 : Yes. Using the cellular phones SMS service, we send a text message that the requested books are ready. The requester gets the first priority for one week to use the books.

L1 : What do you do when the user wants to borrow a book in process?

L2 : If the user requests a rush processing on his/her search result screen by clicking the 'Rush Processing Request' icon, we process the material with the first priority to be ready for use.

상황 15 출판사와의 전화

L : 안녕하세요. 가람출판사죠?

P1: 그렇습니다만, 무슨 일이신가요?

L : 여기는 한국대 도서관입니다. 거기서 ABC 책을 출판하셨지요?

P1: 예 그렇습니다.

L : 서지 데이터 입력을 위해서 그 책의 원저자명과 원서명의 정확한 철자를 알고 싶어서 연락했습니다.

P1: 아, 그렇습니까. 편집부에 연결해 드리겠습니다.

P2: 네, 편집부입니다.

L : ABC 책의 원저자명과 원서명을 알고 싶어서 연락드렸습니다.

P2: 죄송합니다만, 지금은 바로 확인해 드릴 수가 없고, 찾아서 바로 연락 드리겠습니다.

L : 감사합니다. 연락처는 012-345-5678입니다.

P2: 곧 연락드리겠습니다. 안녕히 계십시요.

Cataloging • 정리

L : Hello. Is this Ka-Ram Publishing Co.?

P1 : Yes. How can I help you?

L : This is the Hankook University Library. Does your company publish the book, ABC?

P1 : Yes.

L : We need information about the author and the title of the original book for cataloging.

P1 : OK. I'll transfer you to the Editorial Department.

P2 : Yes. This is the Editorial Department.

L : I'd like to know the original author and the title of ABC.

P2 : I'm sorry. I can't track down the information at this moment. We will contact you with the information as soon as we can.

L : Thank you. Our telephone number is 012-345-5678.

P2 : I got it. I will call you as soon as possible.

상황 16　　💬 일어, 러시아어 번자 입력

L1 : 일본어 자료는 번자하여 입력합니까?

L2 : 일본인 저자명은 일본인명사전을 기준으로 하여 한글화해서 입력하고, 서명은 한자, 일어 모두 책에 나타난 그대로 입력합니다.

L1 : 그럼, 일본어나 한자로도 검색 가능합니까?

L2 : 물론입니다. 한글, 한자음은 물론 검색시 다국어입력이 가능하므로 일어로도 검색됩니다.

L1 : 러시아어는 무엇을 기준으로 번자하십니까?

L2 : 러시아어는 *Great Soviet Encyclopedia* (Macmillan, 1973)을 기준으로 번자합니다.

L1 : 러시아어 검색도 가능합니까?

L2 : 물론입니다. 다국어 입력 기능을 통해 러시아어도 검색할 수 있습니다.

Situation 16　Japanese or Russian Transliteration

L1 : Do you transliterate Japanese works for the cataloging records?

L2 : We transliterate the author's name into Korean using the Japanese Name Dictionary, but for titles, we use the original Chinese or Japanese characters from the books.

L1 : Then can we search by Japanese or Chinese characters?

L2 : Absolutely. You can search Chinese or Japanese works phonetically in Korean, or use the Japanese or Chinese characters.

L1 : How do you transliterate Russian?

L2 : We use the *Great Soviet Encyclopedia* (Macmillan, 1973) to transliterate Russian script.

L1 : Can we search using Russian?

L2 : Yes. The system's support for multilingual inputting enables the user to search in Russian characters.

Library Systems

전 산

한양대학교 학술정보관

7 전산 / Library Systems

U : 도서관의 전산화가 이루어진 과정을 간단히 소개해 주실 수 있으신가요?

L : 전체적으로 세 단계로 구분할 수 있겠습니다. 먼저 도서관 자동화 시스템 구축 시기는 이전의 수작업 중심의 서비스에서 컴퓨터를 이용한 시스템으로의 변환 단계를 말합니다. 기간은 대략 1994년에서 1996년 사이입니다.

U : 다음은 어떤 단계입니까?

L : 두 번째는 디지털도서관 구축기에 해당하는데, 자료의 내용을 인터넷 상에서도 제공한다는 개념으로 시작되었습니다. 기간은 1997~2000년 정도입니다.

U : 주로 어떤 작업이 이루어졌나요?

L : 도서관 자동화 시스템의 계속적인 개선과 학위논문의 원문 데이터베이스를 구축하였습니다.

U : 원문 파일은 어떤 파일 포맷을 사용하셨습니까?

L : 여러 가지 파일 포맷을 시험하였는데, 지금은 PDF를 사용하고 있습니다.

U : 앞으로의 계획은 무엇인가요?

L : 세 번째 단계에서 개인화된 서비스를 도입하여 이용자 편의성 증대를 하는 것을 목표로 하고 있습니다. 또 신기술을 적용하여 모바일 서비스를 확장시켜갈 계획입니다.

Situation 1　Library Computer System 1

U : Could you summarize how Hankook University Library became
　　computerized?

L : It followed three main stages. First, there was a library-automation system
　　(LAS) construction period during when manual-based services
　　transitioned into computer-based services. That was approximately from
　　1994 to 1996.

U : What was the next step?

L : The second stage was the beginning of a digital library when we started
　　mounting the automated system from stage one on the Internet. That was
　　from 1997 through 2000.

U : What types of work were involved?

L : We continued to upgrade the LAS system and digitized dissertations.

U : What kind of file formats did you use for full-text images?

L : After considering various file formats, we chose the PDF format.

U : What are some plans for the future?

L : The third phase is to provide customized services to individuals and to
　　expand mobile library services by adopting new technology.

상황 2　▶ 도서관 자동화 시스템 2

U : 도서관 전산화의 현황을 알고 싶은데요.

L : 저희 도서관은 1995년 국내최초로 GUI, Client/server 환경의 도서관자동화 시스템을 도입하였습니다. 1998년 현재의 도서관이 개관될 때 디지털도서 관도 구축하여 인터넷을 통한 다양한 원문 컨텐츠를 제공하고 있습니다. 그리고 2000년에는 캠퍼스 통합 VOD시스템을 구축함으로써 교내 멀티미 디어 자료의 통합검색 서비스를 제공하고 있습니다. 2010년 이후에는 스마 트폰 보급이 활성화되면서 도서관의 모바일 서비스 구축이 활발히 진행되 고 있습니다.

U : 전산화 작업이 빨리 이루어졌네요.

L : 그런 편입니다. 지난 몇 년간은 한국의 대학들이 도서관 전산화에 집중적 인 투자를 했기 때문에 가능한 일이었습니다.

U : 전산화를 추진하면서 가장 중요한 것은 무엇이라고 생각하십니까?

L : 도서관 전산화는 이용자에게 가장 편리하고 빠르게 정보를 제공할 수 있는 편의성과 신속, 정확성이 가장 중요합니다. 따라서 투자할 때에는 장기적 인 안목으로 시스템을 구축하는 것이 가장 중요합니다.

Situation 2   Library Computer System 2

U : I would like to know the present state of your library computer system.

L : This library introduced the very first library-automation system using GUI
with Client/Server technology in 1995. In 1998, when the new library
opened, we introduced the Digital Library at the same time. Our Digital
Library system provides students and faculty with a variety of resources
on the internet. In 2000, the library built a campus-wide VOD system.
This provides integrated retrieval from multimedia resources. Since 2010,
as the rate of smart phone usage has accelerated, we are focusing on
developing mobile library services.

U : The library automation has progressed quite fast.

L : I think so. It was possible because many universities in Korea have
invested a lot in library computer systems.

U : What are the main aspects of these systems?

L : I would say convenience, speed and accuracy are the main drivers of
library computerization. It enables users to use libraries more
conveniently and efficiently. Thus, we must continue to develop systems
through constant reexamination so that the systems we construct today
will be flexible enough to keep abreast of future developments in society
as well as with new information resources.

상황 3　　도서관 자동화 시스템 3

U : 도서관 자동화 시스템은 어떤 시스템을 사용하시나요?

L : 저희 도서관에서는 1995년부터 전산화를 시작하여 도서관 자동화 시스템 은 ABC라는 상용 패키지 프로그램을 사용하고 있습니다. Windows 3.1에 서 이용되던 ABC 3.0 프로그램에서 시작하여 지금은 5.1 Plus 버전을 사용 하고 있으며, 계속해서 업그레이드를 하고 있습니다.

U : 시스템 관리는 어떻게 하시나요?

L : 시스템 관리는 도서관 직원이 하고, 개발 및 유지 보수는 업체에서 해 주고 있습니다.

U : 전산 관련 담당자는 몇 분이나 됩니까?

L : 팀장을 포함해서 전부 3명이 전산실에서 근무하고 있습니다. 이외에 이용 자 서비스 담당이 2명 더 있습니다.

Situation 3　Library Computer System 3

U : Which system do you use as your library computer system?

L : This library began library automation in 1995. At the beginning, ABC version 3.0 for Windows 3.1 was used. ABC version 5.1 Plus is being used now and we continue to upgrade it.

U : How do you manage the system?

L : Librarians are in charge of management, while vendors provide updates, maintenance and repairs.

U : How many system librarians do you have?

L : Three librarians, including the team leader, are working at the Computing Center. Two other librarians, who are in charge of user services, are also working as assistants.

상황 4 ▸ 학위논문 원문제공 서비스

U : 원문(Full-text) 서버도 있다고 하셨는데, 어떤 서비스를 제공하시나요?

L : 저희 대학에서는 매년 2,000편 정도의 학위논문이 발표되고 있습니다. 이를 원문 DB로 구축하여 온라인으로 제공하고 있는데요, KERIS에서 지원하는 dCollection을 통해 서비스하고 있습니다.

U : 데이터는 어떻게 구축하시나요?

L : 학위수여자가 직접 웹 상에서 논문에 대한 기본정보를 입력하고, 논문책자와 논문 내용이 담긴 PDF파일을 제출하게 되어 있습니다.

U : 저작권 상의 문제는 어떻게 해결하십니까?

L : 논문 제출시 저작권 이용허락서를 받고 있습니다.

U : 그럼 원문은 인터넷에서 모든 이용자에게 제공되는 것인가요?

L : 그렇지는 않습니다. 도서관 홈페이지에서 아이디와 패스워드를 입력해야 원문을 볼 수 있습니다. 그리고 PC에 Acrobat Reader가 설치되어 있어야 합니다.

U : 모든 학위논문이 원문 데이터베이스로 구축되었나요?

L : 현재 1995년 이후의 논문 20,000건 정도를 구축해서 서비스하고 있습니다.

Situation 4 Online Full-text Dissertations

U : You mentioned a full-text server. What kind of services does it provide?

L : Hankook University produces approximately 2,000 dissertations each year. We provide the full-text of these online through the 'dCollection,' supported by KERIS.

U : How do you build a full-text database?

L : The candidates input basic bibliographic information on the web and when they submit their dissertations they include a PDF file.

U : What about copyrights?

L : When they submit the dissertations, they also sign copyright releases.

U : Can everyone have access to the dissertations?

L : Not really. Only students and faculty members who have an ID and password to the dissertations database have access. In addition, Acrobat Reader should be set up on their computers.

U : Do you have full-text for all dissertations?

L : The library provides the full-text for approximately 20,000 dissertations published after 1995.

상황 5   VOD 서비스

U : VOD 서비스라는 게 뭔가요?

L : 주문형 비디오를 의미하는데요, 이용자는 언제든지 원하는 장소에서 도서관 홈페이지를 통해 동영상 자료를 볼 수 있습니다. 저희 도서관에서는 2000년부터 VOD 서비스를 개시하였습니다.

U : 어떤 내용의 자료를 제공하고 계시죠?

L : 주로 교양물과 대학 내에서 생산하는 비디오 자료입니다. 현재 미분적분학 27강좌를 VOD로 서비스함으로써 학생들의 학습활동을 지원하고 있습니다.

U : 도서관에서 자체적으로 비디오 자료를 만들고 계신가요?

L : 아닙니다. 대학 내의 '미디어센터'라는 기관이 있어 직접 비디오 자료를 만들고 있습니다. 도서관에서는 그런 자료를 관리하고 서비스합니다.

U : 최근 한국대학교에서 사이버대학이 개교했다고 들었습니다. VOD 서비스를 통해 사이버대학과 연계하실 계획이십니까?

L : 물론입니다. 사이버대학의 개교로 VOD 제작과 서비스가 활성화될 것으로 기대하고 있습니다.

U : 구축된 데이터 양은 얼마나 되나요?

L : 그렇게 많지는 않고 현재까지 400편 정도의 분량이 구축되어 있습니다.

Situation 5 VOD Service

U : What is VOD service?

L : It's an acronym for Video On Demand. It is a service that enables a user to watch visual resources through the library website. We began the service in 2000.

U : What kinds of resources do you provide?

L : Usually, these are general education programs and video programs developed by universities. For example, you can watch 27 calculus lectures through the VOD service.

U : Does the library develop these by itself?

L : The Media Center on campus produces most VOD materials. The library maintains those materials and services.

U : I heard that your university opened a Cyber University. Will it affect your VOD service?

L : Yes, it will. With the opening of the Cyber University, we expect production and use of VOD materials will become more widespread.

U : How many VOD materials does the library have?

L : Approximately 400 programs have been developed.

상황 6 　모바일 도서관 서비스

U : 모바일 도서관 서비스를 실시한다고 들었는데, 그게 뭔가요?

L : 모바일 도서관 서비스란 핸드폰이나 PDA를 이용하여, 기존 웹에서 하던 검색 및 알림 서비스를 제공하는 것을 말합니다.

U : 아! 이동통신을 이용한 무선인터넷 서비스군요?

L : 네, 한국의 휴대폰 보급률이 세계 최고 수준이기 때문에 도서관에서 2001년부터 모바일 도서관 서비스를 개시하였습니다.

U : 다른 대학도서관에서도 하고 있나요?

L : 그렇습니다. 몇몇 대학도서관에서 하고 있습니다.

U : 단순한 검색만을 제공하고 있나요?

L : 현재까지는 그랬지만 앞으로 반납통지, 예약알림 등의 서비스를 제공하려고 합니다. 또 최근 스마트폰 이용자가 많아지고 있어서 모바일 학생증 및 모바일 웹, 어플리케이션 등 다양한 서비스를 준비하고 있습니다.

Library Systems • 전산

Situation 6   Mobile Library Service

U : Could you tell me what the Mobile Library service is?

L : Users can search websites and utilize the Alert System with a mobile phone or a PDA.

U : I see. It's a wireless internet service to be used on a mobile phone or a personal digital assistant (PDA).

L : Yes, that's right. The distribution rate of mobile phones in Korea is second to none in the world. This library began service in 2001.

U : What about other libraries?

L : Some other libraries also provide the service.

U : Do you provide only a search service?

L : Yes for now, but we plan to provide more services, such as due-date notification, reserved book notification and Short Message Service (SMS). Also, for the increasing number of smart phone users we are thinking of developing a mobile library website, smart phone applications and a mobile ID card.

상황 7   무선 LAN 서비스

U : 도서관에서 무선랜 서비스를 제공하고 있나요?

L : 네, 무선랜 카드가 설치된 노트북을 이용하는 분이라면 기관 아이디와 패스워드를 입력하신 후 인터넷을 이용할 수 있습니다. 랜케이블이 필요한 경우에는 데스크에서 대여하실 수 있습니다. 스마트폰을 이용하시는 분이라면 아이디와 패스워드만 입력하면 됩니다.

U : 도서관 주변에서만 가능한 서비스겠군요?

L : 아닙니다. 현재 캠퍼스 전체에 중계기를 설치하고 있어 캠퍼스 어디서나 이용 할 수 있습니다.

Situation 7 Wireless LAN Service

U : Is a wireless LAN service available in the library?

L : Yes. People with a wireless LAN card installed on their laptop can connect to the internet by using their university ID and password. The service desk provides a LAN Cable too. If you are a smart phone user, just input your ID and password.

U : Does it work only inside the library?

L : No, it should work anywhere on campus because we are installing APs throughout the entire campus.

상황 8 　노트북, 무선랜 카드 대여

U : 도서관에서 노트북을 대여할 수 있다고 들어서 왔습니다.

L : 네. 대출한 책이 연체가 되어 있지 않아야 대여할 수 있어요.

U : 얼마동안 사용할 수 있나요? 무료인가요?

L : 당일 반납하면 무료고요, 다음날 반납하면 사용료 2,000원을 내셔야 합니다.

U : 이걸로 인터넷을 이용하려면 어떻게 하지요?

L : 도서관 내에서는 무선랜이 되니까 무선랜 카드도 받아 가세요.

U : 설치 프로그램은요?

L : 미리 설치되어 있으니까 바로 쓸 수 있습니다.

U : (잠시 후) 이 노트북으로는 인터넷이 안되는데요.

L : 아마 이전 사용자가 임의로 네트워크 설정사항을 변경한 모양이네요. 여기 매뉴얼을 보시고 다시 설정해 보세요.

U : 고맙습니다.

Situation 8 · Checking out Laptop Computers and Wireless LAN Cards

U : I've heard that I can borrow a laptop computer.

L : As long as you don't have any overdue books, you may check one out.

U : How long can I check it out for? Is this free?

L : It's free if you use it for a day or less. 2,000 won will be charged for the next day.

U : Could you tell me how I can get connected to the Internet?

L : Why don't you borrow the wireless LAN card, too? You can use it in the library.

U : How can I install the program?

L : You don't have to. It has been set up already.

U : (After a while) The Internet is not available now.

L : I guess the previous user changed some settings in the computer. Why don't you set up a new network setting with this manual.

U : Thank you.

상황 9   CD Net

U : CD-NET이라는 게 무엇인가요?

L : 원래 CD는 한 사람이 이용할 수 있는 제품인데, 이것을 네트워크 상에서 여러 사람이 동시에 이용할 수 있도록 지원하는 시스템입니다.

U : 이런 게 있는지 몰랐는데 어떻게 해서 가능한가요?

L : 동시 이용이 가능한 프로그램이 개발되었거든요. 여기에는 서버에 있는 다수의 CD 드라이버에 단품 CD를 장착하는 방식과 CD의 내용을 서버의 하드 디스크에 옮겨 데이터를 제공하는 두 가지 방식이 있습니다.

U : 그러면 CD-Net을 통해 제공되는 데이터베이스에는 어떤 것이 있습니까?

L : 국내외에서 널리 이용되는 학술정보 CD-ROM 데이터베이스를 전 분야에 걸쳐 다양하게 제공하고 있습니다. 현재는 법률, 역사, 규격 자료가 주를 이루고 있죠.

U : 그렇다면 온라인 DB와 다른 점은 무엇인가요?

L : 서버를 도서관에서 가지고 있으므로 제공하는 DB의 네트워크 상황에 따라 접속속도가 좌우되는 온라인 DB보다 안정성과 속도 면에서 유리하다고 생각합니다.

Situation 9 CD Net

U : What is the CD Net?

L : Originally, CDs are designed for a single user. The CD Net service connects users on the network so that multiple users can use the CDs at the same time.

U : That sounds interesting. How does it work?

L : There are two different types of softwares. One is to load CDs into a multiple CD driver. The other is to transfer CD contents onto a hard disk server.

U : What kind of resource is provided by the CD Net?

L : You can access any academic CD-ROMs that we own. Law and history databases and other standard resources are frequently used.

U : How is it different from online databases?

L : Since we can control the CD Net server locally in the library, it is more stable and faster than online databases.

상황 10　　PC

U : 도서관에는 PC가 상당히 많네요.

L : 저희 도서관은 총 400대의 PC를 보유하고 있습니다. 검색전용은 약 300대 정도이고 나머지는 교육용과 사무용입니다.

U : 전부 네트워크로 연결되어 있나요?

L : 그럼요. 도서관에서 제공하는 각종 서비스와 인터넷을 이용하실 수 있습니다. 그리고 기본적인 응용프로그램들이 모두 설치되어 있고요.

U : 관리는 어떻게 하고 계세요?

L : 소프트웨어가 손상된 PC는 '하드보안관'이라는 하드디스크 복구프로그램을 설치해서 몇 초 내에 복구할 수 있습니다. 또 하드웨어 손상은 수시로 학교 A/S 시스템에 따라 처리하고 있습니다.

U : 학생들이 많을 때는 시간제로 이용하게 되나요?

L : 특별한 제한이 있는 것은 아닙니다. 자율적으로 운영하고 있는데 별 문제는 없습니다.

Situation 10　　PCs

U : It's amazing that your library has so many computers.

L : The library has 400 computers. 300 of them are for public use and the others are for library instruction and staff use.

U : Are they networked?

L : Yes. Patrons can access all library services and the internet. Users also find convenient the applications installed in each computer.

U : How do you manage them?

L : Each computer has the Hard Disk Driver Sheriff, which recovers software errors in seconds. The University Computing Center examines computers regularly to prevent hardware damage.

U : Are there any time limits when other users are waiting?

L : There are no time limits, but we have not experienced any big problems yet.

상황 11 　 노트북 이용코너

U : 노트북 사용자를 위한 자리가 있나요?

L : Information Commons에 노트북 이용자를 위한 코너가 마련되어 있습니다. 현재 100석의 좌석이 있고, 전원과 네트워크를 제공하고 있습니다.

U : 네트워크는 어떻게 연결을 할 수 있습니까?

L : 네트워크는 각 좌석마다 적혀있는 IP, Gateway, DNS 주소를 개인이 가지고 있는 노트북에 설정하시면 됩니다.

U : 현재 포트만 나와 있는데, 네트워크 선도 이용할 수 있습니까?

L : 신분증을 카운터에 제출하시고 선을 빌릴 수 있고요, 나중에 반납할 때 신분증을 찾아가시면 됩니다.

U : 열람실에서는 노트북을 사용할 수 없나요?

L : 가능합니다. 열람실 자리마다 전기 콘센트가 설치되어 있거든요. 하지만 네트워크는 사용할 수 없습니다.

Situation 11 Laptop Computer Users

U : Is there any space for laptop computer users?

L : You may go to the Information Commons. There are 100 assigned seats for laptop computer users with power sources and network ports.

U : How can I get connected to the network?

L : After setting up an IP, a Gateway and a DNS address, which are written on the desk, you can use the network.

U : How about a network cable? There is nothing but a port.

L : You are able to check out a network cable with your ID. You will get the ID card back when you return it.

U : Can I use my laptop computer in a study room?

L : You may. You can plug it in any study room, but you cannot use the Internet.

상황 12   Audio 이용코너

U : 오디오자료 같은 비도서자료를 열람할 수 있는 곳은 어디인가요?

L : Information Commons에서 이용할 수 있습니다. 그곳에는 50대의 오디오 장비가 있어 이용자들이 자유롭게 이용할 수 있습니다.

U : 주로 어떤 용도로 이용되나요?

L : 어학 공부용으로 이용을 많이 하고 있습니다.

U : 오디오 장비는 도서관에만 있나요?

L : 아닙니다. A/V센터가 별도의 건물에 따로 있습니다.

U : 비도서 자료도 개가식으로 이용이 되나요?

L : 부분개가제입니다. 비디오테잎은 개가제이고 나머지는 파손을 방지하기 위하여 폐가식으로 관리됩니다.

U : 비도서자료도 검색할 수 있나요?

L : 그렇습니다. 도서관의 모든 자료가 MARC 데이터로 구축되어 있어 검색이 가능합니다.

Situation 12　Audio Center

U : Where can I use audio materials?

L : You can use them at the Audio Center in the Information Commons. There are 50 desks equipped with audio systems.

U : What is the Audio Center used for?

L : Usually students who study foreign languages use it.

U : Do you have any other audio centers besides in the main library?

L : Yes, we have a main A/V center in another building.

U : Are non-book materials kept in the open stacks?

L : Some of them. Videotapes are in the open stacks section, while other non-book materials are in the closed stacks section.

U : Can I search them?

L : Yes. All resources in the library are cataloged.

상황 13 　　비디오, 위성방송 이용코너

U : 검색을 해보니 비디오라고 표시되는 자료가 있던데, 어떻게 이용하면 되죠?

L : Information Commons에 TV, 비디오, DVD가 1세트인 비디오 시설이 있으니까, 자유롭게 사용하시면 됩니다.

U : 제가 가져온 비디오도 볼 수 있나요?

L : 물론이죠.

U : 혹시 도서관에서 위성방송을 볼 수도 있나요?

L : Information Commons에 가시면 위성방송도 볼 수 있습니다. 그곳은 어학 공부를 하는 이용자들에게 인기가 높습니다.

U : 위성방송은 어떤 채널을 볼 수 있나요?

L : 국내방송은 물론 미국 CNN, 중국 STAR TV, 일본 NHK, 이탈리아 RAI, 프랑스 TV5, 스페인 TVE, 독일 DWTV 등등 40여 개의 채널을 보실 수 있습니다.

Library Systems • 전산

Situation 13　Video and Satellite Broadcasting Center

U : I got a search result that is identified as a video. How can I use that?

L : Each video station at the Information Commons has a TV, a video player and a DVD player. You can use any of the video stations.

U : Can I watch my own video?

L : Yes, you can.

U : I'm wondering if I can watch satellite broadcasting, too.

L : You can watch them at the Information Commons. It is very popular among students who study foreign languages.

U : Which channels are available?

L : You can watch 40 channels, including domestic channels, CNN (US), STAR TV (Chinese), NHK (Japanese), RAI (Italian), TV5 (French), TVE (Spanish), DWTV (German) and so on.

상황 14   비도서자료 대출

U : 비도서자료 대출은 어떻게 하나요?

L : 비도서자료 대출업무는 Information Commons에서 하고 있습니다.

U : 비도서자료 가운데 어떤 것이 대출되나요?

L : 비디오, DVD, CD, 오디오테잎 등이 대출 가능한데 일반 책자자료와는 별도의 규정 아래 대출되고 있습니다.

U : 도서와 비도서자료의 대출 자료수가 별도로 관리되나요?

L : 그렇습니다. 예를 들어 학부생의 경우 도서 5책, 비도서 5개를 대출 할 수 있습니다.

U : 관외대출도 되나요?

L : 악보와 몇몇 자료를 제외하고는 가능합니다.

U : 이용자가 직접 자료를 고를 수 있나요?

L : 일부 가능합니다. 저희는 개가식과 폐가식 배열을 병행하고 있습니다. 고가의 자료는 폐가식으로 보존하고 있거든요.

Situation 14 — Checking Out Non-book Materials

U : How can I check out non-book materials?

L : You may check them out at the Information Commons.

U : What kinds of non-book materials can I borrow?

L : You can borrow videotapes, DVDs, CDs and audiotapes. But, we have different check-out rules for non-book materials.

U : Do you mean that books and non-book materials have separate check-out policies?

L : Yes. For instance, undergraduate students can borrow up to five books and five non-books.

U : Can I check them out of the library?

L : Yes, except for musical scores and some special materials.

U : Can users browse the materials by themselves?

L : Users can only browse some of the materials because this room has both open and closed stacks. Precious and rare materials are kept in the closed stacks.

상황 15 CCTV

U : 이곳에는 고가의 장비가 많이 있는 것 같은데, 시설 보안은 어떻게 합니까?

L : 코너별로 CCTV를 이용하여 보안관리를 하고 있습니다.

U : 저기 위에 동그란 것이 있는데 그건 무엇이지요?

L : 그것이 바로 CCTV용 Dome camera입니다.

U : 녹화를 하시나요?

L : 물론입니다.

U : 실제로 도난사고가 발생하나요?

L : CCTV를 운용하고 있어서 그런지 그런 일은 없었습니다. 사실 이런 장비를 둔 것은 보안상의 문제를 예방하는 데 의미가 있답니다.

U : 그렇군요.

Library Systems • 전산

Situation 15   Closed-Circuit Television (CCTV)

U : There is a lot of expensive equipment here. How do you manage
    security?

L : There are closed-circuit televisions (CCTVs) set up around each corner.

U : What is the round-shaped object on the ceiling?

L : That is the Dome camera for CCTV.

U : Do you record?

L : Yes, we do.

U : Has anything been stolen?

L : Not really. I think the CCTV contributes to preventing minor crimes.

U : I see.

상황 16   항온항습기

U : 서버가 있는 시스템실은 어떻게 관리됩니까?

L : 시스템실은 항상 일정한 온도와 습도가 유지되어야 하기 때문에 시스템실에는 2대의 항온항습기가 설치되어 있습니다.

U : 왜 항온항습기를 2대나 설치하셨나요?

L : 1대가 고장이 날 때를 위해서입니다.

U : 좋은 생각이네요. 항온항습이라고 하셨는데 온도와 습도를 어떤 수준에서 유지하시나요?

L : 온도는 항상 섭씨 23-27도 사이, 습도는 50% 정도로 유지하고 있습니다.

U : 시스템실에만 항온항습기가 있나요?

L : 네, 그렇습니다. 나머지 실은 공조기를 통한 공기 순환을 시키고 있습니다.

U : 희귀서나 고서는 따로 관리하지 않습니까?

L : 그런 자료들을 위해서는 별도로 특별한 설비 시스템을 고려하고 있습니다.

Situation 16 Temperature and Humidity Maintenance

U : How do you maintain the server room?

L : We must keep the temperature and humidity constant in the server room. There are two machines to control them.

U : Why do you have two machines?

L : In case one of them is broken.

U : Good idea! What is the appropriate temperature and humidity?

L : About 23-27 degrees Celsius, and 50% humidity is suitable.

U : Do you have this kind of machine only for this room?

L : Yes. Diffusers control the temperature and humidity of the other rooms.

U : What about rare and ancient books?

L : We are considering getting a more powerful system for them.

상황 17 　♥ 무정전시스템

U : 갑자기 정전이 되었을 때에는 시스템을 어떻게 보호하십니까?

L : 정전에 대비해서 무정전시스템을 설치하였습니다.

U : 무정전시스템이 무엇인가요?

L : 정전이 되더라도 30분 정도 전기를 제공하는 장비입니다.

U : 그럼 30분 이상 정전이 지속되면 어떻게 되나요?

L : 그럴 때는 자동 Shutdown 기능이 수행되도록 되어 있습니다.

U : 무정전시스템의 또 다른 기능이 있습니까?

L : 원래 무정전시스템은 외부로부터 들어오는 전압을 고른 전압으로 걸러주
　어 고가의 민감한 장비들을 보호하는 역할을 합니다.

U : 그럼 총 몇 대의 UPS를 쓰고 계십니까?

L : 서버 1대당 하나의 무정전시스템을 쓰고 있으니까 총 11개를 사용중이네요.

Situation 17   Uninterruptible Power Supply (UPS)

U : How do you protect computers from a sudden power outage?

L : In case of an emergency, we have the UPS system.

U : What is the UPS system?

L : It is a machine that supplies electricity for half an hour.

U : What if the power outage lasts more than half an hour?

L : In that case, the automatic shut-down program will be activated.

U : Are there any other functions of the UPS?

L : Basically, the UPS protects our expensive and fragile machines by regulating high voltage from sources.

U : How many UPS machines do you have?

L : There are 11 UPS machines, one UPS per server.

상황 18 　　보안

U : 해킹과 바이러스를 어떻게 대처하고 계신가요?

L : 네트워크 속도가 빨라지면서 그런 문제에 자주 일어나고 있는데요, 운영체제를 지속적으로 업데이트하고 서비스를 하지 않는 포트는 닫아서 보안성을 높이고 있습니다.

U : 혹시 방화벽 프로그램을 사용하시나요?

L : 예, 그렇습니다. 방화벽 프로그램을 설치하여 비정상적인 접근을 차단하고 있습니다.

U : 방화벽으로 충분한가요?

L : 완벽하지는 않지만 모니터링을 하면서 취약점을 파악하고 있습니다.

U : 바이러스에는 어떻게 대비하십니까?

L : 아시다시피 예방이 최선이죠. 도서관 네트워크는 학교 전산센터와 이중라인으로 연결되어 있어서 항상 만약의 사태에 대비하고 있습니다.

Situation 18  Security

U : How do you prevent computer hackings and viruses?

L : As network speed increases, such problems occur more frequently. We enhance security by updating the OS on a regular basis, and shutting down Internet ports not in use.

U : Do you use a firewall program?

L : Yes, and by using that program, we prevent illegal access.

U : Does the program provide complete protection?

L : We don't think it's absolutely perfect, but we're monitoring constantly.

U : How do you protect against viruses?

L : As you know, prevention is the best policy. Also, the library networks are connected with the Computing Center by substitute lines on campus in case of emergency.

상황 19 백업

U : 상당히 많은 데이터를 보유하고 계신데, 백업은 어떻게 하고 계십니까?

L : 시스템에 대해서 설명할 때 말씀 드렸듯, 현재 백업만을 위한 전용서버를 이용하고 있습니다. 한 달에 한번 전체 백업을 하고 매일 한번씩 변환된 부분에 대한 백업을 하고 있습니다.

U : 백업은 언제 누가 하나요?

L : 야간에 백업 작업이 자동으로 이루어지도록 서버에 세팅을 해 놓았습니다. 다음날 직원이 백업 수행 여부를 확인합니다. 그리고 조만간 학교 전산센터와 이중백업도 할 예정입니다.

U : 백업서버의 용량은 어떻게 됩니까?

L : 11 TB 정도입니다.

U : 백업은 신규데이터 입력보다도 중요한 것 같습니다

L : 그렇습니다. 도서관은 무엇보다 데이터가 가장 중요하니까요.

Situation 19   Backup

U : The library holds a great amount of data. How do you back up your
    library data?

L : We have a dedicated server for the back-up. We do full backup once a
    month and update every day.

U : When, and who does the backup?

L : Backup is done automatically during the night. The backup server is
    self-controlled. The next day, a librarian will check if the backup was
    done properly. Soon, we will implement a cross-backup with the
    Computing Center.

U : What is the capacity of the backup server?

L : It is about 11 TB.

U : I think backup is sometimes more important than inputting new
    information.

L : I agree. Data is the most valuable asset of the library.

상황 20 ▶ 불법 소프트웨어

U : 불법소프트웨어 설치 문제가 전세계적으로 큰 이슈가 되고 있는데, 어떻게 대처를 하고 계세요?

L : 도서관에서는 공식적으로 라이센스 계약이 된 제품이거나 프리웨어 제품 들만을 설치하고 있습니다.

U : 이용자들이 불법소프트웨어나 파일을 설치하면 어떻게 하죠?

L : 가끔씩 그런 일이 있는데, 하드웨어보안관 프로그램을 이용해 불법프로그 램 설치 사용을 방지하면서 동시에 불법 소프트웨어 삭제도 같이 하고 있 습니다.

U : 설치 자체를 막을 수는 없나요?

L : 여러 가지 방안을 검토했지만, 현재의 관리 여건으로 설치 자체는 막을 수 는 없을 것 같습니다. 제 생각엔 이용자 각자가 저작권의 중요성을 깨달아 야 할 것 같습니다.

Situation 20   Illegal Software

U : Illegal software is a big issue worldwide. How do you prevent its installation?

L : Every program that we install in the library is either licensed or freeware.

U : What if users install illegal software or files?

L : Sometimes they do. The Hardware Sheriff Program, however, prevents computers from illegal programs being set up and also deletes them regularly.

U : Can you prevent the installation of illegal software?

L : I'm afraid not. Technically, no one can hinder users from copying and installing illegal programs. I believe that users should recognize the importance of the copyright.

상황 21 ♥ 디지털 콘텐츠 구축

U : 꾸준히 전산화 작업을 진행해 오셨는데, 현재 콘텐츠 구성이 어떻게 되어 있습니까?

L : 정확한 통계는 통계자료를 확인해봐야 알겠지만 대략적으로 말씀 드리면, 학위논문 원문 50,000 여건, 잡지기사 35,000여건, VOD 4,000편 정도가 디지털 도서관 사업으로 구축되어 있습니다.

U : 많은 콘텐츠를 확보하셨네요. 서지 데이터는 얼마나 구축하셨나요?

L : 현재 장서량은 약 200만 권 정도인데, 고서를 제외한 거의 모든 서지 데이터가 구축되어 있고 이를 홈페이지에서 검색할 수 있습니다.

U : 왜 고서는 서지 데이터로 구축하지 않았나요?

L : 저희가 사용하는 시스템이 아직은 고서 MARC을 지원하지 않기 때문입니다. 그러나 곧 새로운 시스템으로 업그레이드하여 고서 MARC도 구축할 예정입니다.

Situation 21   Digital Content

U : Could you describe the digital content of the library?

L : I have to look at statistics for the exact information, but I can give you some estimates. For our digital library project, we uploaded 50,000 dissertations, 35,000 articles and 4,000 VODs.

U : That is a lot. How about a bibliographic database?

L : The library now holds 2 million volumes. With the exception of classical works, almost all of our holdings have electronic bibliographic records. Users can search the library catalogs.

U : Why did you exclude classical works?

L : The current system doesn't support MARC for the classics yet. Pretty soon, the new system will incorporate them as well.

상황 22　　Institutional Repository (IR)

U : IR이 뭔가요?

L : IR은 기관 디지털 기록보존소(Institutional Repository)를 의미하는데요, 기관에서 생산한 논문, 보고서 등을 디지털화하여 보존하는 것입니다.

U : 그렇다면 Open Access와 관련이 있는 건가요?

L : 그렇습니다. 최근에는 많은 대학들이 학술연구 성과에 대해 IR을 진행하여 제공하고 있습니다. 서울대학교의 S-space나 KAIST의 KOASAS처럼 말이죠. 광의로 보면 KERIS의 dCollection도 IR이라고 할 수 있습니다.

Situation 22   Institutional Repository (IR)

U : Could you explain IR?

L : IR is the abbreviation for 'Institutional Repository.' IR is an online locus
for collecting, preserving, and disseminating materials in digital form.

U : It means that there's a link between IR and open access. Is that so?

L : That's correct. These days, many universities provide open access to
institutional research output such as dissertations and research journal
articles by self-archiving. For example, there is the 'S-space' of Seoul
National University and 'KOASAS' of KAIST. In a broad sense,
'dCollection' of KERIS is another example.

상황 23 | 도서관의 Social Network Service (SNS)

U : 도서관에서 공식 트위터를 운영한다고 하니 의외네요.

L : 도서관은 책과 이용자를 연결하는 역할을 하는데 트위터로 이용자분들과 가까워질 수 있다면 좋지 않겠어요?

U : 그리고 보니 트위터에서 도서관소식을 들을 수 있어서 좋아요. 좀더 편하게 질문을 할 수도 있고요.

L : 저희도 이용자분들의 이야기를 자주 듣게 되어 많은 도움이 됩니다. 도서관에서 홈페이지 외에 블로그도 운영하고 있으니 방문해주세요.

U : 블로그에는 어떤 내용들이 있나요?

L : 책과 서비스 관련한 유용한 정보와 함께 도서관에서 진행하는 각종 행사사진과 영상들을 담고 있어 재미있을 겁니다. 주기적으로 이벤트도 진행하고 있습니다.

U : 재밌겠네요, 꼭 방문해볼게요.

Situation 23   Social Network Service (SNS) in the library

U : I'm kind of surprised our library manages an official Twitter account.

L : The library plays a role in connecting resources and users. So it's better to get close to users with Twitter.

U : Come to think of it, it's good to know about library news through Twitter. Also, I can ask a question easily.

L : It's also very helpful for us to hear user suggestions. Also, our library manages not only a website but also a blog, so please drop by.

U : What kind of content is on the blog?

L : There are all sorts of pictures and videos of events hosted by the library and useful information about books and services. It is very interesting. Besides, that we hold events periodically.

U : That sounds interesting. I'll certainly visit.

상황 24   링킹 솔루션

U : 논문을 찾고 있는데 전자저널을 쉽게 검색하려면 어떻게 해야하죠?

L : 링킹솔루션을 활용하여 검색해보셨나요?

U : 아니요 설명해주시겠어요?

L : 간단히 말해서 검색된 전자자원의 모든 정보를 한번에 보여주는 것입니다. One Stop 서비스를 지향하는 것이죠. 서지정보를 입력해서 원문을 빨리 찾을 수 있을 뿐 아니라 자관 구독여부 및 저널의 SCI 등재여부를 조회할 수도 있습니다.

U : 하지만 메뉴가 익숙하지 않아서 불편하네요.

L : 이 서비스는 구글이나 네이버의 학술검색을 이용할 때도 유용합니다. 간단한 환경설정만 해주면 검색결과에서 우리도서관 구독자원을 표시해준답니다. 홈페이지에 있는 매뉴얼을 보고 설정해주시면 됩니다.

U : 참 편리하겠네요. 고맙습니다.

Situation 24 Linking Solution

U : Is there any easier way to search for an e-journal article?

L : Do you know about linking solution?

U : No, could you explain that?

L : In brief, linking solution shows all e-resources at once. It is a one-stop
service, so to speak. Through bibliographic data input, you can get to
full-text databases and determine whether the article is available either in
our library or SCI.

U : I see, but the interface looks very complicated.

L : Not really. This service is really helpful because it can be connected to
Google Scholar (or Naver Scholar). By a simple setting, they display the
results with our library's holding information. To find the setting, check
the library website.

U : Sounds good. Thank you.

부 록

● ● ●

공지 / E-mail 영어 예문

1. 방학 중 대출 기간 연장

Due date extension service on summer vacation

Due dates for checked out books will be extended until the end of vacation.
Please refer to the notice below.
- For undergraduate students
- During Jun 17 — August 13
- Due date extended to 25 days
  * Questions or inquiries : 02-3290-0001, circulation@hankook.ac.kr

2. 도서관 자료 리콜 서비스

Library begins Recall Services on Oct. 1, 2008.

Recall Services : A recall is a request to the library to ask another user who has
an item checked out to bring it back to the library by a specified date. Place a
recall to get access to a book or other item within a defined time period.
When the item is returned, you will be notified to pick it up.
- Recall Item Limitations
  - Only one copy of foreign books may be requested.
  - Only a book on which more than one half of the loan period remains for
    the current borrower can be recalled.

- Users are limited to two active recall requests and one recall request per book.
- How to Place a Recall Request
  - Place an online Recall Request at the library website.
  - When the library notifies you, you must pick it up within three days.
- Current Borrower
  - The current borrower must return a recalled item within 7 days from the date the recall notice is sent.
  - In the case of a temporary return, the item will be available for a 5-day period only.
  - Recalled books may not have an extended return due date.
    * Full return : The book is returned by the current borrower.
    * Temporary return : The current borrower wishes to re-check-out the item after the user who requested the recalled book uses it for 5 days.
- Penalty
  - If available items are not picked up more than two times or if recalled books are not returned within the due date more than two times, your use of Recall Services will be suspended for 6 months.
- E-mail, SMS Services
  - The current borrower will receive a recall notice indicating that the item has been recalled and must be returned.
  - When the book is returned, the recall requester will be notified and the item will be held at the Circulation Desk for three days at any Hankook University Library you choose.
  - The date the item will be available to be re-checked out will be given to the current borrower who requests a temporary return.

• Check Recalled Book Progress

  – The recall requester can check the progress of a recalled book at the Library Homepage → My Library → Recall System

3. 비도서자료 반납 시 주의 사항

Request for considerate use of library materials

Dear Library Users,

It has been observed that many movie DVDs, music CDs and magazines have gone missing from the library during the last two months. In the case of DVDs and CDs, it is often found that discs have been taken out and their containers left behind.

We therefore ask your cooperation. Please take materials out through the proper check-out procedure and put the discs back in their containers after using them in your personal laptop within the library.

Thank you for your cooperation.

4. 도서관 자료 연체 정책 변경

Changes in overdue policy

To increase the availability of library collections, the following changes are being implemented in the Overdue Policy for long-term overdue items.

- Effective date : April 15, 2011
- What is a long-term overdue item?
  - An item (book or multimedia material) that is 60 days or more past due
- Long-term overdue fines
  - A long-term overdue item is treated the same as a lost item.
  - A borrower may ① replace the item or ② pay for the item.
- Restrictions on borrowers with long-term overdue items
  - Borrowers will be restricted from accessing the library and using library services (e.g. checking out library materials, using library facilities, inter-library loans, and accessing e-Journals) until the overdue item(s) is(are) returned or paid for.
- Contact Information
  - Tel : 02-3290-0000, E-mail : circulation@hankook.ac.kr

5. 도서 연체 안내 (e-mail)

Dear _____

You have overdue library material. Please confirm your loan status details below.

Title	Call No.	Registration number	Due date
Developmental biology	571.8 G466d9	121207237	2nd May 2011

As you will be unable to have any certificates printed by the Hankook University until you return all materials and restricted from checking out library materials, please return all materials to the library ASAP.

Please let me know if you have any questions. (Tel : 02-3290-0000, E-mail : circulation@hankook.ac.kr)

6. NDSL 서비스

NDSL Guide

NDSL (National Discovery for Science Leaders) is an integrated science and technical information retrieval system, providing more than 60,000 journals from Korea and abroad and full-text services by bibliographical information search (45,000,000 articles included in 200,000 proceedings). It also provides international patent information and connecting service to relevant articles and corroborative facts. (※ Service is provided in Korean only.)

International students are welcome to use it for free so create your own personal ID and Password on NDSL (http://scholar.ndsl.kr/) as a domestic user. When you join NDSL, please put Hankook University Library for "소속기관(Sosok Kigwan)" and Student No./Employee No. for "학번/사번(Hakbon/Sabon)".

7. 전자자료 공정 이용

Attention to Using e-Resources

Recently, the library has received an increasing number of warnings from publishers due to illegal downloading of e-journals. Since the e-resources of the Hankook University Library are protected by copyright, reasonable use for research and educational purposes is allowed. Therefore, we have established the Policy for Acceptable Use of Electronic Information Resources in order to protect the majority of users and to guarantee e-Resources services. We ask you to comply with this policy.

- Maximum downloading per day
  - 30 articles, from the same publisher, downloaded to the same PC or IP number
- Criteria for defining abuse
  - Downloading the entire contents of a particular issue
  - Systematic printing or downloading of e-resources within a short period of time
  - Saving excessive amounts of e-resources beyond research boundaries
  - Using saved or printed material for commercial purposes
  - Downloading e-resources using another person's ID or password
  - Allowing off-campus access by careless management of personal or public servers
- Sanctions for violation of e-resources policy
  - Suspension of library privileges for 6 months, such as library access, borrowing, library website login, purchase request, request for document

delivery service or interlibrary loan, and off-campus access

• Violators shall pay fines requested by the publisher.

8. 신입생 오리엔테이션

Library's Spring Orientation Campaign kicks off February 23

The Hankook University Library has all of the information resources you
need to get the school year started. Find it all — at anytime and from anywhere.
What better time to explore what the Library has to offer than during
orientation? From February 23rd to March 31st, the Hankook University
Library will be offering three orientation sessions : Tour, Getting Started
Workshop and Finding the Right Resource Workshop. These initiatives will
help new and returning students get a head start on discovering the Library's
vast resources. Students who attend all three orientation activities will collect a
FREE USB bracelet and be entered in a draw to win an iPad.

For more information, visit the Library's orientation website at :
http://library.hankook.ac.kr/education/list

9. 이용자 교육

Library Instruction Schedule for August 2011

The Hankook University Library will provide user instructions to enhance user library resource utilization ability. All sessions will be conducted in Korean. The schedule is as follows :

- For Graduate students

    8.17 (Wed) 13:00－15:00 How to write references (APA & Chicago Style)

    8.18 (Thu) 14:00－16:00 How to use SCIE, Citation Indexes DB

    8.26 (Fri) 14:00－16:00 EndNote Basic

    Location : Seminar Room #501 (5th floor, Science Library)

- For Undergraduate students

    8.24 (Wed) 14:00－15:00 How to use library services

    8.25 (Thu) 14:00－15 :00 How to research information for reports

    8.26 (Fri) 13:00－14:00 Basic Search Databases

    Location : Library Instruction Room (6th floor, Main Library)

- Registration/Cancellation : Login to the Library website → Library services → Library instruction

- Contact ： Lee, Koryo (02-3290-0001, library@hankook.ac.kr)

10. 전자학술정보 이용자 교육 (E-mail)

[Library] Online DB Workshop on AAA

Dear Library Users,

The Online DB Workshop will be held this Friday, Jul. 25, 2011. Please participate in the Library Workshop to enhance your research skills. If you'd like to participate, register at the library website or send an e-mail to me (library@hankook.ac.kr). The workshop is first-come, first-served.

- Subject : _____

- Venue : _____

- Time : _____

- Date : _____

- Number of Places Available : _____

- Instructor : _____

Printed handouts and brochures will be distributed during the workshop. Also, complimentary gifts will be given to five attendees. Please let me know if you have any questions.

Thank you.

11. 원문복사 무료 서비스

Free!! Library's Document Delivery Service

Library users can request our domestic as well as overseas partner institutions for photocopies of resources that are not held by the Hankook University Library. The library provides materials requested by DDS (Document Delivery Service) free of charge as follows :

Eligible	Details

Graduate/ Lecturer	− Up to 15 cases per semester
	  * Overseas DDS is limited to 5 cases.
	  * ProQuest Dissertation & Theses (PQDT)
	    is limited to 1 case.

Eligible	Details
Faculty	− Up to 120 cases per year * Overseas DDS is limited to 20 cases. * ProQuest Dissertation & Theses (PQDT) is limited to 2 cases.

※ An additional notice may be posted if the DDS policy changes.

12. E−DDS

E-DDS with Interlibrary Loan fees supported by KERIS

   KERIS (Korea Education and Research Information Service) supports Interlibrary Loan fees. E-DDS, International Document Delivery Service through KERIS, receives fee support as of 2009.
  • Support Policy : ₩17,000 support for 1 item, with a limit of 15 items for professors and 10 items for graduate students annually.
  • Guidelines for E-DDS Services : http : //cat2.riss4u.net/edds/guide.html
  • Contact :
    − KERIS ILL Management Team, 02-2279-8767~8
    − For E-DDS user verification : The Library ILL Section 02-3290-0001, library @hankook.ac.kr

13. 상호대차 서비스 개선

Interlibrary Loan Service has improved

The Interlibrary Loan Agreement between our library and the Koryo University Library took effect in January 2009. Users can borrow books held by the Koryo University through ILL Services. (Agreements with other 10 domestic university libraries have already taken effect).

• Eligible : Faculty / Lecturer / Graduate
• Loan Policy : 3 books, 10 days (renewable once)

To promote the Interlibrary Loan Service, the library will provide ILL document delivery charges for domestic ILL (except for quick-service) and return shipping charges for overseas ILL.

14. 상호대차 온라인 신청

Interlibrary Loan Requests Forms Now Online!!

Can't find what you are looking for in our library catalog? Fill out an Interlibrary Loan Request (ILL) form and we will be glad to request it for you from another library. These forms can be found at the ILL Desks of the libraries or now on our website at library.hankook.ac.kr. Just under the Library Catalog search button at the bottom of the page, you may click where it says "Request ILL", fill the form out, and send it. We will then contact you by e-mail when your item has arrived.

15. 상호대차 서비스 잠정 중단

Suspension of Interlibrary Loan between the Seoul and Busan Campuses

Interlibrary Loan between the Seoul and Busan Campuses will be suspended for the time being due to the renovation of the Busan campus library. Library materials from the Seoul Campus can be supplied to the Busan Campus library, but library materials from the Busan Campus cannot be provided to the Seoul Campus library. Your cooperation and understanding will be greatly appreciated.

• Period of Suspension : October 5th, 2009 — January 31st, 2010

(The above length of period is subject to change depending on the status of the renovation process.)

16. 상호대차 의뢰 (E-mail)

Dear Sir/Madam,

I am a librarian of the DDS/ILL section of the Hankook University Library in Seoul, Korea.

One of my patrons requested a Ph.D. dissertation from Tel Aviv University in Israel. Please refer to the following bibliographical information :

Title : Structural analysis of the human foot in standing posture.

I searched for it via OCLC First search and found that JNUL is the only library that owns that item. However, it was impossible to request a copy or loan through OCLC.

Could I request a copy or loan through JNUL's Interlibrary Loan service? If possible, please let me know the estimated cost and payment method. Your assistance is most appreciated.

Thank you.

17. 상호대차 신청 접수 (E-mail)

Dear Colleague,

Thank you for your request.

From our catalog, it seems that we have a copy for loan.

We can lend the book for the sum of : $30.00.

Payment may be made with invoice.

Please confirm.

Best regards,

18. 상호대차 배송 방법 문의 (E-mail)

Dear Zmira,

Thank you for your reply by e-mail on December 1.

As the patron needs them quickly, he is willing to pay extra for express mail or FedEx. Please let us know the charges, including express mail or FedEx, and how many days we have to wait until we receive it. It would be grateful if we could receive it by December 10.

I really appreciate your help.

Best regards,

19. 상호대차 배송 방법 안내 (E-mail)

Dear Mr. Lee,

Payment for FedEx is about $130.00. They can deliver it in 4 days.

Registered air mail takes about 10-14 days.

Does your University have an account with FedEx? Please supply the number.

If not, we can pay FedEx here, provided that you reimburse us.

Please let us know soon; there is a flight tomorrow at 14 : 00.

We have to call FedEx to collect the book.

Best regards,

20. 상호대차 자료 분실 확인 요청 (E-mail)

Dear Librarian,

This is an inquiry about the ILL request that you have ordered from us : ILL #7338000.

This book was mailed to your library January 17, 2010, but according to the OCLC request number it has not been received to date. We have checked our Canada Postal Service tracking information, and it shows as having been delivered to your library February 14, 2010. Would you please check to see if it has just been misplaced, or possibly shelved with your books in error?

Thank you very much for your attention to this matter, and I look forward to hearing from you shortly.

Sincerely,

21. 상호대차 자료 분실 여부 조사 회신 (E-mail)

Dear Sir/Madam,

We received your e-mail last Wednesday and investigated ILL #7338000

Please refer to the following notes about ILL #7338000 :

Date	Note
Jan. 12	Made ILL request #7338000.
Jan. 27	Check the shipping date from OCLC FirstSearch.
Apr. 25	Received a claim from user and made another request via OCLC
Apr. 30	Received an e-mail concerning record status from the University of Alberta

Since the date of shipment, January 27th, we have been looking for the ILL parcel from our University Post Office, but we could not find any sign of it at all. According to the Post Office, the only way to track your ILL parcel is by EMS invoice number. Please let me know the shipping company you used and the EMS invoice number (or registered mail number). I will contact the shipping company office in Seoul, Korea and investigate thoroughly.

I'm looking forward to hearing from you and I really appreciate your help in advance.

Best regards,

22. 상호대차 자료 오배송 확인 (E-mail)

Dear Librarian,

    After tracing the EMS number through Korea Post, we finally found that your parcel had been delivered to KyungHee University, not Korea University. This is most surprising as, apart from the postal code, the addresses of the two Universities are profoundly different. Please refer to the following address :

	Korea University	Kyung Hee University
Address	Korea University Library reference service/1, 5-Ga/Anam-dong/Sungbuk-Ku/ Seoul/136-701/South Korea	Kyung Hee University Library/ Hoegi-dong/Dongdaemun-gu/ Seoul/130-701/South Korea

    As you see, there is no point of similarity apart from the postal code. My guess is that the address was probably misplaced because both universities are very well-known in Korea.

    I just made a phone call to KyungHee University and requested a search. I will let you know as soon as I hear any news from KyungHee University.

Best regards,

23. 원문복사 의뢰 (E-mail)

Dear Librarian

We are trying to obtain a copy of the following article :

(our reference 674-11473)

Hankook Univ. Medical Journal

Article : Effect of renal sympathetic nerve stimulation on regional renal haemodynamics

Year 2001

Volume 7th

Page(s) 201－205

Author HM Yang, et al

Are you able to provide us with a copy? If not, do you know what library might be able to help us?

With very kind regards,

24. 원문복사 제공 (E-mail)

ILL No. CS2011007 (ref. 674-11473)

Dear Librarian,

Attached to this e-mail is the document you requested and invoice from the Hankook University Library. The total charge is 1 IFLA voucher. Please send us the charge to the following address :

Koryo Lee

Reference Services Dept.,

Hankook University Library

Anam-dong Seongbuk-gu,

Seoul, 136-701

Korea

Best regards,

25. 신입생 도서관 투어

Take a guided tour of Hankook University Library!

Are you a new student or a returning student who gets lost in the Library? Join the Library Tour and find out how to access library resources and services that will help make your school life a success.

For international students, we offer Library tours in English on two dates : March 18th (2 p.m.) and 24th (2 p.m.).

During the tour, attendees will take a walk through the libraries on the main campus, visit locations of major services, and learn how to make the best use of library facilities.

The 50-minute tour will start at the gate of the main library. A souvenir will be given to all attendees.

To reserve a space, please send an e-mail to library@hankook.ac.kr (Tel : 02-3290-0001) or just show up!

26. 시험기간 중 열람실 연장 개방

Midnight Hours in the Library

The library will be having extended hours until exams are over.
- Duration : December 7th (Mon)~18th (Fri), 2011
  (We will resume regular hours on December 18th closing)
- Opening hours : 05:00 to 24:00
  (Opening and closing time extended 1 hour each)
- All study rooms in the main campus library will open as above.
  (Study Room at the Science Library, 1st fl. will be open 24 hours.)

27. 방학 중 도서관 이용시간 변경

Library Hours during Summer Vacation

During summer vacation, library hours will be arranged as below.
- Period : Monday, June 20~Friday, August 19, 2011
- Opening hours : 09:00~19:00 (Mon. —Fri.)
  09:00~13 : 00 (Sat.)
 * Study rooms will open as usual.

28. 도서관 리모델링으로 인한 서비스 변경

Scheduled Renovations for the Science Library

The Science Library will conduct renovations from July 10 to August 20.
During that period, library services will be limited as follows :
- What will be renewed?
- Old shelves and desks will be replaced.
- Lighting systems and library facilities will be rearranged.
- More multimedia PCs will be added.
- RFID system will be installed.
- Library operation plan
  - Librarians will operate "closed-stack services." Users can not enter the book stacks. (But the Library website will be available.)
  - For Loans & Returns, please ask the librarians located at the temporary help desk in the lobby.
- Hotline
- Koryo Lee library@hankook.ac.kr, 02-3290-0001

29. 명절 공휴일 휴관

Library Holiday Closings

All libraries will be closed during the Chuseok holidays on September 12th and 13th, 2011.

- Study rooms will open as usual.
- During the period, borrowed book return dates will be automatically extended.

30. 입시로 인한 도서관 임시 휴관

Notice of Library Closure due to the 2011 Entrance Exam

The 2011 essay examination for Hankook University entrance will be held on Oct. 1st (Sat.) in all buildings within the campus. All Libraries will be used as examination halls as 44,000 examinees will be taking the exam simultaneously. Accordingly, the library study rooms will close from Sept. 29 (Thu.) to Oct. 2nd (Sat.) We appreciate your cooperation and understanding in this regard. Any inquiries should be directed to Administrative Services at (02-3290-0001, 0002)

31. 도서관내 소음 발생 자제

Attention!

Recently, there have been some concerns about the NOISE level in the library (for example, talking too loud, answering cell phones and listening to music on high volume).
Please be considerate of other library users by being as quiet as possible

부록

inside the library.

Thank you for your cooperation.

32. 도서관 내 음식물 및 음료 반입 제재

Food and Beverage Policy in the Library

According to the library management policy, consumption of food and beverages is prohibited in the library.

- Allowed : Covered plastic bottles, thermos bottles and tumblers.
- Banned : Cans, uncovered packs, take-out containers, paper cups, cups with straws and glass bottles.

The policy will be applied with a three-strike rule from July 1st 2010. After the third offense, use of any libraries on campus will be prohibited for a month. Inspections will be conducted at the entry gate, and reinforced by random checks inside the library.

The cooperation of users is highly appreciated.

33. 도서관 좌석배정 시스템 도입

Library Seat Allocation System Installed

To streamline the operation of the Study Rooms, a seat allocation system has been put into effect.

- When : From November 24, 2011
- Where : Reading Rooms in the Main Library
- Seats can be used for up to 4 hours
- Extensions can be made one hour prior to expiration. Up to 6 extensions can be made per day.
- During exam periods, the seat allocation system will run on exam schedules.
- Procedures :
  - Place your ID-card/mobile pass/Library Membership Card onto the ID reader
  - Select the seat you want
  - Take a printed ticket
    * If you finish before your allocated time expires, please log-out and free the seat for new users by placing your ID-card or mobile pass onto the reader once again.
    * Suggestions and Inquiries : kor@hankook.ac.kr   02-3290-0001

34. 설문조사

Law Library Student Survey

The library wants to know what you think about our space, classes, reference and circulation desks and more. Your feedback is especially important now as the Law School is preparing to undertake a redesign project to improve how the building meets your needs. It should take you 5-10 minutes to take the survey, which is available here.

After you take the survey, you can enter a drawing for a reserved study carrel for Fall semester 2011. Thank you for your time and feedback.

35. 근로학생 모집

Working in the Library

Are you a looking for part-time work?

The Library has some shelving positions to assist in keeping the collections in order. If you are interested, please complete the application for employment and send it to library@hankook.ac.kr.

36. 도서관 시스템 및 홈페이지 개편

Library Website Upgraded

The Library upgraded the Library website and information system last June. The newly upgraded Library Information System has been optimized to Internet Explorer 7.0 or above, and it also supports other web browsers such as Google Chrome, Firefox and Netscape. If you are using the 6.0 version of Internet Explorer, you may not be able to utilize the system properly. Therefore if you are currently using an Internet Explorer version lower than 6.0, we recommend upgrading your version of Internet Explorer to at least 7.0

or using another web browsers such as Firefox or Chrome.

For installation support, please contact the IT Help Desk (Main Library 1F) at 02-3290-0001 or send an e-mail to library@hankook.ac.kr

37. 도서관 영문 홈페이지 오픈

Hankook University Library English Website Now Open

On October 15th, the Hankook University Library launched its English-version websites. We invite you to view them at the following addresses, and hope that you will find the new sites to have new and improved site features.
- Hankook University Library (English) : http://library.hankook.ac.kr (→ Click 'English')

If you have any questions or comments, please contact us at library@hankook.ac.kr (02-3290-0001) or contact a library service desk.

38. 도서관 트위터 오픈

Hankook University Library is tweeting

Follow us for the latest library news and tips to help you succeed at HUL. We'll be tweeting about library events, training, services and information resources. Please feel free to tweet us with any questions or suggestions - we'd love to hear from you!

Follow us here : http://twitter.com/HULibrary

39. 긴급 보수공사로 인한 도서관 홈페이지 일시 중단

The library website will be unavailable for 15 minutes from 5 : 30 p.m. on Monday, December 13th due to urgent maintenance.

40. 정전으로 인한 도서관 홈페이지 일시 중단

Shutdown of the Library Website

Please be advised that the Library website will be temporarily closed due to a scheduled power shutdown inside the campus.
- Time of Power Failure : Feb. 14 (Sat) 13:00 − 15:00
- Time of Website Shutdown : Feb. 14 (Sat) 12:00 − 17:00
- All services provided by the Library Homepage will not be available during the power shutdown.
- More Information : Office of Information Systems (Tel : 02-3290-0001)
  * The above shutdown time is subject to change depending on operation status

41. 학위논문 제출 안내

Graduate students who are scheduled to graduate in Feburary 2011 should refer to the following guidelines for submitting theses and dissertations.

- Submission of Thesis/Dissertation in PDF file
  - When : January 20~January 31, 2011
  - How : Go to the library website (http://library.hankook.ac.kr) →
    "Library Services" → "Online Submission of Thesis/Dissertation"
- Submission of Thesis/Dissertation in Hard Copy
  - When : February 07~February 11, 2011
  - Where : Central Library Rm #205
  - Required Documents :
    A. Four hardbound copies of your thesis/dissertation
       (One of the copies should have the thesis/dissertation approval sheet signed by all members of the advisory committee)
    B. Agreement to Disclose Electronic Thesis/Dissertation with your signature (which may be printed out after online submission is completed)
- Print out the Certification of Thesis/Dissertation Submission in the library website after the hard copy submission, and then submit the Certification to the Office of Academic Affairs in each college and/or graduate schools.
- For further questions regarding the thesis/dissertation submission, please contact : Koryo Lee (Tel : 02-3290-0001 / E-mail : library@hankook.ac.kr)

42. 교외접속 서비스 개선

Open-Link Now Available for Off-Campus Access to the Library

Open-Link is now available to library users. Open-Link is a quick, easy and convenient method to access library subscription databases off-campus. Unlike the conventional proxy service, it requires no prior computer or browser set-up. All users need to do is to log in using their ID and password when prompted. Users will be asked to log in only once per browser session.

To use Open-Link for accessing databases when off-campus, use one of the library's online tools, such as the Library Catalog, and Find an e-Journal. The easiest place to start is with the search options on the Library homepage.

Open-Link will not replace the proxy service. Users who don't go through the library website can continue to use the proxy service exactly as they have in the past.

For more information, please visit the Off-Campus Access page or FAQ.

편집 후기

다반향초(茶半香初)

공적이든 사적이든 삶에 지치고 때론 매너리즘에 빠져 헤어나지 못할 때, 다반향초와 같은 사람에 대해 생각해 봅니다. 나는 지금 잘 살고 있는 것인가? 내가 하고 있는 지금 일도 그러한가? 그러지 못할 때가 더 많았는데, 개정판 작업역시 지금에서야 '아쉬움'이라는 표현을 쓰게 합니다. 다만 매너리즘 극복을 위해 새로운 것을 경험한 것으로 개인적인 위안을 삼고자 합니다.

사서들도 영어를 배울 수 밖에 없는 주변 환경이 독자들로 하여금 이 책을 선택하게 할 것입니다. 부디 그 향기가 끝까지 함께 하시길 바라겠습니다.

끝으로 편집을 위해 노력해 주신 사서실무영어회화 개정위원회 위원님들과 즐거웠던 시간을 고이 간직하며, 특히 고려대학교 서진영 부장님, 오태호 선생님께 감사의 말씀을 전합니다.

● ● 경희대 황일원

출판을 앞둔 시점에서 장고의 작업을 몇 마디로 요약한다는 것은 어려운 일입니다. 초판은 도서관계의 고전으로써 손색이 없을 정도로 훌륭하지만, 학술교류협의회 사서 선생님들의 힘을 빌려 새로운 책으로 거듭나게 되었습니다. 마치 오래된 예술 작품이 복원가의 손을 거쳐 새로 태어나듯, 최근 트렌드를 반영하고 새로운 내용을 더하여 일대 화학변화를 일으켰다는 생각이 듭니다.

우선 작업을 위해 동고동락하셨던 사서실무영어회화 개정위원회 소속 사서선생님들께 진심으로 감사의 말씀 드립니다. 함께한 시간은 각별한 체험이었습니다. 비록 저의 역량은 매우 보잘 것 없었지만, 위원회의 격려와 도움 속에 유종의 미를 거둘 수 있었습니다. 아울러 무한한 신뢰와 믿음으로 격려해주셨던 서진영 부장님, 도서관 입사 동기 국종건 김다영 선생님, 중앙대학교 문헌정보학과 동기 및 선·후배님들, 작업과정에서 많은 영감을 주셨던 KDI 국제정책대학원 최성진 팀장님과 신윤정 선생님, 어둡고 힘든 시간 속에서 항상 빛이 되어 주신 부모님께 지면을 빌려 거듭 감사의 말씀 드립니다.

● ● 고려대 오태호

초판의 간단한 수정작업 정도가 될 것이라고 하여, 가벼운 마음으로 작업에 참여하였다. 하지만!!! 볼수록 바꿀 내용이 많이 보이고, 실용적이지 못한 내용들과 근 5-6년간 새롭게 생겨난 도서관 서비스가 얼마나 많은지 수정할 것 투성이지 않은가!! 참여한 5개 대학 선생님들의 열정 또한 대단하여 수 차례 회의를 거치면서 목차를 뜯어고치고, 불필요한 내용은 삭제, 신규내용은 추가 등등을 거쳐 드디어 완성본이 나왔다. 단순히 영어회화 책자라는 것을 뛰어넘어 업무적으로도 많은 지침이 되고 배움이 되는 작업이었음에 감사함을 느낀다. 열띤 열정으로 함께 하신 선생님들, 특히 고생이 많으셨던 고려대 서진영 부장님, 오태호 선생님께 감사함을 표하고 싶다.

● ● 성균관대 민경승

When in Rome, do as the Romans do.

'로마에 가면 로마법을 따르라'는 말이 있음에도 불구하고 많은 외국인들이 한국에 와서도 한국어를 시도조차 하지 않고 당당하게 영어로만 얘기하곤 한다. 세종대왕님이 만드신 훌륭한 한글을 세계인들이 사용한다면 얼마나 좋을까만은, 현실이 그렇지 않으니 우리가 세계 공용어라 할 수 있는 영어를 배우지 않을 도리가 없다.

바쁜 업무를 핑계로 시원찮은 원고를 넘기고 나서 후회막급이었지만, 부족한 실력을 한탄하기 보다는 이번 작업을 함께 한 좋은 분들과의 만남에 의미를 두고자 한다.

● ● 연세대 채정림

영어회화집이 발간될 수 있도록 도움주신 관장님과 선생님들께 감사드립니다. 선생님들의 아이디어 덕분에 도서관실무에 활용할 수 있는 수준 높은 책이 나올 수 있었다고 생각합니다. 이 책이 국내도서관의 외국인 이용자서비스의 질을 한 단계 높이는 계기가 되길 바랍니다. 1년간 함께 작업을 했던 사서실무 영어회화 개정위원회 위원선생님들도 수고 많으셨습니다. 감사합니다.

● ● 한양대 안신섭

이 책자가 우리 도서관계에 조금이나마 도움이 된다면 그것으로 충분합니다. 사서실무영어회화 개정위원회 위원 여러분들 고맙습니다. 감수를 담당하신 고려대학교 국제어학원 관계자와 USC 이선윤 선생님께도 감사 드립니다.

…부족함은 미래를 위한 기약이라 위안하며…

● ● 고려대 서진영

글로벌 사서를 위한 **도서관 영어회화**
Essential English for Global Librarians

초판 1쇄 발행 | 2012년 4월 30일
　 2쇄 발행 | 2013년 11월 15일
지 은 이 | 학술정보교류협의회
편집위원 | 서진영(고려대학교 도서관, 편집위원장), 황일원(경희대학교 중앙도서관),
　　　　　 오태호 (고려대학교 도서관), 민경승(성균관대학교 학술정보관),
　　　　　 채정림(연세대학교 중앙도서관), 안신섭(한양대학교 학술정보관)
감　　수 | Sun-Yoon Lee (Korean Studies Librarian, Korean Heritage Library,
　　　　　 University of Southern California)

펴 낸 이 | 배정민
펴 낸 곳 | 유로서적
편　　집 | 공감인(IN)
디 자 인 | 미학

등　　록 | 2002년 8월 24일 제10-2439호
주　　소 | 서울시 금천구 가산동 329-32 대륭테크노타운 12차 416호
　　　　　 TEL: (02) 2029-6661
　　　　　 FAX: (02) 2029-6664
　　　　　 E-mail: bookeuro@bookeuro.com

ISBN 978-89-91324-49-7 (93010)